THE TRAGIC HISTORY OF ESOTERIC CHRISTIANITY

Sean Byrne

THE TRAGIC HISTORY OF ESOTERIC CHRISTIANITY

THE CHURCH'S WAR AGAINST THE SPIRIT OF SOPHIA

AGE-OLD BOOKS

DEDICATED TO
ALL TRUE SEEKERS OF THE SPIRIT

Copyright © Sean Byrne 2001

Published by: Age-Old Books,
                37 Cultra Avenue,
                Holywood,
                Co. Down,
                BT18 0AY

The moral right of the author has been asserted.

ISBN: 0-9540255-0-4

A catelogue record of this book is available from the British Library.

Printed and bound in
Holywood, Co.Down N. Ireland by
Priory Press

CONTENTS

Acknowledgements
Preface i
Introduction ii

PART ONE
The First Millennium: A Struggle For Unity

1. The Importance Of Sophia To The First Christians 5
2. The Perennial Wisdom-Philosophy And The Coming Of Christ 13
3. A Vessel Is Prepared In The East 22
4. The Rejection Of Sophia 32
5. The Forging Of An Orthodoxy 38
6. The Birth Of The Heretic And The 'House-Arrest' Of The Spirit 50
7. The Holy Land Of Erin Comes To The Rescue 66
8. Rome Rules…Or Else! 88
9. The Spiritual Flower Of Christ Versus 'The Dogma Machine' 105
10. A Tragic Denial 114

PART TWO
The Second Millennium: A Legacy Of Conflict

1. The Holy Grail And Esoteric Christianity 127
2. The Albigensian Holocaust 142
3. The Dangerous Secret Of The Knights Templar 153
4. The Spirit Of The Rose Cross 164
5. From Heretic To Devil 175
6. The Truth About The Alchemists 182
7. The Artists Keep The True Spirit Alive 188
8. The Dark Age Ends And A New Age Begins 199
9. The Third Millennium: Pointers 216

    Postscript 220
    Appendix 221
    Notes to the text 227
    Select bibliography 239

ACKNOWLEDGEMENTS

The publisher wishes to acknowledge the following publications, extracts from which are quoted herein; Edouard Schure: *The Great Initiates*, Steiner-books, 1976. T.W.Rolleston: *Celtic Myths and Legends*, Studio Editions, 1994. Rudolf Steiner: *Mystery Knowledge and Mystery Centres*, Rudolf Steiner Press, 1973. Alexander Carmichael: *Carmina Gadelica*, Floris Books, 1992. Jacob Streit: *Sun and Cross*, Floris Books, 1993. A.E.Waite: *Alchemists Through The Ages*, Rudolf Steiner Publications (USA), 1970. *Wordsworth's Verse*, Faber and Faber, 1971. Johann Wolfgang von Goethe: *Faust*, Sphere Books, 1969. W.B.Yeats: *Collected Poems*, Macmillan and Co., 1952.

PREFACE

While the contents of this book concern themselves, as the title suggests, with Christianity as such, it should be noted from the outset that the word Christianity and the term 'the Church' are nevertheless used in a much broader sense than is usual. The latter term particularly has such a huge range of interpretation that it is part, at least, of the purpose of this book to clarify its *fundamental* meaning.

Any reaction therefore to the many and deep criticisms levelled against the Church in the course of the book should take this into consideration. For although, because of these criticisms the book *may* appear to be written from a perspective outside the Church, it is nevertheless intended as a contribution to the Church's necessary spiritual renewal.

Also the term 'orthodox' is used fairly loosely in order chiefly to indicate those forces which provided the Church, essentially a spiritual entity, with its vital temporal footing in the world.

Alldates in the book are *Anno Domini* (A.D.), i.e. *after* the birth of Christ, unless otherwise stated.

Also the word 'he' is sometimes used in the generic sense in which it refers to mankind at large, and therefore includes the feminine.

INTRODUCTION

Esoteric Christianity differs from mainstream or conventional Christianity in a number of significant ways. One is that it exposes much fundamental and relevant information and knowledge pertaining to the essence of Christianity which, whether by accident or design, has never gained a wide currency in the Church. For from about the middle of the 4th century onwards, precise knowledge of the spirit or the spirit-world, a knowledge upon which Christianity was actually founded, was discouraged, later to be actively suppressed, and eventually almost totally to disappear from public view.

Another factor, allied to the latter one, which seperates Esoteric Christianity from orthodox Christianity is that it places Christianity itself into a much deeper and wider historical context than is usual. In doing this it also reveals Christianity as a religion which, though centered upon the historical Event of the Incarnation, actually is rooted in a spiritual tradition much more ancient than this.

Esoteric Christianity can thus be said to be 'perennialist' in nature. This means among other things that it represents that aspect of Christianity in general which can trancend what conventionally seperates it from other religions. For Esoteric Christianity gives a Christian expression to something which is in fact a universal experience. And that is the thirst for true knowledge of the Divine Spirit, knowledge of man's true origins and make-up, something which has always, from time immemorial, expressed itself as a desire to know that Being we, for simplicity's sake, always refer to as God.

It can thus be truely said of Esoteric Christianity that it represents a path which makes the realization of this aspiration possible for all people no matter who, what, or where they are, for it points the way to that secret yet accessible wisdom of God the soul of man invariably longs to acquire. And though it does this by placing the figure of Christ at its centre, Esoteric Christianity nevertheless can be truely said to represent the deepest yet common core of *all* true religion. This somewhat paradoxical statement will become clear in the course of the book. Indeed in this latter perhaps lies Esoteric Christianity's greatest virtue! For living as we do in a time when a superficial or even fanatical fundamentalism in faith and beliefs is on the increase in many places, the spirit of Esoteric Christianity offers a way of circumventing or transcending these unwelcome trends. For it offers the possibility of avoiding the dogmatic intransigence established religions often display in high, or even low places, while yet having the advantage of remaining true to all of these religion's spiritual core. Furthermore Esoteric Christianity establishes a spiritual Way or path which those of doubtful or even of no religious persuasion at all may well be able to relate to, for while retaining what is most essential to the practise of religion and spirituality generally, it yet of necessity does not demand of its adherents any obligatory or cultic practises, which latter often indeed do as much to divide people from one another than to unite them. For Esoteric Christianity gives expression to *perennial* truths which constitute the very essence of every human being's true make-up. And these are truths which must of necessity go to the inmost heart of all spiritual matters. In doing this Esoteric Christianity provides the soundest basis possible upon which religious, ethnic and especially purely human barriers, of whatever kind, can come down and become entirely a thing of the past. It is thus a path of great promise!

And all this is possible because at the centre of Esoteric Christianity ultimately lies the knowledge of an art, a science even, which contains the very essence of what is most needed in the world: the art or science of true healing.

This healing is possible because Esoteric Christianity offers the tools, the techniques of an essentially spiritual or divine art which is nothing less than the Spirit of pure enlightenment and knowledge. It is, or was, a Spirit which lived once very vibrantly throughout the Church, especially during the time of Christ's physical presence on the Earth and for a couple of centuries afterwards. The Church itself was, one can justly say, born and grew up to a degree out of it, and it provided also the foundation of all that came afterwards. This early foundational period is now generally known as the time of The Gnosis.[1]

After this time however this Spirit rapidly diminished and for complex reasons was eventually almost completely snuffed out. This was a tragedy of the first degree!

Tracing the reasons for this tragedy, as this book attempts to do, is thus also an attempt describe the history and demise of the human/divine spirit itself! The issues are indeed very complex, but the book attempts to simplify them for the average person so that in understanding their essentials a 'grass roots' movement of the individual human spirit may contribute to a much needed renewal of the broader Spirit of the Church itself and thereby lead it forward in its essentially healing mission to the Earth once more.

And the book attempts to define the necessary framework within which this great work can be gradually accomplished.

PART ONE

THE FIRST MILLENNIUM:
A STRUGGLE FOR UNITY

HAPPY HE
WHO HAS PASSED
THROUGH THE MYSTERIES;
HE KNOWS THE ORIGIN
AND THE END
OF LIFE.

Pindar

3

Chapter One

THE IMPORTANCE OF SOPHIA TO THE FIRST CHRISTIANS

In attempting to understand both the original essence of Christianity and the salient features of its spiritual, as opposed to its purely temporal, history, it is necessary to call attention to two general aspects of it. One is that from its very beginning Christianity had two distinct 'flavours' which can be essentially characterized as an Eastern and a Western one. Another key point to be kept in mind is the importance ascribed in the early Church to the *feminine* aspect or concept of God. In the East this was summed up in the Being known as 'Sophia'. In the West, where early Christianity came to its greatest flowering in the Irish Celtic Church of the 5th to the 8th centuries, the same Being was recognized as an aspect of the ancient Goddess Brigid.

These points are important because they have a direct relationship to the balance, purity, brilliance, and strength of the spirit of the early Church. But also, and equally importantly, they relate directly to why this spirit was subsequently largely quenched!

For the overall religious tradition out of which Christianity was conceived and into which it was born and had subsequently to find its feet, i.e. the ancient Mosaic/Judaic one, had little place in it for the feminine, especially in its divine aspect. This however was not the case with the so-called gentile religions which surrounded the Jews and of which they were so suspicious and even fearful. For in these the feminine, or one can say, the soul or naturalistic aspect, held much greater sway than the purely intellectual, spiritual, or 'logos'[2] element such as the Jews cultivated. Similarly if we look at the situation in the West we find also that the feminine played a very important part in the religions of the time, as even a cursory knowledge of the myths and legends, often the basis of these various cults, will show.

So when Christianity eventually came to Ireland, it found waiting, so to speak, a maternal embrace, something which it was in effect largely denied within the tradition out of which it was born. Furthermore this feminine atmosphere actually remained very strong in Hibernia compared with other places in the then known world. The reasons for this of course are several, but nevertheless had very much to do with the fact that the Hibernians actually never came under the direct restrictive influence of the Patristic Roman world with all its attendant trappings of male aggressiveness and militaristic imperialism, etc. Yet all of these latter, in truth spiritually repressive influences, played very strongly into the early Christian drama in Palestine where the presence of Rome was all-embracing.

Quite apart from all of this however the ancient monotheistic tradition cultivated by the Jews and out of which Christianity emerged after the Incarnation, had always been a purely male orientated one. This is very widely known and an easily recognized fact. But partly because of the light in which Christ came to be seen in early Christianity regarding the feminine as a divine aspect of the Godhead, the Church soon began to take on a wholly different character to Judaism.

THE GNOSIS

The reason why this feminine element entered into Christianity at all of course is that from the very beginning, Christ was seen to represent something new, exciting, and totally different in religion generally, something which seemed to both transcend and at the same time unite elements that were previously divisive in the spiritual life of man. And this perception was very much to do with the familial or community aspect of early Christian life. For as the New Testament is at pains in many places to point out, there can be no Christian life at all without community life, and in the early Church this ideal was truely lived. And this impulse for family and community is of course, it need hardly be said, far more naturally a feminine one than a masculine.

It has to be remembered too of course that early Christianity in Palestine manifested itself as one of the main tenets within a confluence of diverse religions and philosophical systems which flourished in the general area of the Middle East between approximately the Ist century B.C. and the 3rd century A.D. and which has come to be known as The Gnosis.

Initially however Christianity of necessity was seen to form part of the Judaic culture generally. But what is most important to understand in relation to how Christianity began to assert its fundamental difference from the gentile-fearing Jews, is that at the centrepoint of the thriving Gnosis was in fact a spiritual Being who represented none other than the feminine aspect of the supreme Godhead itself. And the name which was given to this Being was Sophia. The early Christian Church thrived on this Sophia because she had the power, so natural to her gender, not only to break old moulds, but to do so in an entirely wise and enlightened fashion.

Furthermore Sophia occupied a primary place in the consciousness, hearts and souls of the first highly inspired followers of Christ because she combined into one those twin aspects of divinity most essential to the pursuit of any spiritual path of knowledge that leads to God. And that is Wisdom and Love which together represent 'philo-sophia', or philosophy. (In Greek 'phileo' means love and 'sophia' means wisdom. And to the Greeks, it must be pointed out, philosophy was not the abstract pursuit which we have come to know it as. For to them 'philosophia' was a living or divine spiritual Being, a Goddess in fact. And both Phileo (Love) and Sophia (Wisdom) are essentially and fairly easily identifiable as being purely feminine.)

Now all of this figured very strongly in the spiritual dynamics of the formation of the early Church. As the Church developed however, much of the old patriarcal Judaism and its law-orientated and custom-ridden influence inevitably lingered on within it. Though now transformed and in possession of a new Christian countenance, patriarchism nevertheless, as time passed, tended to increasingly oppress the wonderful new, fresh, pure and feminine power. For this patriarchism was something which ran very deep indeed and could hardly but at some point have become the cause of tension and conflict within the emergent froms of the early Church. We may thus easily imagine the kinds of social and personal difficulties which erupted as the ancient male-orientated traditions, customs, and attitudes became challenged within the new Sophia-infused milue. And we can furthermore very easily imagine tempers and emotions running high as the aggressive male element once more tried to gain the upper hand after the initial flood of Sophia-inspired freedom had subsided. For this indeed is what happened! There is much in the letters of the New Testament to indicate in fact that these kinds of problems existed even from the very beginning.

The Sophia power was novel, strong and widespread. It promised much possibility for change, perhaps far too much for some, and was thus perceived as something of a threat also. As it turned out, these forces of Reaction gathered themselves slowly but surely within the growing Church, and at length they in fact gained the upper hand. And soon a rehashed patriarchism was fast emerging as the new Church's strongest power. Moreover it was a power exceedingly conscious of its own far-reaching possibilities within the new institution and was nothing short of hell-bent on consolidating itself there.

A FOUL CRIME

Everyone knows just how deeply the antagonisms between the sexes can run! But when feelings like these are hitched onto spiritual and political causes, they can give rise to crises that reach far beyond the personal and can even effect the course of history itself.

And the depths of jealousy and spiritual hatred which this masculine Judaic/Roman consciousness could inspire against the spirit of Sophia is well illustrated and symbolized by one of the Church's earliest and foulest of crimes. This concerned the sagacious and beautiful philosopher Hypatia.

Let us briefly consider her case therefore, for it indicates well just what was happening in the Church at this time.

By the 5th century the Sophia-loving Gnostics were actually well and truely rooted out, and in the emerging Church the new style of a purely Christian patriarchism which the Gnostics' defeat was fast breeding, began in earnest to bite the bullit of feminism. Attitudes were becomingly increasingly hardened, intolerant, and even fanatical.

Hypatia was in fact one of the most renowned and influential teachers in the famous neo-platonic School of Alexandria where the last vestiges of the Gnostic wisdom obviously still lingered and had the power to provoke bitter dispute between factions engaged in what was fast becoming a battle for the very survival of the true sophiacal spirit of the early Church. And because Hypatia could evoke, through her eloquence and vast learning, and also (one can easily imagine) even through the very contours of the lips which formed her inspired words, a powerful image of the sublime Sophia herself, she fell foul of the anti-feminists of whom the zealous Church Father St. Cyril was undoubtedly the most vicious. For it was he, history tells us, who out of a great hatred, orchestrated and incited a crazed mob to perform a deed more ugly than one can imagine and destroy this lovely vessel of inspired wisdom and purity!

8

Cyril was Bishop of Alexandria at the time in question. And, obviously incensed that one of her gender could achieve such fame, authority, and spiritual influence as Hypatia undoubtedly had in the city where he himself was busily consolidating and strengthening the growing and highly patriarchal Roman-inspired Church, he resorted to the foulest of all tactics to rid himself of her. For into the minds of a carefully selected band of the fanatical rabble who lived in the outlying districts of the great city, he implanted seeds of spiritual hatred against Hypatia, and these he carefully nurtured until the time was ripe for his vile plan to take effect. Then at the appropriate moment, and on foot of a certain signal from Cyril, this mob was incited to such a pitch that they attacked Hypatia, 'dragged her off the street and into a church and there stripped her naked and hacked her to death with oyster shells, after which she was torn to pieces and her limbs carried to a place called Cineron and there burned to ashes (415 A.D.)'.

Such was the tragic fate of one of the brightest jewels of neo-platonism. (Cyril, it is interesting to note here, wrote very many books on theology and against heresy, and was one of the chief architects of the eventually triumphant Roman orthodoxy!).

Though by the time of Hypatia's prominence Alexandria and her famous School were long in decline, something due largely to the Roman occupation and influence of which Cyril was a prime representative, the School and the city were nevertheless still a matrix of the deepest religious, philosophical and spiritual fervour. But it was also a milue in which the proud and growing young Christian Church felt itself constantly threatened by what it increasingly regarded as heretical beliefs and practises. It thus felt the need to define, formulate, and defend its own particular beliefs ever more clearly and sharply over against whom it deemed to be, rightly or wrongly, its opponents. And the manner in which it set about doing this is undoubtedly connected with the male dominated culture in which it was trying to grow. But though it is not here suggested that Cyril's was the *principal* method of achieving it, nevertheless the Church's orthodoxy gained momentum far more through the masculine power of 'theologia' than through the sublime and richer influence of 'philosophia' and her inspired neo-platonists. Unable therefore to properly incorporate this feminine spiritual wisdom into its doctrines and dogmas, the Church as a result became ever more temporally inclined and power-orientated, more male dominated and heretic-fearing. And in this atmosphere the gentle and maternal spirit of Sophia gradually lost it's power and influence in the

Church and sadly eventually faded almost completely from its sight to be cultivated only by those espousing that form of Christianity which we here call esoteric.

THE ANCIENT MYSTERY RELIGIONS AND THEIR RELEVANCE TO CHRISTIANITY

One of the main, if not in fact *the* main reason why Sophia, as representative of the Eternal Feminine, played such an important role in The Gnosis was her primary connection with the very ancient Mystery Religions of mankind. And because Christianity arose directly out of Judaism, a religion whose deepest wisdom can in turn be traced directly back to these ancient Mystery Religions, it is necessary to have some knowledge of them if we wish to understand just where in fact the original Spirit of Christianity came from and what it stood for. Before we try therefore to expose more fully this Spirit of early Christianity, let us pause briefly to look at this particular Mystery phenomenon of the ancient world.

Now it is true to say that nearly every ancient culture and nation had its own Mysteries or Mystery Religion. Whether a nation or a tribal grouping was primitive in the extreme or whether it reached the sophisticated heights attained by say the ancient Egyptians, religion was always the form in which man's most basic cultural and civilizing tendencies were experienced, expressed, and fostered. Needless to say these Mysteries differed widely in style and content and actually acquired their particular characteristics according to the folk who adhered to them or the geographic location in which they manifested. There was however at least one fundamental principle which underlined and was common to all of them. And this, significantly, is a principle which even still holds good today, for it has a psychological validity appertaining directly to man's religious impulse, though in our own time it of necessity takes on a very different character. What we refer to is the principle of *initiation*.

It will thus be seen when investigating these old Mysteries that they will invariably have an outer as well as an inner form. The outer forms were chiefly those rites, ceremonies and practises performed publicly and in accordance usually with the rhythms of the changing seasons and so on. The inner forms however were always enacted in strictest secrecy. And the overall form was perpetuated by the leaders of the Mysteries who periodically seperated out from the masses some few individuals of exceptional promise, expressly to initiate them into the secret meanings of the various religious practises which, though known to all, were rarely understood. These festivities and sacred observances were always of course arranged and orchestrated by the leaders of the Mysteries. The ordering of the community, through the exercise of religious, mystical or even magical power over the mass of people, was of course the motivation of the Initiate. It was after all his perogative! For he was the one with the great power of the inner knowledge at his disposal.

Thus it can be said that initiation always signified the existence of a hidden or secret civilizing knowledge. But even more importantly it pointed to the manner in which this knowledge was acquired. This is also the reason why the ancient religions are known as the Mysteries. Now those who passed the necessary initiatory tests and thus acquired the Mystery knowledge, were known by different names in different cultures and religions; i.e. priests, priest-kings, hierophants, druids or shamans, etc. However the generic name which can cover all of these is that of 'initiate'.

So it was that in this manner the initiates nearly always became a powerful grouping in ancient societies. And in the most advanced of these societies, nations, or tribes, there can be no question at all as to the initiates' primary and formative influence. Thus if we trace the Semetic current of mankind back to ancient Egypt we find flourishing there, even four thousand years before our own era, one of the world's most sophisticated of initiation-based cultures.

MONOTHEISM - THE KEY SPIRITUAL CONCEPT

Here we have, if you like, the method by which all civilization on the Earth gradually arose. Before civilization proper, man lived in a kind of dream-like half-earthly half-cosmic condition where he felt just as much at home with the gods as he did on the Earth itself. It may have been inwardly paradisial; outwardly however his life was often instinctive, brutish and tribal, and if he was going to evolve beyond this, things just had to change! Thus out of the primeval and mysterious depths of time when man begins his fascinating and often tortuous journey on the face of the Earth, historians can, through studying the mythic content of the Mysteries, give us some little taste of the cosmic consciousness of the ancients and their grand initiation wisdom.

And what a consciousness it was! For, as the old stories and myths invariably show us, the soul of the ancients was imbued with a fabulous knowledge of gods and goddesses, of spiritual and elemental beings, a consciousness filled to the brim with wild and passionate life, and one which came, of course, to its greatest expression and clarity in the souls of the initiates and their disciples.

As the aeons passed and great cultures and civilizations rose and fell, they invariably made both an impact upon the larger consciousness and culture of mankind and also left, especially through their religions, some traces of their wisdom and knowledge to those who followed, so that even we to this day may still examine these with profit.

But though the Eleusinian, Samothracian, Hibernian, and various other Mysteries all have played their part in the development of human culture and consciousness, it was the Semites who bequeated to our modern culture its most singular, salient, and beneficent spiritual feature. For it is to these peoples, especially those who elaborated the great spiritually based culture and civilization of ancient Egypt, that we owe our knowledge of the primary spiritual concept of *monotheism*.

Monotheism is, one could say, the very first theological pillar upon which the Christian religion is or was raised. And of all the ancient religious traditions it was in the temples of Egypt that this concept was most highly developed and elaborated. It was upon the recognition that there was fundamentally only One, though often an unknown, God, behind the many others who invariably vied for their attention and allegiance, that the Egyptians built their civilization. For through this concept, and the unifying effect it had on their consciousness, the Egyptian Initiates achieved for their civilization its great sophistication. With this key in their possession the Egyptian priest-initiates could unlock the ordered spiritual power necessary to control and channel the often chaotic pantheism and polytheism which was in fact the most pronounced feature of the various tribes within their jurisdiction. And in this way the Initiates could promote their civilization and cause it to evolve in whatever way they desired.

Chapter Two

THE PERENNIAL WISDOM-PHILOSOPHY
AND THE COMING OF CHRIST

Although monotheism has come to us via the line of descent described briefly in the previous chapter, i.e. through the Semites and the Egyptians, then via Moses and the Jews* into the beginnings of Christianity, it must be pointed out that at the heart of all the great Mysteries of antiquity this concept also lived. It may indeed be said that monotheism represents the very core of the ancient and perennial wisdom-philosophy[3] and that it is in fact the foundation of an esoteric doctrine which is common to all great religions. It is true of course that it takes on different forms according to time and place. But although it is elaborated here in this book under the name of Christ, the merely outward name should never be an obstacle to realizing the sublime inner truth in it all.

Now it is perhaps understandable that conventional Christianity will proudly and resolutely proclaim its God, Jesus Christ, as the *only* God, or the *only* Son of God, etc. Such a practise is after all of the very nature of what we call monotheism. What is generally missing however from such a proclamation is an informed understanding of how it differs from other versions of monotheism. And uninformed overemphasis of this type of proclamation may, more often than not be merely divisive as far as getting to the heart of the matter of the One universal God is concerned. Thus as far as the truely brotherly and sisterly implications of the concept of monotheism can be made to apply practically in the world, an empty or a fundamentalist insistence on a single name without the necessary wisdom-informed elaboration of its true meaning, will merely add to the existing divisions. And the danger of this mis-emphasis on the part of conventional Christianity is something which in fact only an understanding of Esoteric Christianity can make fully apparent.

The questions involved here are of course highly complex. These however, it must be noted, were the very same kinds of questions which the early Gnostic Church tried to tackle. But unlike in our time, it tried to do this in a meaningful and comprehensive way. And we may thus designate these considerations as 'perennial' for they call into question the Godhood or

* This is described in more detail in the next chapter

Divinity of Christ himself and in doing so highlight the need to properly address and define Christ's relationship to other messianic figures, avatars, etc.

The Gnostic Church however actually thrived on this kind of debate and did so because of its essential spirit of goodwill towards the Incarnation. And it was only gradually that this spirit of goodwill began to give way towards a much more hard-headed and dogmatic approach to the whole question, or set of questions. Moreover it was this dogmatic tendency that actually represented those forces at work within the Church which moved to outlaw Gnosticism as such.

Now from an esoteric point of view this was a fundamental error! For essentially what this outlawing of Gnosticism and the promotion of dogmatism did was try to reduce the relevance of the Incarnation to a mere matter of words or definition of terms. And this was in direct contravention of the essence of the Incarnation which should not at all in fact be reduced to merely human definitions or word-formulas.

St. Paul makes this very clear in his letter to the Galatians (see Galatians 1:10-12). The spiritual essence of the Incarnation lies in the fact that it actually *happened*; it is not therefore so much a teaching as a fact of spiritual life! That is the point!

THE MUMMIFICATION OF THE TRUTH

It can be therefore said that intellectualism, dogmatism, and so forth, often do nothing more than fudge the real issues of importance. For there is a real sense in which the Church tried, after the light of The Gnosis was quenched, to put the living truth about Christ into a mere set of formulas, articles of faith, and so on. It did this because instinctively it knew the truth had to be preserved *some way* for future generations. But in doing so it also in a sense mummified the living truth into laws and lifeless word -formulas. These formulas have of course their part to play in the Christian religion, but their danger is that they appeal only or usually to the head of man, to intellectual types, to the exclusion of the common man, and often to the detriment of the deepest needs of all.

Now Esoteric Christianity has the possibility, the means, to address these deeper needs which, from a spiritual, as well as a physical point of view, are in essence to do far more with real blood and real flesh than with mere words!

We shall later be looking at this blood aspect of the Incarnation much more closely (see page 138) but suffice it is to say here that with even a cursory knowledge of the often absurd debates that go on, and have gone on in the past regarding the nature of Christ, that this in itself indicates the manner in which the spirit of the early Church inevitably and so sadly got lost to the common man or woman.

So briefly stated, in the early Church all of the trends indicated in the foregoing eventually shook themselves out into the structures of the emerging orthodoxy, something which essentially depicted the triumph of a male orientated intellectualism over a female, and much more soul-orientated spiritualism[4].

THE DIVINE TRINITY

But before proceeding further into the history of the deep esoteric spirit, we will have to consider another important doctrinal issue which also figured strongly in the early Church. And this is the question of the Holy Trinity. We need to address this, however briefly, because it is a fundamental issue towards which we will have to gain a positive relationship if we are to fully comprehend the true nature of both Esoteric and conventional Christianity. The Trinity may be represented in fact as the second theological pillar upon which the Church itself was actually raised in the world. Thus a study of the early Church will also reveal its preoccupation with this controversial doctrinal issue. It is important because it is an issue that is both directly connected with monotheism as such, as well as being a fundamental plank of all the ancient Mystery wisdom teachings. Unlike the later elaboration of the Christian Trinity however, the ancient Mystery teaching of the trinitarian nature of the Godhead was a doctrinal concept that incorporated both the masculine and feminine principles, (as well of course as the issue of their fusion, i.e. the principle of sonship as such).

Now what is central to an understanding of the history of Esoteric Christianity is that this exclusion of the feminine element from the Christian Trinity was entirely bound up with the defeat of Gnosticism in the Church proper, as we shall presently see.

Trinitarianism as such regarding the Godhead was always known and taught by the initiates of old even long prior to Christianity. For it is a universal principle and what is more is an entirely logical outcome of the more fundamental teaching of monotheism. Thus its correct formulation, and the full understanding of its application, lay at the very heart of the Mystery wisdom, its learning and teaching. And early Christianity, knowing Christ as it did to be in a direct line of descent from the ancient Mysteries, inevitably therefore grappled with this problem of the Trinity also. Indeed one can say that this issue lay at the very heart of all the heated Gnostic controversies in so far as it was the mediating Being of the Three who comprised the Trinity, the divine Sophia, who, as the archetypal feminine, was battling to have her rightful place in the emerging orthodoxy acknowledged, something which, as we have already seen, she patently failed to achieve.

ISIS, OSIRIS AND HORUS ~ THE EGYPTIAN TRINITY

It is therefore necessary to briefly consider this whole question of the Trinity in order that we have some appreciation of the sort of intellectual and spiritual milue which formed the backdrop in which the young Christian Church attempted to assert her independence over all other groups and cults actively seeking followers at this time of The Gnosis.

Now the trinitarian concept of the Godhead is complex and can of course be understood or studied on many different levels. We will try therefore to simplify some of these for clarity's sakè before proceeding. Firstly, the Trinity is, as we have said, directly related to monotheism. For, stated very briefly, whether one views the problem philosophically, theologically or even mathematically, once the essential unitary nature of God becomes recognised and yet also his Creation as being something substantially identical yet separately manifest, he must of necessity have had to draw something out of himself, i.e. the One must have become Two; and if these Two are to remain truely united they must of course do so by virtue of a third principle. This is the most simplistic of all expressions of the idea or concept of the Three in One and the One in Three, the spiritual Trinity as such. And from here it can take on the most varied of forms. But in the mythological traditions of the ancient Mysteries, out of which Christianity developed it, its at once most popular, profound, and also most easily assimilated version, is the well known Egyptian Trinity of Isis, Osiris and Horus. For the primal consciousness of the Egyptians hovered around this mythological family of Father, Mother and Son in the very same way as the Christian consciousness revolved or still revolves around the Holy Family.

Now while this is an obvious and fundamental analogy, it is however one whose Christian significance can only be understood if the relationship to the Egyptain model is properly elaborated. For in doing this we are enabled to gain an insight into the vanished Sophia spirit. Thus in the Christian theological Trinity the feminine aspect of the Godhead is significantly almost non-existent, despite the fact that Sophia is nothing less than a Greek philosophical and conceptual development of the spiritual reality which, for the Egyptians, lay behind their Goddess Isis! We thus come to the real truth of the matter underlying the trinitarian controversies in the young Church.

For the hard-headed theologians who gained eventual power over the Gnostics at this time when the ancient Mystery connection with Christianity was still being energetically thrashed out, did so precisely on account of their ability to theologize Sophia and her Mystery *out* of the newly evolving Christian idea of the Trinity! She was simply eliminated! And this is also the primary indicator why Christianity became eventually such a legalistic, tradition-rooted, dogmatic and male dominated religion, so very far removed from the fresh and spiritually infused movement it was intended to be by its Sophia-inspired initiator, and actually was at the beginning.

The modern spiritual demise of Christianity is of course directly related to all of this! This is also the reason why Sophia, knowledge of whom has continued to be cultivated in Esoteric Christianity down the centuries, must be allowed back into mainstream Christian consciousness if the Christian religion is to become filled with the spirit once again as it was so abundantly in its beginnings.

Leaving aside however this direct Sophia connection for a moment, if we are to attempt a genuine portrayal of this spiritual demise of the Church, we must to begin with also have some pretty clear idea of just what it is we are talking about anyway when we use a term such as spirit. For this is a very precious word of our language, but one which, unfortunately, together with love and a few others, has a kind of common currency which greatly undervalues or even belies its true meaning.

We must therefore outline, for clarity's sake at least, a general definition of this word, spirit. Yet while being general it will nevertheless also be one which will allow its deeper meaning to unfold as the principal tenets of this book are developed and are (hopefully) grasped by unprejudiced readers. For it will be seen that no true understanding of this word is actually really possible at all, and thus no conceptual framework can ever truely evolve within which a genuine spiritual renewal can be fostered, unless or until the word spirit is properly grasped. And this can be done only when spirit itself is considered within that framework which, as we have already indicated, lies at the very heart of all Mystery and wisdom knowledge, i.e. the trinitarian framework. Let us therefore examine this problem briefly with this in mind.

BODY, SOUL AND SPIRIT - THE HUMAN TRINITY

Every normal adult is aware of him or herself as being, or possessing, a physical body. This goes without saying! Most people however will also fairly readily acknowledge that they possess a soul as well, though this word has lost the clarity it once possessed in ascribing to man a purely spiritual, as distinct from a merely material or natural, being. Thus many people nowadays prefer to use the word 'mind' or even 'consciousness' instead of soul. Only a few however will be able with any degree of certainty or articulation to espouse the possession of 'a spirit' or 'spirit' as such. Though the word 'spirit' itself, as we have already said, is widely used in common language, and not just in relation to religious matters, the possession of it by an individual in the same concrete form as the body, or in the same easily identifiable aspect of mind or soul, is in fact rarely admitted to, and if it is, even more rarely understood.

So without entering into the heady ontological complexities in which it is possible to indulge here, on a more down-to-earth level it can easily be seen that with modern man the problem of the 'spirit' is largely a conceptual one[5]. This however, to an earlier form of consciousness, even one as relatively recent as the early Christian consciousness, was manifestly *not* the case. For then man lived in a much closer and simplified affinity with his God or gods than we could ever wish, or indeed even want, to. This intimacy however did not prevent man from expressing his understanding of this relationship with his God or gods in a very profound manner indeed. Quite the contrary. For he was in fact capable of an erudite, concise, and very much to the point expression of it. Moreover it was a relationship he always characterized in trinitarian terms, terms which in fact our modern language can easily be seen to correspond to body, soul, and spirit. For through a constant study of the manner in which this communion with their

18

gods actually took place, the Initiates were also able to identify, in the most basic of its governing aspects, how spiritual, or indeed any kind of knowledge at all, arises.

Moreover they knew that the framework needed to express this spiritual/religious knowledge had of necessity to take on a trinitarian form. For the Initiate's entire knowledge, wisdom, and teaching, was based firstly on their awareness of God as divine *spirit*; secondly on their own seperate physical presence as *body*; and thirdly of that which mediates between these two polar, yet directly connected spirit and physical realities, their own *soul*. And all three they knew were interconnected in the most intimate and complex of ways.

Now this, briefly stated, indicates the methodology used in this book also. Thus it will be seen that an increasing clarity can and will prevail regarding the psychical aspect of religious matters generally if this method is rigorously adhered to. For the method has the finest possible credentials and is indeed firmly rooted in the spiritual history of mankind himself, notwithstanding the fact that knowledge of it has been snowed under by centuries of Sophia-starved intellectual wranglings, mostly between men.

Now the truth of all we are getting at here can be best illustrated and fully appreciated by looking at one of the greatest Initiates of all time, one who nevertheless enjoys the advantage of having lived within the fairly narrow limitations of our recorded Western history. This is the universally famous sage, Pytagoras.

PYTAGORAS

Pytagoras (d. circa 500 B.C.) was one of the very earliest of the great classical Greek philosophers. He acquired his renowned and vast wisdom in many ways, not the least of which was a life of deepest meditation and reflection. But he was also an extremely active person. And in his time he travelled extensively throughout the ancient world absorbing everywhere he went the essence of the then extant Eastern Mystery teachings (or more precisely, what was left of them, for by then they were, for various reasons, very much in a state of decline). Now he eventually settled in southern Italy and there he formed a sort of (for that time) modern Mystery centre.

Pytagoras was in many ways a transitional figure in that he represents a bridge between the old Mystery wisdom cultivated secretly in the temples from time immemorial, and a new style of 'academic'[16] learning, much more openly practised. This latter phenomenon was in fact something which can be attributed to the Greeks generally and which they inaugurated around this time. As such it was a new and vitally important departure for the human spirit. For it was an activity with the deepest and most far reaching of consequences for human evolution, and which we have come to know simply as *philosophy*.

Pytagoras was at the forefront of this movement. He was thus in his teachings doing something quite extraordinary and revolutionary for his time! For he was attempting to give conceptual expression to what formerly was taught in the Mysteries only in a pictorial way through myth, symbol and the like. He was thus, we may say, one of the prime initiators of our modern civilization in that he set in motion what was in time to become one of our greatest assets, the art of pure conceptual thinking as such. For whereas formerly pictures, images, or indeed real visions of the gods and goddesses were the keys to unlocking the enigmas of spiritual, psychical and physical reality, in Pytagoras' system all is reduced to *Nous, Thumos* and *Phrenes*, three Greek words which we can still work with today as relating to body, soul and spirit, for they are universal concepts.

Needless to say Pytagoras's teaching was vast and his wisdom very profound indeed. His trinitarianism however, we must note very carefully, is its most fundamental and basic characteristic. And though it is possible to piece together many of his teachings through Plato and others, this Mystery wisdom of Pytagoras was by and large either lost or discarded along with all the rest of the ancient wisdom teachings, by the time orthodox Christianity had finally and completely defeated Gnosticism in the 4th century. It is a loss which we still suffer from very much! For one of its most obvious effects is that it denies human beings access to the only true method which empowers them to conceptualize or even see 'spirit' as such.

KNOW THYSELF

Now this loss of the power to conceptualize 'spirit', or rather more accurately, the historical process to which it has succumbed and which needs to be understood in order that it be fully activated again in our own time, is part of the whole purpose of this book through the reading of which hopefully a clearer understanding of the whole problem will emerge. Here however it is necessary to merely establish the fact that the trinitarianism invariably discernable at the heart of the ancient Mystery Religions was a wisdom and spirit-filled expression and recognition of how God images himself forth into the visible and physical world, and especially into the being of man himself. For in the Mysteries, knowledge of God and knowledge of man were intimately and inextricably linked together. The inscription 'KNOW THYSELF'[7] was always the key rule, the very password of the ancient temples, and this in itself indicates very clearly how the triune concept or image of God was the very same foundational framework for the initiates' image and knowledge of man and the world also.

For in the ancient initiation-knowledge, man in his deepest and truest image was always understood as not just a being comprised of terrestrial body alone, plus a soul which gives it consciousness and life, but also of a divine spark of true *spirit*. Man was thus conceived of in his deepest sense as a cosmic being, a microcosmic replica of a macrocosmic reality, God. And the universe itself was seperated from neither God nor man. All three were reflections, in varying degrees of perfection, of one another, with the universal feminine soul as the great cosmic mediator.

So with these primal thoughts in our mind regarding the fascinating but flickering mystery of the human/divine Spirit, we will now begin to trace a) its marvellous igniting within the crucible of early Christianity; b) its almost complete snuffing out by the advance of orthodoxy; and c) its continuing glow within the hidden mantle of Esoteric Christianity.

Chapter Three

A VESSEL IS PREPARED IN THE EAST

Christianity grew, as we have noted, out of the ancient Mystery knowledge, a tradition of cosmic wisdom practised from time immemorial in the secret sanctuaries and temples of the Initiates. Now this knowledge reached a very high point of sophistication in ancient Egypt, as even a cursory look at its religion and mythology will prove.

The influence of Egyptian mythology and theology on early Christianity is in fact quite well established historically. But in so far as we are trying to circumscribe the unique spirit of early Christianity as such, this Egyptian influence can only be understood and fully appreciated when it is seen how the nation or religion of Israel acts as the link or as a bridge between these two cultures, i.e. between the very ancient one of Egypt and the newly emerging one of Christianity. And we will in turn be able to gain our best insight into this process when we understand the role in it of the great prophet Moses.

As a priest of the Egyptian Mysteries of Osiris, Moses[8] had been initiated into the deepest and most sublime wisdom available to man in the then civilized world. His destiny indeed marked him out as one of the greatest seers mankind has ever known, a destiny which he fulfilled primarily through his inspired application of the Mystery principle of monotheism. For 'through him this principle, hitherto concealed beneath the triple veil of the Mysteries, issued from the recesses of the temple and entered into the domain of history. Moses was bold enough to turn the loftiest principle of initiation into the sole dogma of a national religion, and yet so prudent that he revealed its consequences to none but a small number of initiates, imposing it on the masses by fear. In this the prophet of Sinai had evidently far-sighted views which looked beyond the destinies of his own people. The universal religion of mankind was the true mission of Israel, a mission few Jews, except their greatest Prophets have understood'.[9]

For almost singlehandedly Moses conceived of and hammered together out of the nomadic tribes of Semites who were enslaved during his time in Egypt, a people and a nation capable and worthy of hosting an event as supremely significant for the whole of mankind as the Incarnation.

THE STORY OF MOSES

The fascinating and supremely heroic story of Moses himself can be pieced together chiefly from the Old Testament as well as other minor sources, all more or less historical. But the story of his conception and gestation of the Jewish nation, its fierce struggles for birth and survival in a hostile environment, and its eventual establishment and prosperity, all of which were due to his vast and wisdom-filled influence, is nothing if not archetypal. It is nothing in fact if not a universal or epic image depicting in a sense the struggle of Everyman as he tries to make his way through the darkness of the material world with its manifold allurements, enticements, and deceptions, and towards the healing spirit-light of the pure vision of his God.

And all of this great task filled Moses with not only a god-like zeal, but also a great sadness.

For what he saw, did, and heard during all the years of his momentous work, coupled with his initiated eye of seership which could stretch his vision way forwards into the distant future – all of this gave to Moses enough insight into the flickering loyalties and passions of man to know how desperately these people needed the authority of the God he had revealed to them. And he also needed to constantly work upon the inculcation of this authority if they were going to remain on the straight and narrow path, and fulfill the mission he had carved out for them. And a great worry and sadness undoubtedly issued from such a vision, for when he was gone, when he was no longer with them in the flesh, what would become of these tribal people, his very own spiritual children? Who but himself was capable of wielding a rod as powerful, as judicial, and as wise as the one he possessed? It was indeed a burden of great care producing a sadness worthy of a god.

Just before he died however Moses received what was undeniably the most comforting of all his many spiritual revelations. For then there was revealed to him a secret, a knowledge which seemed to his restless soul more subtle and sublime than if all the many pearls of wisdom he had yet acquired were rolled into one dazzling piece: For in his old age Moses learned the great news from God that One was coming who would complete the magnificent work he had begun and into which he had poured the vast resources of his great soul and spirit. 'Then the Lord said to me, I will raise up for them a prophet like you, one of their own race and I will put my words into his mouth and he shall convey all my commands to them'. (Deut.18:17-18). And this is precisely what Moses needed to know. He could thus die in the peace of knowing that not only his own work and the work of his nation would in time be fulfilled, but that the work of every man and woman on the face of the Earth was to become capable in time of its proper spiritual fulfillment. For in this revelation Moses had become prophetically aware of the future Incarnation of the Christ on Earth.

Now when this eventually came about some thirteen hundred years after the death of Moses, the concept of monotheism had been firmly and fully entrenched in the psyches of the Israelites. Moreover it had become, as Moses well foresaw, the very lifeblood of the Jewish Nation as it struggled to retain its spiritual coherence and dignity in the face of great secular temptations, constant persecutions, and even wholesale captivity and enslavement. Monotheism nevertheless did manage to survive, and in doing so the crystal clear spiritual light of true religious idealism was kept burning in the world.

From the beginning Moses had laid down the Law of God to the Israelites with all the sterness of a caring father who struggles to bring dignity, purpose, and hope to a large family of unwieldly or wayward children who would otherwise be scattered upon the winds of worldly dissipation without ever achieving anything of worth in life. So in their own very best interests he made God the most important thing in their lives.

This God, Jehova, was undoubtedly a stern God, one the people feared as well as respected. He was however largely perceived by the people as a male God, a Father God, a bit, one could even say, like Moses himself! For if Moses was going to rule this unruly lot, he knew instinctively that he must utilize the masculine and forceful power of the purely male *spirit* itself as opposed to the much more gentle feminine and earthly orientated one of the soul as such.[10]

THE FATHER SPIRIT

This was surely a hard choice for him! But it was one he felt he had to make. And so the trinitarian nature of the monotheistic Godhead, incorporating as well as spirit, both the soul and the earthly nature herself, barely figured in the Mosaic religion. For there was, as the Word of the

Mosaic Law revealed, only *one* God and absolutely no other. It was a religion of, the application of monotheism, *par excellence*. As such it evoked only the Father spirit and it was his worship only that was duely imposed on the whole of the simple tribal people of Israel. Moses was in fact applying in an acutely singular fashion, the specifically spiritual power of his God which he nevertheless knew himself to be trinitarian in nature. But he wished to establish on the firmest possible ground the presence on the Earth of this Spirit with whom he communicated so intimately, even if it were the case that he should reveal only *one* aspect of the totality of its divinity. He had very specific and crystal clear reasons for doing this. For he knew he was, via the Jewish Nation, preparing a vessel for nothing less than the incarnation of the divine Word itself. This Word had been prophetically revealed to him, and through its revelation he actually gained all his power, and it stood as the reason behind all his actions.

To the cosmic or astrologically determined consciousness of the wise ancients, including Moses, it was towards the sun that they always looked when seeking the abode of this Divine Word. The sun in fact was always regarded as the abode of the highest of all of the ancient divinities. And here of course was a masculine Being *par excellence*. Here was a God who had been regarded from the very earliest of civilizations on Earth, beginning from Vedic times in India and onwards, as representing the magnificent and solar power of the divine Word and who thus, and precisely because of this, was always conceived of and given expression to, in the most sublime, profound, and loftiest of all possible terms.

And it was this same divinity whom the early Christians called the Logos (= Greek for Word), seeing in him the full trinitarian revelation of the Godhead. It was indeed in this manner that the hope of Moses found its fulfillment in early Christianity.

THE SOLAR LOGOS

Now it should be carefully noted in attempting as we are here to behold the tangibility, the reality, of the spirit of Esoteric Christianity, specifically what part the heavenly body of the sun plays in it. And there should be no misunderstanding here! For we refer openly to the fact that this star, our sun, had a direct spiritual baring upon the genesis of Christianity, and represents in fact the key to understanding the new-risen bodily nature of man, inaugurated at the first Easter.

Some people may find such a notion somewhat alarming or disturbing. But this is usually only the case with those who consciously or (usually) unconsciously cut themselves off from a relationship with Nature beyond one of a most dense or superficial kind. It is sadly a common condition nowadays and one which can only be properly addressed by a conscious effort to re-awaken the dormant senses of man. When this is properly done, and in a balanced fashion, the soul-filled reality of 'mother nature' soon awakens in the individual also.

Now this kind of soul and sun-filled thinking and feeling the early Christians willingly and enthusiastically practised and absorbed, and integrated it fully into their new religion. And specifically regarding their understanding of the overwhelming importance of the sun, this is something which is indeed very evident from the Gospel itself. In fact the very opening sentence of the most profound, spiritual, and esoteric of all the Gospels, St. John's, refers to this solar deity: 'In the beginning was the Word (Logos)'. [11]

The ancient religions are of course all renowned for their worship of the various planetary deities. Each tribe or grouping had, for whatever reasons, its own peculiar or particular favourites. As the aeons passed and mankind progressed however, it was to the sun more than any other planet or heavenly body that man gradually turned to offer his purest sacrifices and perform his most instructive rites of worship. This was an inevitable but yet a slow turning, involving a multiplicity of factors, climactic and geographic, as well of course as purely psychic and psychological ones.

Nevertheless the Solar Logos has long figured in mankind's religious consciousness. For, beginning in India even thousands of years before the rise of the great classical Egyptian civilizations, the universal power of the sun and its God had already been well recognized.

KRISHNA

It was through the great Indian avatar Krishna at the very dawn of man's civilized life on earth, that a mighty revelation of God in his solar Logos aspect had been first established. 'Krishna reveals to men the idea of the divine Word; never more will they forget it. (........) After Krishna, there passes a powerful radiation, so to speak, of the solar Word, through the temples of Asia, of Africa, and of Europe. In Persia we have Mithras, the reconciler of the luminous Ormuzd and of the sombre Ahriman; in Egypt, Horus, son of Osiris and Isis; in Greece, Apollo, god of the sun and of the lyre; Dionysos, who roused souls to life. Everywhere the solar god is a mediatorial god, and the light is also the word of life. (........) It was by Krishna that this idea entered the ancient world; it is by Jesus that it is to shed its rays throughout the whole Earth'.[12]

Now we have seen that Jesus enters the world through the Judaic nation and its religion. And so if we try to relate all of this to the still later and gradual emergence specifically of the spirit of Christianity, we must do so by asking: How can we identify precisely the way in which this Solar Logos power enters the Judaic stream of wisdom? For our answer to this question we must turn to Moses once more.

It is through him that we can observe this solar power strongly at work. For in the manner in which he received his mighty and far reaching spiritual revelations can be seen the unmistakable drawing nearer and nearer to the Earth of this sun spirit, a process which culminated eventually in the Incarnation itself. Perhaps the famous incident of the Burning Bush in the Old Testament is the best illustration of this. For in this scene from the Book of Exodus (chapter 3) God appears to Moses as a fire or an unquenchable flame. And to the all-embracing spirit and cosmic consciousness of Moses, a flame which spoke spirit revelations of the mightiest kind could be nothing if not the reflected microcosmic image of the real and macrocosmic Sun God!

And when this Spirit reveals in the same episode to the perplexed Moses that his (God's) name was or is the word, I AM, (see Appendix 1), we can see foreshadowed in this highly instructive Old Testament episode the essence of what was later understood by the first Christians as the 'Word becoming flesh' in the Incarnation. For the Incarnation was or is, conceived of as being nothing less than that spiritual/historical event by which each and every indivdual human being became empowered to recognise in himself, in his or her very own flesh and blood, the reality of an indwelling God. In other words the Incarnation empowers us through our I AM centre to be able to participate in the Being of God. And this is the reason the God of the Old Testament speaks thus.

Now this crystal clear and pure knowledge of the sun or the Solar Logos nature of Christ was very alive in the early Church, as the most spiritually significant of the Gospels (St. John's) prove.[13] For the relationship of the sun and the Father aspect of the Godhead was still very clear in the minds of these early Christian initiates, something due principally no doubt to the Mosaic Mystery tradition.

And in highlighting the sun nature of Christ's divinity, in so far as the solar God and the divine Word were seen as synonymous, the whole question of just who Christ was, was thus brought entirely into focus, if not absolute resolution, in the early Church. In the early Christian consciousness the fact the solar light becomes identified with divine light, or 'enlightenment', is not in truth very difficult to understand. For, given the less abstract (in relation to our own) form of consciousness they possessed, a consciousness which was still very much coloured by a spiritual wisdom which saw far more than a mere ball of fire in the sky when it beheld the sun, it is in fact entirely to be expected that they would have been able to see in the teaching, in the very Being of Christ, a reflection of, if not the actual sun's light. For they experienced through him a light which gave to them a spiritual clarity of consciousness far greater than any they had ever yet experienced.

For these early and highly learned initiates and philosophers who meditated deeply upon the Incarnation, found in it nothing less than *the* most significant contribution ever possible to be made to the overall development of human consciousness as such. And they could indeed envision the spiritual implications of this great event of the Incarnation and its universality as plainly as they beheld the very sun in the sky! For the fact is that the concept of the divine Logos, as they came to see it in its embodiment in the Incarnation, carried or carries this whole process of the development of human consciousness a huge step further along its proper evolutionary path by injecting into it a new and mighty soul/spiritual impulse! Thus their faith, their knowledge, and especially their spiritual vision could allow them to indeed 'see' the very Word incarnate.

THE LIVING WORD

The Word however, it must be said, is always in the early Christian consciousness, the spiritual and Living Word and never the merely mechanical and law-dominated one which we are normally accustomed to use. Thus we can understand how and why Christ is seen in St. John's Gospel as both the Living or divine Logos and also the Word made flesh.

Herein also we can grasp the kernel, and can feel the whole heat of the debates that raged about Christ and his origins within The Gnosis. For back then (as indeed they are still now), the very direct questions were continually being asked and needed equally direct answers: Who was he? Where did he come from? By whose authority does he speak?, etc. Unlike nowadays however when we have so many other things to distract our minds, these were they very hottest questions of the day during the time of The Gnosis and, it should be noted, not just for the philosophers and theologians, but for everyone. Now the cannonical Gospels indicate clearly this perplexity about Jesus, but do so however mainly on behalf of the Jews. But the Gospels, it must be remembered, are as much *archetypal* as they are historical, and the Jews' questions in this sense merely represent questions that everyone had, or still have the right to ask. And in The Gnosis these questions actually constituted the pervading spiritual atmosphere. For everyone then suddenly felt, given the very nature of the Incarnation, that they had the authority to open their mouths about spiritual matters, speak up, and throw in their tuppenceworth! And some, because they were bold and daring enough, went on even to develop their own, often idiosycratic versions of the Gospel.

We can nowadays barely sense the subtleties and intensity of these controversies that raged in and around Palestine at this time! For, given the small amount of relevant documents that have survived, and also taking into account the breath and depth of wisdom that is lost through translations (from the Greek mainly), we merely get a faint hint, through even the best exegesis, of just what was actually going on in the minds and hearts of the people at this time and place.

However, all of these controversies regarding Christ, his origin, etcetra, eventually got somehow hammered out and into the early theological concept of the Christian Trinity. What is more pertinent however from the point of view of our present study is that the eventual formulation of this still current Christian Trinity is in fact utterly tied up with the expedient means by which Gnosticism was finally defeated within the orthodox Church. For the intellectual sharpness of the Christian Trinity was achieved at the expence of the central yet expansive Sophia Mystery which represented in fact the hallmark, nay, the very essence of Gnosticism. And this loss of the generous and all-embracing Sophia wisdom to the Church also indicates clearly why Christian theologians invariably get the Logos and the Sophia concepts, as aspects of the Godhead, (a knowledge that was

29

so important, exact, and alive in early Christianity), very much mixed up! And it must be said that philosophical clarity will only prevail here when correspondences are sought and found between these Greek concepts in the Gospel and the lost trinitarian Mystery wisdom.

THE INCARNATION

This is a work however which calls upon and evokes the substantial spirit of Esoteric Christianity through which true knowledge of the Sophia-Christ Mystery has been, and still is, kept alive in the world. We shall later follow the fascinating vissisitudes of this Spirit in the outer history of the Church. For though it is a fact that we must regard it as esoteric, this spirit and the wisdom and knowledge it bestows, has nevertheless managed to survive in the world, something due no doubt to its own great inner power and resilience. For the cultivation of it gives living, genuine, and vibrant insight into not only the sun origin and mysterious significance of the Christ Being himself, but it also reveals the Incarnation in its most profound and spiritual depths. In doing this it draws out of the Incarnation its unique I AM nature, and gives to the student a sensation, if not in fact a tangible vision, of the reality of Christ's continued Presence in the world. And in this latter of course lies, has indeed always lain in the Church, the very keynote of the Incarnation's significance, whether esoteric or exoteric.

* * *

It was the perceived *uniqueness* of the Incarnation which had set men's spiritual aspirations aflame in Palestine at the beginning of our era. Now this religious fervour was something which took place not only in the first couple of centuries after the Incarnation's actual occurrence, but also, and very revealingly, in the century or so before it too. For an event with such implications for the whole future of mankind as the Incarnation can justifiably lay claim to be, must of its very nature be capable of sending, via the medium of the Earth's finer substances to those capable of receiving them, currents of its foreknowledge. Thus it was that wise men, soothsayers, sensitives, and inspired clairvoyants of greatly diverse character, religious background, and spiritual training, could not but divine something of its impending import. Through their extrasensory faculties or sciences of divination, they could not but determine that some happening, if not in fact *the* most decisive event ever to take place in the history of mankind, was approaching, or indeed had actually occurred! And all of this activity was quite apart from the solid and orthodox prophetic tradition of Israel itself which had for many centuries been predicting the advent of One whom it saw as not only its own Saviour but also the Suffering Servant of all mankind. Thus it can be seen that in this unique Event of the Incarnation there is embodied the culmination of the esoteric and messianic thread of hope that ran or runs not only throughout the whole of the Jewish tradition from Moses onwards, but one which also ran or runs into the deepest spiritual aspirations and intuitions of men and women everywhere.

Chapter Four

THE REJECTION OF SOPHIA

The Incarnation lays claim to uniqueness on very many different levels! No one with even a little knowledge of it can deny that! What we are here endeavouring to establish however are those tenets within it, knowledge of which have to be cultivated if its perceived uniqueness is to be integrated into the Church in its full spiritual richness. This was, after all, the very process which constituted the chief dynamic of the Gnostic Church before this great effort was so tragically truncated. It is however a process that can and indeed must be revived if the Church is to be renewed in the way that it not only longs for, but actually can achieve, once a clarity is reached regarding its errors of the past.

But this in its turn can only begin to be achieved if and when the Incarnation is seen in its true and proper perspective and in its most instructive character, which is as a continuation of the ancient Mystery tradition, albiet in a modern form.

Now when the early Christians began to first organize themselves into groups on a large scale, the divorce, referred to earlier, from the ancient Sophia-inspired Mystery wisdom certainly allowed the body of the Church to establish itself as the entirely new spiritual and religious entity which it could validly lay claim to be in so far as it placed the Event of the Incarnation at the centre of all its teachings. It wanted, and rightly so, to establish itself as something totally new and different from all other cults contemporary with it. And of necessity it attempted to do this on many different levels, intellectual as well as practical.

But in the most important aspect of this work, in the formation of that primary image without which no religion can exist at all, i.e. its image of God, the Church made its biggest (to date!) mistake. For in creating on the one hand a purely theological and entirely male-orientated trinitarian God-image, and then in compensation for the obvious feminine deficiency within this image, and, (merely as an afterthought) promoting a Marian cult quite seperate from the Godhead, the Church could not but cause a split within its spiritual consciousness. In other words, if its image of God, an image which should, after all, by Biblical definition contain the *whole* of man's existential experience[14], effectively excluded at least half of this experience (the female half!), how could this God not but cause a split in man's spiritual consciousness? However if the Church was to incorporate properly the feminine element into its image of the Godhead it should not have broken its connection with the ancient Mysteries in the manner in which it actually did! For this wholeness in both the image of God and its temporally reflected reality in the Church's body, was something which ideally speaking, could or can only be achieved through a properly constituted and holistically disseminated trinitarianism, as understood from time immemorial by the Initiates.

As the Church evolved however, there came, as a result of the defeat of Gnosticism and the rejection of knowledge *per se* that this very defeat implies, a total splitting off of the knowledge of God from the reality of the Church's day-to-day existence. And it can or could be no other way! For unless this Mystery knowledge of God and the manner of its correct dissemination is understood, the Church must of necessity remain truncated, even headless, blind to all intents and purposes unto the shining light at its centre, the spirit-Mystery of its founder!

JESUS: A NEW KIND OF HUMAN BEING

The very early Gnostic Church gained its individuality and much of its vitality precisely because it had possessed this wholeness of spiritual perception and vision. For these very early saints and followers of the new Way could conceive of Christ not only as a human representative of the Father spirit whom Jesus's ancestors, the Jews, had for so long worshipped, but they could also behold in him something entirely new, health giving, and spiritually uplifting, an almost unfathomable quality they had never witnessed in anyone or anywhere ever before. He was quite simply a totally different kind of human being; for everything he did and said, from the manner of his dealing with the religious customs and conventions of his time, to his attitude towards, and handling of children; but most especially in his relationship with women – all these spoke tremendously of his great difference to his contemporaries. And the reason he could be so shockingly 'loose' in his behaviour was because he had been able, with angelic complicity, to incorporate fully into his being, the, to the Jews largely unknown, feminine aspect of the Godhead. For the Sophia spirit was, and is, of the very essence of enlightenment. And though he speaks, through the Gospels, of the Father in much more overt tones (for this Father God was, strictly speaking, the only one the Jews knew about anyway!), Christ's knowledge of the Sophia Spirit was not at all in question to the Gospel's writers. Our familiar cannonical Gospels indicate this in various ways. But in the early Church, where the use of symbol was both highly selective and vitally significant, the use of the *dove* as indicating the culmination or completion of Jesus's spiritual initiation, is the most precise indication possible of his intimacy with the Eternal Feminine. For the dove was always that by which the ancient Mystery wisdom indicated the soul or feminine aspect of the trinitarian Godhead. And it will be remembered that it was the Spirit, in the form of a (white) dove, who decended upon Jesus at his baptism by John in the Jordan just before he (Jesus) began the momentous three years of his ministration of this Spirit on the Earth and in the flesh.

So once the unique nature of Christ as the very Word incarnate began to circulate in Palestine in the aftermath of the Incarnation, there began inevitably to group around it men and women from all kinds of backgrounds and cultures and of every degree of initiation, wisdom, and knowledge, or even of none at all. Nevertheless it was of course the learned ones who possessed the capabilities of giving direction to this great new spiritual movement.

And many of these people were of necessity thoroughly acquainted with, if not actual initiates of, the ancient Mystery teachings.

Now it should be noted that the term 'initiate' by this time did not have the same weight as it would have had in similar circles at a time when the Mysteries were much purer in their spiritual content and were not as diluted as they had become by the beginning of our era. Indeed pagan initiation by Jesus's time had taken on at least as much the philistinic attraction of political expediency as it had of spiritual enlightenment! Nevertheless the knowledge possessed by the early Christians who had converted from the older Mysteries was vital to the formation of the new young Church's vibrant spiritual content.[15]

THE DELICATE MAGIC OF THE EARLY CHURCH

Thus the magic of the very early Gnostic Church was very much to do with its infusion by a tradition and a trinitarianism as old almost as mankind himself. It was a tradition possessed of a wisdom of infinite depth, coherence and beauty, for it was based on a precise, even mathematical cosmology, which knew or had known at first hand the spiritual entities which originated and animated every single body in the universe, from the Initiate's own, to the Earth itself, to the ones magnificent beyond all imagining revolving in the heavens.

Of course it was a gigantic task the Church had here in trying to bring all of this to bear upon the Incarnation, not least because the Mystery traditions had by this time almost vanished themselves anyway! For it was merely echoes of this wisdom that was resounding in the early Church. The most astute of its converts nevertheless knew at least the essence of these traditions of which the trinitarian concept of the Godhead, inclusive of its feminine aspect imaged forth in man, was primary.

And despite the fact that these enlightened people were usually anathematized by orthodoxy in the end, it was nonetheless their work and effort that ensured the injection of the pure spirit into the Church at all in the first place. And the survival of this spirit, even in the very limited manifestation it now displays, continues to rely to some extent upon them!

The Gnostic's key to spiritual knowledge lay in their understanding of the principle or power of initiation as such, and for these early Christian initiates, what was most remarkable of all about the Incarnation was that it had achieved something on the broad stage of human history that had previously been capable of achievement or permissible only within the highly secretive confines of the initiation temples. For in the ancient Mysteries the neophyte or initiand (i.e. one who is to be initiated) always received his initiation and his deepest spiritual inspirations in more or less out-of-body states through a direct contact via the soul with the divinity, who afterwards nevertheless always withdrew from him. The new initiate could then go out into the wider world once more and duely impart, in correct measure, to his flock, what he had mystically learned. In that spiritual event which came in time to be regarded as, or called, the Incarnation however, something entirely new was perceived to have entered into this whole precess. For here the divinity came to be regarded as having decended directly, via John's baptism, into one Jesus of Nazerath, one held to be human by all means, but one who had also possessed the astounding capability of hosting the divinity in such a manner that it could actually remain with him fully consciously, and moreover go with him in the fullest physical sense out into the world, passing with him even through the gate of death!

Now this was unheard of in the Mysteries before Jesus. Apart from anything else, the very idea of a God dying was a totally and utterly new one. For it was neither thought possible nor necessary for this ever to happen. In the divine sacrifice however which constituted the most fundamental aspect of the Incarnation, it became increasingly obvious that this was the extraordinary way, indeed the *only way* in which man himself could ever now progress and hope to be raised to greater heights, even to godhood, in the future.

The physical as well as the spiritual consequences of this Event were thus seen to be of the most extraordinary and miraculous nature. Not only that, but the whole initiation process was thereby seen to have moved to an entirely new level in that the personality, even the very physical body itself, was given an emphasis it never had or needed before in initiation rites and practises. It was in fact the outwardness, even the historicity, of the whole process of gaining or perceiving the spirit that was now being emphasised, something which gave initiation a completely new dimension compared to the former method of absolute inwardness and secrecy practised in the confines of the old temples.

Something of universal importance, something which had a direct relevance to every human being of whatever race, religion, colour or creed was thus seen to have occurred. For initiation was now conceived of as being accessible to everyone and not just to a chosen few, as had always been the case in the past. *Now*, it was perceived, everyone could have 'gnosis', could know God for themselves. That or this was the real secret of the Incarnation. And when the word of it spread, inevitably spiritual turmoil was the result!

THE CHURCH TOUGHENS UP!

And indeed, that turmoil was the primary feature of The Gnosis is very well known! It was also however that very same feature of the times which impelled the growing Christian Church into a spurning of Gnosticism as such. For although the early Church Fathers may have been aware in varying degrees of initiation, of just how the Incarnation was an inevitable outcome and development of the ancient Mystery tradition, they could also see that if the Church did not become properly constituted, in a temporal way at least, it had no hope at all of surviving, spiritually or otherwise, as an institutionalized force in the outer world, something which they of course felt of necessity it should be. It was in the process of achieving this latter purely temporal goal however that the Mystery knowledge eventually became totally seperated from the established Church, and in time almost entirely lost to it as a vital and spiritually nourishing force.

So although it is easy to ascertain that in the Gnostic Church there was a widespread acceptance of the fact that the Incarnation Event constituted a grand renewal of the Mystery tradition, it also has to be accepted that this awareness gradually and sadly diminished as time went on. Rather than having the implications of this manifold connection with the ancient wisdom elaborated and clarified so that it could foster a rich spiritual consciousness within its congregations, the Church developed rather into a dogmatic and theocratic institution.

For in many respects it merely reinstated, with a slightly altered constitution, the exoteric aspect of the old law-ridden Mosaic religion which it was the Church's very initial inspiration to overcome or remove.

So from the defeat of Gnosticism onwards, what constituted the spiritual element in the Church took on a very different guise. For in truth spirituality then was split off from the mainstream activity of the Church and gradually became merely a sort of sidelined branch of it. In time it proved to be nothing less than a breeding ground for all kinds of strange activities, for the cultivation of what someone once disparragingly termed 'mystic mud', and it was a splitting that also proved a surefire strategy for the eventual establishment of mere superstition as the only real spiritual element in the lives of many ordinary folk. And the great catastropy was that eventually, pursuit of the true Mystery spirit became an object of fear, suspicion, and even outright hatred, something to which the primary dynamics of Medieval history especially, gives us ample testimony.

The true Spirit of God in man of course cannot ever be put down. And this is especially the case from the time it achieved its unique and powerful uplift via the Event of the Incarnation. The existence of Esoteric Christianity is proof of this.

Chapter Five

THE FORGING OF AN ORTHODOXY

In our own day, history, in a spiritual sense, is actually repeating itself. For it is obvious that a grassroots change in attitude is afoot nowadays regarding the spirit and spirituality generally. The very deepest of questions are stirring within the hearts and souls of growing numbers of people from all walks of life. And matters pertaining to the soul and spirit being of man are increasingly felt to be central to the proper resolution of so many of our modern world's ills. However dimly, inarticulately, or naively it might sometimes be felt or expressed, there is nevertheless a real and perceptible movement towards a resurrection or re-definition of this body of sublime wisdom and knowledge with which the ancients were so familiar.

In the world generally, but also within the body of the Christian Church itself, there are indications which are strongly suggestive of a call back towards this lost or forgotten knowledge. The growing interest in early Celtic spirituality is one, perhaps the most potentially promising, of all these signs. For following fast on the heels of the upsurge of interest in all things Celtic, the early Celtic Church itself is gradually being discerned as having been infused with some vibrant, almost magical, spiritual power which in a very short space of time is seen to have transformed the existing pagan Celtic culture of old Hibernia into a new, vital, and Christianized force.

For it is becoming increasingly obvious to historians, academics and others that that which lived in the ancient soul of Ireland and which had, through the power of the Incarnation, become infused and invigorated with a mighty new spiritual impulse, provided the chief foundation upon which the light of learning and civilization generally was kept alive in Europe at a time of ever increasing chaos and darkness.

We have been indicating hitherto briefly and in general terms the reasons for this cultural decline in the early centuries of our era. And these can be summarized and simplified by highlighting the defeat of the ancient light-filled esoteric knowledge in the East by the 4th century, as well as the growing Barbarian invasions which caused chaos and the eventual break-up of the Roman Empire. There were also of course other less obvious factors.

But all of these adverse conditions constituted the chief grounds for the development of a hardheaded and repressive Roman Christian orthodoxy which, as the centuries passed, became ever more dogmatic and militant. And the end result of all this was a slow but sure sinking of Western civilization into a confused social stew of superstition, intellectual dogmatism and spiritual darkness, i.e. into what are generally regarded as the Dark Ages.

THE MAGIC OF IRELAND

From time immemorial however the island of Ireland was known to have possessed a strange, magical, and light-filled quality. So much so that even the hard and matter-of-fact consciousness of the Roman Emperors and their cohorts always hesitated when they came to the thought of hauling this mysterious outpost into their Empire. And the result was that the Romans never darkened the doors of old Hibernia, and it was thereby left to its own cocooned but spiritually productive mystical destiny. And this most surely was the work of a benign Providence!

For the soul of the country thus remained, as far as the ancient wisdom was concerned, pure and relatively undisturbed, and the might of Roman legalism and its attendant militarism was never allowed to blemish it. It was as if a garden was being preserved by a wise working of Providence in which the seed-Word of the Gospel could in time find its most fertile soil. For the Hiberno-Celtic soul was one that had been thoroughly suffused, perhaps more than any other folk-soul on the whole of the Earth, with the sublime fragrance of the ancient wisdom, so much so that the land of Erin had acquired in ancient stories and legends the reputation of being nothing less than a piece of Paradise itself! It can thus be imagined how this island had become by the time of Christ a well-formed vessel into which the new outpouring of the spirit into the world through the advent of the Incarnation, could flow. And when this began to actually happen, it was duely received there and integrated into the soul of the nation with a powerful strength and grace. In this way the Incarnation imparted to the soul and spirit of the people of Erin, a resilience and a quality of endurance unmatched in its purity. Indeed many sense this Hibernian spirit even in our own day as still possessing something of its original grace and magical essence. And the current general upsurge or renewal of interest in the ancient spirit, especially that of the Celtic Church, indicates this very strongly.

A great spiritual search is in progress! And one of the most instructive and revealing aspects of this search, especially as it relates to Esoteric Christianity, is in how it teaches the seeker to observe this spirit to have been so vibrantly alive and thriving within cultures and traditions so totally different from one another as the ancient Celtic one was from the ancient Palistinian! Moreover it is this very universality that speaks the promise that this spirit of true love and cosmic wisdom can be revived once more in our own time.

For it was the same all-inclusive Spirit of the Incarnation that can be seen to be at work here in the Irish soul in the 5th to the 8th centuries, that was also at work in the Eastern Gnosis, a few centuries earlier.

Though obviously having its prehistory in, and being nurtured and elaborated through the more or less direct influence of the purely Eastern Mystery wisdom-traditions, this Spirit however took an incredibly strong root in the fertile ground of the Celtic soul of the Irish.

The forces inherent in the Western hemisphere are, generally speaking, always of a harder, rougher or more earthy nature, in contradistinction to the 'etherial' East. It can thus be said that this incarnational spirit underwent a strengthening in its transplantation from the East into the Western Celtic consciousness. For here in this green Isle it germinated, grew and blossomed at a time when it had been well-neigh obliterated in the East. Further, one can see how this spirit even took on a more formed life in the Celtic West. For after its initial incubation in the East where it had shone gloriously for a couple of centuries, it is nevertheless seen by the 4th century to have almost completely wilted away there under the influence of an alien power. Now this was the power which had been concentrating itself in and around the military might of Rome, and was something which had been developing for many centuries, even prior to the Incarnation. And it was the selfsame power which was set to become the foundation of the future Church's Western orthodoxy.

We will in a later chapter be looking much more closely at this aspect of our spiritual history and the vital part played in it by the Celtic Church, all of which in truth set the stage and defined the content, of even our current orthodoxy.

SAUL OF TARSUS

Now however we must shift our focus somewhat. For in order to gain an understanding of the complex web of forces at work in this forging of an orthodoxy, we need to look closely at the Mystery nature of a hugely important post-incarnational event in the East. For this was a pivotal event, as a result of which, what was eventually to become this aforementioned Roman Western orthodoxy, managed to establish itself at all in the first place. For the manner in which this shift towards the West actually took place is, though quite paradoxical, very revealing both as to how the Church became established, but also how it in effect came to reject the spiritual core of its true mission in the process.

What we will look at now therefore, in order to illustrate this clearly, is the famous and dramatic conversion to Christianity of one of its greatest initial opponents and haters, one Saul of Tarsus, later to be known as the great St. Paul.

For apart from Christ himself it is to this particular individual that the Church looks as the supreme elucidator of its spiritual mission and purpose in the world.

Now it is hardly necessary to recount here the details of St. Paul's initiation into the Mystery nature of Christ.[16] For it is an event that has in the course of time actually taken on an archetypal dimension, something which nevertheless does nothing to diminish the impact and implications of its purely *historic* actuality. We will however outline its essential features in an attempt to highlight its importance as the key transitional event which cleared the way for the new spirit-light of the Incarnation to radiate outwards from its cocooned or crysallis-like beginnings in Palestine and into the world in its full colour, brightness and purity, unimpeded by any kind of antiquated or religiously orientated customs. For this latter possibility indeed posed a great initial danger to the radient power of the Incarnation, given the strength of the tradition and culture in which it was enacted, and by virtue of which the very 'crysallis' was in the first place able to form at all.

So let us imagine this impeccably Jewish Saul riding high on his horse one day towards the town of Damascus, carrying with him the legal instruments necessary to eliminate as many as possible of the (to him) absurd and highly disruptive sect (the Christians) which had recently arisen in Judaism and had been fast gaining converts from the orthodox faith. It was a very deep and powerful faith we must remember, the observances of which Saul meticulously kept and whose customs, beliefs and legalities he was totally dedicated to upholding, down to the last jot and tittle. Saul, a man of the highest possible standing and learning within his long, proud, and deeply religious culture, was no doubt infuriated by these wierdos in Damascus, and gladly accepted the work of getting rid of them there, or anywhere else for that matter! For they were teaching what sounded to him like absolute blasphemies, and were saying things and evolving practises which seemed, apart from penetrating right through to the very heart of all that he held most zealously to be true about God and the world, nevertheless could be nothing but the most malignant types of inventive nonsense. For they were spreading stories abroad which, although they claimed them to be the absolute truth, must, to any sensible person, be nothing but the purest of pure fiction! And fiction was something Saul had very little time for at all, whatever form it took! For he was, true to the finest qualities of his forebares, a man, in all matters, of purest fact, and this was most especially the case when it came to matters concerning God and his holy Law. What these people were spreading abroad simply couldn't be true! That the one they claimed as their God, a mere carpenter from Nazareth by all accounts, had actually arisen from the dead, indeed! What absolute and utter nonsense! He, Saul, was going to make plain to them the real truth and was, in no uncertain terms, going to put them straight about religion, resurrection, God, Holy Writ and especially the Law of Moses!

Providence however, as it often does in even the most meticulously laid plans, intervened. And Saul's fearsome will and determination was to be turned right around and redirected towards, for him, the most unlikely and unexpected of goals.

Now, the duration or outwardly visible signs of the actual conversion or initiation experience of Paul, where he was struck from his high horse to the ground by a blinding light, accompanied by other phenomena, this should be of little consequence to anyone who is trying to assess it from the purely *spiritual* point of view. What should really only matter from this point of view is the actual *inner* content of the experience as such.

And it is this latter chiefly we shall try to do here, however tentatively. It has to be tentative. For by their very nature spiritual or religious experiences can be extraordinarily subtle as well as being, of course, deeply meaningful for the individual concerned, and as such do not yield themselves to easy or generalized interpretation.

However, in this special case of St. Paul's we have one which is particularly significant and instructive (in so far as we can at all evaluate it). For as well as its undoubted impact upon Paul himself, it was also one which was to have the most profound influence on the whole future development of Western history. For this single episode in the New Testament in truth represents the very fulcrum through which the Christian faith becomes established in its own right in the wider world, and not merely as another sect within Judaism, something which it was in fact in danger, or actually in the process, of becoming. This is a view widely accepted by Christian historians of all types regarding Paul and his initiation.

Thus that Paul's conversion was of a most extraordinary nature there can be no doubt at all! (At the same time it must be pointed out that Paul's is only one, albiet the best known, of a great variety of extraordinary events indicated in the New Testament, relating the manner in which growing numbers of people of all types and classes, of greatly varied backgrounds, cultures and temperaments, were drawn to Christ soon after the first Easter Sunday morning. For people everywhere were being moved to the very depths of their being by the news of the Incarnation. And more than anything else it was the individualized aspect of the way in which the Incarnation initiation began to work in the world that was its most significant and essential characteristic. It had the power to touch and influence people in the most extraordinary and diverse of ways).

ST. PAUL'S INITIATION

In ascertaining the spiritual importance of St. Paul's initiatory experience however we have to be aware that it was of such an order that not only did it have the effect of instilling within him the great power necessary to the laying of the foundations of the new Church, something which, a few years after he had fully assimilated the experience, he set about doing with an almost superhuman zeal and energy! But his experience also gave him the inspiration necessary to communicate vitally through his inspired writings something of the real spiritual essence of Christ to peoples as greatly differing in soul and character as we are from say people of one thousand or two thousand years ago, or as different in temperament and manners as say the Chinese are from Irishmen. Paul's letters appear as fresh, subtle and alive today as when they were first written nearly 2000 years ago!

It is obvious therefore that Paul has much to teach us regarding the true nature of the Christ Mystery and that furthermore he must be given very careful consideration in any study such as we are undertaking here. So what we must first be quite clear about is that Paul's experience on the Road to Damascus was in fact nothing less than a true initiation, in the deepest possible meaning of this term. It was in fact a genuine initiation into the Christ Mystery. And he gives us a real hint as to how this spiritual event took place in his soul and body in those places in his writings where he refers to this new Mystery of Christ. This is something which he does most openly and directly in his famous letter to the Colossians. We thus may come to understand that Paul's 'secret' can be nothing less than an absolute initiatory certainty that his God had shaken off his own ancient and tightly guarded Mystery nature, emerged from the secrecy of the temple, and had in fact incarnated into the earthly world! Not only that but Paul could see that his God, whom he had up to this point known only in a predominantly intellectual, faithful, mystical, or some other more or less abstract way, had assumed a living and vibrant form, an immanent Presence and tangibility in the world, through none other than this very Jesus that he (Paul) had been up to then so totally dismissive of!

It was a most extraordinary and shattering realization! For he could now clearly see, (and this is evident not necessarily from his account of his initiation, but from his writings generally), that this Jesus Christ had been able to miraculously unite himself with what we may call the very bio-etheric stuff of the Earth itself; and moreover that he did this in such an all-embracing fashion that it was no longer possible to truely know one's own bodily self in one's ordinary awake consciousness anymore without acknowledging the astonishing fact that, in one's deepest conscious essence, somehow one had become identical with this Christ!

That Paul experienced all of this can be, without question, deduced from his writings, which are quite literally, saturated with the Spirit of Christ. For coming to the fullest possible realization of this sun-filled transformation of the Earth, meant also for Paul that his very own inner being itself underwent a veritable transfiguration. From there on it is evident he could no longer conceive of his own, or indeed any mortal or earthly body, in any other way than that of a living temple of the Christ Being. It was *the* most astonishing revelation possible for Saul and one we can share with him through his wonderful letters in the New Testament, the study of which are in fact necessary to any full and thoroughly modern Christian initiation.

Thus on the Road to Damascus we can say that the powerful monotheistic spirit of Paul's noble race, a spirit which indwelt and motivated him so singlemindedly and zealously, was in fact Christened through him! Prior to his initiation, the Incarnation was something Paul simply could not believe, for he had no reason to. In his initiation experience however his spiritual faculties were opened and activated in such a way that no amount of reasoning power, no law, dogma, or ancient doctrines, however much he believed in them, could deny the reality of what he now beheld. This Jesus Christ was indeed alive! He had seen him, spoken to him, touched him! There was absolutely no doubt whatsoever about his living Presence, however extraordinary this may have seemed.

Now there are with regard to Paul's initiation both parallels with the ancient Mystery initiations as well as radical departures from them, which mark out Paul's as one in which a most remarkable transition actually took place. For on the one hand, when we examine it in the light of the ancient Mysteries, it can be seen that there were compressed into this dramatic incident of Saul's conversion the principal features of all classic initiations where the disciple is led to the God through a death, or out-of-body experience, and then, some time later, returns or is 'reborn' again as a totally new man. This was the universal standard of initiation in the old temples. And one of the most significant outcomes of it was that always afterwards the disciple could no longer conceive of himself in the manner in which ordinary mortals conceive of themselves and their moral relationship to the world. The new initiate's experiences then were such that all matters concerning faith, beliefs and dogmas, all rules and regulations of whatever kind were simply swept aside, their usefullness having now been organically outlived by the power and privilige bestowed on the disciple by the actual initiation itself. This can easily be intellectually comprehended. For at the point of initiation the disciple no longer merely believes or knows. Then he truely *sees*. He has achieved gnosis, *per se*. His prior merely intellectual knowing which he acquired as a neophyte has now become actual spiritual seeing! He has ascended, in short, from the status of neophyte to that of Initiate! And in achieving this full degree of initiation, the God duely bestows his own immortality upon him. In this way the old mortal Saul became the reborn spirit-filled and re-named Christian Initiate, Paul.

Apart however from these classic similarities to older forms of initiation, Paul's experience is also different in many respects. And the most obvious of these is the manner in which he was able to achieve through his initiation the knowledge and awareness that not only did the God, the Christ Being, take absolute possession of his own (Paul's) soul and spirit, but this spirit took possession of his *body* too. Moreover he saw that this was also something which, to an equal or lesser degree, could now apply to everyone under the sun! Thus when Paul reveals his 'secret' to the Colossians that 'Christ is in you', he literally means, and is absolutely certain of, precisely that! And all of his instructions, admonitions, prayers and blessings throughout his letters in the New Testament are inspired attempts to encourage his congregations to awaken to this awsome yet wonderful reality. Christ has done an immense spiritual Deed for you, was Paul's basic message. Now you yourself must do the rest.

It was, he tried to indicate in accordance with his own initiation, as if a spiritual lightening flash had impregnated the entire physical universe and everything in it now possessed the possibility of a divine renewal through the Incarnation.

And so it was in this way that a consciousness of the global Church of Christ began to awaken, first in Paul, and then in the hearts and souls of Christ's first followers. And through his tireless missionary journeys, his sermons, talks, and especially for us, his letters, Paul set the tone of this new Church and tuned its pitch to the highest possible spiritual and moral standards.

It was in this way that early Christian orthodoxy, as a power in its own right, independent of the Jewish one in which it was conceived and gestated, arose directly out of Paul's initiatives which were in their turn born *in toto* out of his all-embracing Damascus initiation. The later highly dogmatic Christian orthodoxy that superseded Paul's early free spiritual one was not of his making. For the emergence of this later Roman orthodoxy can be traced directly back to the fact that the link with the ancient Mystery knowledge was conveniently forgotten about or indeed totally severed from the Church's early consciousness, posing as it did in its Gnostic individualism a threat to the centralist designs of the emerging theocracy.

Paul himself however was acutely aware of the need to acknowledge and maintain this vital link with the ancient Mystery wisdom. And this is most evident from the manner in which he approached the wise men of Athens with his revolutionary insights.

For when St. Paul, in the course of one of his great missionary endeavours, was preaching in this ancient city, his words were met with the greatest of interest, especially by the philosophically and religiously-minded people there. And they took to listening to him to such an extent that he was eventually given the great opportunity to address their famous philosophical court, the Council of the Areopagus, one of the most distinguished assemblies of the old Greek world which met on the Hill of Mars.

Now the men of this gathering presented Paul and his insights with a great challenge indeed! For undoubtedly they would have been thoroughly familiar with all the extant Mystery wisdom and knowledge of the day, with all the theologies and philosophical systems available in the world at that spiritually and culturally vibrant time and place.

And the manner in which Paul met this challenge is most significant, because he felt compelled, through the power of his own particular initiation into the spiritual Presence of Christ in the world, to draw attention to the fact that now all Mystery or initiation knowledge had been totally renewed. Not only that, but even those aspects of it which were hitherto not understood, now stood fully revealed in and to the world. And all of this was due to the person of Jesus Christ and his supreme act of sacrifice. Paul expounded his teaching very ingeniously by drawing his distinguished listeners' attention to the fact that the 'unknown God' of their own religions,[17] the One but secret God who stood behind all the most ancient of the Mystery religions of the world, is none other than Jesus Christ himself!

Now it was obviously *this* aspect of Paul's knowledge more than anything else which most excited, fascinated and stirred the Athenians into giving him a greater hearing than he might otherwise have got. For in it they deeply sensed that, if true, it represented something important, vital, and essentially new in the spiritual life of civilized man. The hidden and secret God of the Mysteries was finally revealed, Paul was brazenly telling them! There is no more need of images of him other than the one you can learn to see with your own inner eye, the eye of your heart, of the soul, the eye in fact of purest Sophia-imbued spiritual love. The old ways of secret magical initiation, confined to a chosen or specially selected few, are truely over, he was saying. A new era in the history of the soul of man was beginning. Now each man can learn the truth about the One God and even see him for himself imaged forth to the world in the One man who stood, lived and died as a representative both of God himself and of all men for all time: the Godman Jesus Christ.

But although the Athenians were thoroughly interested in Paul's teaching they were also astonished and totally dumbfounded when the kernel of it finally became fully apparent to them, the axis upon which it rested, or the centrepoint around which it revolved and without which it fell utterly and totally apart. The spirit of the Athenians was indeed willing to listen, debate, speculate and argue, but in the final analysis their capacity for faith was too thin and lacked the flesh or blood-warmth to accept the core truth of St. Paul's proclamation, i.e. the astonishing reality of the Incarnation itself as the apotheosis of the power of love. For this indeed was its real kernel! Love however, to these learned gentlemen, represented something entirely different from what Paul had to reveal about it. And this was where the real difficulties lay. Sophisticated argument and debate was something the Athenians were no doubt very good at and loved to indulge in. But the idea of 'love incarnate' was something they had much difficulty with.

THE GOSPEL OF LOVE

Paul's Gospel message however, which he proclaimed out the warmth of a purely Sophia-inspired knowledge of the spirit, which he had gained in a manner that gave him the status, authority and power of a real Initiate of old, was as much about the simple practise of spiritual love as a prerequisite to the gaining of the new spirit-vision, as it was about anything else. Paul's teaching deeply emphasised that love alone was the route now to be taken by those who wished to acquire knowledge of God. More than anything else he stressed that love was the tremendous and primary power it was now necessary to cultivate in order to open up the vision in the soul of God's countenance revealed to the world through Jesus Christ. Thus Paul's teaching was far more to do with this love-imbued simplicity of soul than with the intellectual power inherent in a knowledge cultivated for its own sake, or for the sake of material or temporal advancement. It was a teaching that was at once both spiritually profound and humanly simple, and in this combination lay its great power, wisdom and wide appeal. It was in fact a way for shepherds as well as kings, as the Gospel's Nativity story beautifully and very clearly indicates. The life of feeling was thus to be raised to a level on par with, if not actually higher, than the life of thought itself. It was however this dual nature of it which also constituted the tricky ground on which the men of Athens stumbled. For simple shepherd-like loving humility was hardly a feature that figured prominently in the hearts of these serious-minded and sophisticate statesmen.

The writer of the Acts however, was inspired to draw attention to this episode in Paul's life because he knew, like Paul himself, that the new Way of the spirit ushered in through Christ, only made sense when knowledge of it was linked and even integrated very consciously with the Mystery wisdom and temple knowledge that existed in the world from the remotest aeons of antiquity. Because of this the learned men of Athens certainly sensed 'something' in Paul's teaching, but they lacked either the simplicity or the wisdom, (or both), to be moved by the Gospel in any significant way.

However not all of them were of such a hardened disposition. Perhaps not in Athens, but in other places many, of the 'initiates' were won over to the Gospel and they soon constituted in fact a significant part of the early congregations of the new Church of Christ[18]. In Athens however we know from the Acts of the Apostles that at least one distinguished initiate was converted by Paul. And indeed it was this one vitally important individual who proved to be instrumental in maintaining for the later Church the crucial link with the ancient Mystery wisdom which was so much a feature of the very early Church.

The individual to whom we refer is known to us as Dionysius the Areopagite (so named because he was a member of the above mentioned Areopagus Assembly), and his significance in the history of the Church is almost of an order equal to that of Paul himself, although as yet this is not generally recognised. Nevertheless an acceptance of the relevance of Dionysius to a proper understanding of the relationship between the ancient wisdom and the new Christian Way is gradually growing, and as it does the stature of Dionysius increases accordingly. For more than anyone else, even more than Paul himself in a certain sense, it is through Dionysius (who became Paul's pupil) that this link is most cogently established. And as such a link becomes more and more necessary for the Church to recognize, so too will the place of Dionysius in it gain its deserved and proper recognition.

Chapter Six

THE BIRTH OF THE HERETIC AND
THE 'HOUSE ARREST' OF THE SPIRIT

We shall in a later chapter deal more thoroughly with the question of Dionysius the Areopagite (see p 106 ff). Here however it is necessary to establish a way of recognising those forces which, after Paul's initial foundational work had been done, there soon began to arise within the body of the Church, forces which worked quite contrary to the pure, open, and free spirit of Paul and the other early initiates.

Now this repressive trend within the new Church showed itself from a very early date and has, needless to say, a very complex genesis. And it would be all too easy to form misguided opinions and conclusions about it, and, as so often happens with those who produce or acquire misinformation about Christianity generally, evolve personal attitudes to Christ which in reality amount to nothing less than a throwing out of the baby with the bathwater! A certain emotional tolerance which takes into account the all too common weaknesses inherent in human nature, and which it is the very business of religion and spirituality to sensibly manage, must come into play here. And it is only possible to be tolerant in one's attitude to this repression, early institutionalized in the Church, if one attempts to gain a sense of not only the magnitude of the perceived implications for the whole world occasioned by the Incarnation, but also for the great practical and intellectual difficulties attendant upon its proper elaboration and evangelization. Now these in fact are the very kinds of tensions which constituted, one can say, the fundamental dynamic of The Gnosis. So let us therefore look more closely at all of this.

Once the word of it began to spread, the Incarnation quickly became the centre-point of a kind of spiritual vortex towards which every conceivable philosophical, theological and mythological interpretation of the world and man became drawn, and against which all extant Mystery knowledge and wisdom generally, soon came to be measured. Individuals and groups of great diversity thus began to emerge and engage themselves actively with it all over the Middle East.

Now in our own day we have become very used to the concept, indeed the proliferating reality, of religious cults and sects of all kinds. However, in the time of the early Gnosis, into which the light of the Incarnation shone without any questioning at all as to the reality of the unifying, healing, and loving spiritual Presence it bequeated, the divisive nature which *we* naturally associate with sects as such was hardly a factor in the spiritual thought and lives of those who were following the new Way. However, given the very imperfect nature of human beings, and the conflicts that nearly always lie buried within even the most spiritually developed and outwardly placid of souls, it was inevitable that once the initial light of the Incarnation began to fade somewhat, and the pure spiritual balm of its healing became clouded, the inevitable differing interpretations of the nature of Christ would have the effect of stirring up these inner psychic difficulties.

So, conflicts, personal arguments, antipathies, even downright hatreds soon began to show their all-too-human and ugly faces in the light of the Incarnation, from which nothing after all, according to the Gospel, was to be hidden anyway. And when psychological and psychic conflicts such as these are harnessed onto the spiritual potency of an event as profound and meaningful for man and the world as the Incarnation in fact was, it is perhaps inevitable that our spiritual history would have had to witness a most extraordinary eventually. And that was the birth on the human level of beings which are, ideally speaking, purely spiritual or demonic in origin or kind! For this is precisely what begins to happen in the early Church! Out of the spiritual cauldron which constituted The Gnosis, and into which every imaginable magical and mythical potion was being stirred, there was born a veritable monster, that most despised of all human types ever to exist - the heretic! And the birth of the heretic can in fact be taken as that psychic event which marks the beginning of the end of what may be prosaically called the honeymoon of the Incarnation. For by managing to give a human countenance to this ideal and conceptual device of the demonized human being, the new Church derrogated unto herself a deified, theocratic and spiritual power which was nothing less than universal. Sadly however, it was also in the manner of this derrogation, i.e. in the methods the Church used to enforce this unilateral assertion of spiritual authority, that the initiatory and spiritually potent kernel of the Incarnation itself, i.e. the freedom to *choose* one's individual relationship to the Christ, was to be made totally illigitimate. A centralized and deified spiritual authority was emerging with an enormous and fearful power for both good *and* evil and one simply *had* to obey this............or else! (The word heretic, it should be carefully noted, actually means 'to choose'!) Freedom of the spirit was thus fast becoming a thing of the past!

FAITH V KNOWLEDGE - THE PERENNIAL DILEMMA

Now all of this speaks of what may be referred to as 'temporalism', at the expence of 'spiritualism'[19] being that force by which the Church was gaining ground in the world as a new religious and, actually unique, institution. As indicated earlier, the Church had some way to find its own very clear identity as an organized power in the world in contradistinction to every other spiritual grouping of which there was a great proliferation at this time. For coming to the realization, however imperfectly, of the meaning of the Incarnation, and subsequently and inevitably speculating as to the manner of it's proper evangelization, this was something which taxed every soul who was drawn to Jesus Christ, in the deepest and most inward of ways. On a basic level this meant of course communion and community. On another level however it also meant teaching, learning and instruction. And understandably many voices were beginning to assert themselves with varying degrees of intensity and often with very particular viewpoints, emphasis, and practises to legitimize, within this thriving spiritual milue.

There was however one overall linking characteristic in all of these various teachings and practises. And that was that they were invariably attempting to elaborate the ancient wisdom in the light of the Incarnation and to integrate this elaboration into the new vision which the Incarnation inspired. This of course was a spiritual work *par excellence*, and a work also indeed of knowledge, or of pure 'gnosis'. Gnosis in this sense was therefore seen to be something quite distinct from faith as such. The problem here of course was nothing new. It is in fact a perennial problem regarding religion: the polarity of faith v knowledge. It was sharpened here however in the Gnostic Church because of the presence in it of the by now well developed Greek philosophical way of thinking. For knowledge had, or has, always far more to do with thought than with feelings. Faith or feelings however were not a problem at all in the early Church. One could say in fact that turning 'shepherd-like' in faith towards Christ was a relatively simple matter in many ways. Christ after all was just another name for God in the minds of ordinary people.

However, if the new faith was going to be a strong one, the reasons for turning to Christ had to be clear, especially given the milue in which the new Church was being formed. As such the new faith demanded great articulation on the part of those who would wish to become the leaders or elucidators of this growing trend towards belief in Christ as opposed to other deities. However, it soon came to be observed by the more serious minded and erudite of souls who were working with Christ, that whereas the Gnostic aspect of the new religion led far too easily into airy-fairy speculation about this, that, and every other blessed thing, the faith aspect was a much more practical and down-to-earth affair. Faith as such had thus much more appeal and far greater possibilities as an instrument, a tool, or a power by or through which the newly emerging and necessary Church institutions could be forged. To these realists faith was in fact seen to be far more containable in its dynamics than knowledge or gnosis. And this knowledge aspect, it was construed, would be far better left to those who could be trusted to properly dispence it in the overall interests of the growing Church.

It was thus through the restrictive tendencies characteristic of less spiritually adventurous and more worldly orientated souls who advocated such a path, that the young Church was able to establish its identity by a gradual eschewing of the Mystery knowledge. Gnosis in other words, was abandoned in favour of a far more faith-orientated constitution, a faith allied now alas to the predominantly temporal vision which followed as a matter of course upon the abandonment of the spirit-imbued Mystery knowledge.

Though in time the writings of St. Paul actually took the status of scripture and were eventually even to become the largest single part of the official New Testament Cannon, the great irony is that the Church formed itself into its deified universality and global catholic unity by effectively sidelining the importance and meaning of their primary content! It may be of course that there was no other way to forge this unity! This however does not alter the ambiguity inherent in the whole process. For the superiority of Paul's initiatory authority shines through so strongly in his writings that they could not or cannot possibly be ignored by anyone who desires true knowledge of the Incarnation. Yet what Paul was essentially saying all through his writings could not but in a sense give rise to the very kinds of speculation that the Church wished to stamp out! For Paul was in truth endeavouring always to point out the way in which each individual could attain or aspire to the grand initiation he himself had received. The very manner and method by which he had come to know Christ meant that he could not but do otherwise. So in many ways he was, (to bluntly turn around one of his own very well known phrases), a bit of a spiritual thorn in the flesh of the Church!

The unity eventually attained by the Church in this less than straightforward fashion in its dealing with the initiate Paul and his writings, could therefore of course only be a temporary one, somewhat artificial, surely temporal, and most certainly not of a truely spiritual nature. The subsequent history and current state of the Church prove this beyond dispute. The great mystery indeed of Christianity surely has as much to do with the fact that it still exists in the world at all as something of a coherent or clearly identifiable spiritual force after two thousand years of its confused, traumatic and turbulent history, as it has to do with the miraculous nature of the Event which constitutes its spiritual core! This strength and continued relevance of Christianity to the world, in its turn, is certainly due in no small measure to the fact that the Christ Being continued and still continues to empower individuals in truely esoteric, inward or even mystical, as well as of course in more outward, ways. And Paul's writings have very much to do with this!

For the attraction and spiritual superiority of Paul's letters lie precisely in the fact that they highlight the essential and necessary mystical core of Christianity, while yet combining this with the wide-awake clarity of a pure conceptual thinking. In reading Paul's letters one cannot but be struck by the manner in which he struggles to awaken people out of an older, more symbolic type of consciousness, and into one based on a clear perception of the *word* as such. In this sense we can say that, for his time, Paul was being thoroughly scientific. Furthermore Paul's writings form a perfect balance to the somewhat allegorical, often parabolic, or even symbolic, nature of the Gospel stories themselves. We need have no qualms in asserting therefore that any future re-integration of the Mystery nature of Christ into the body of the Church's teachings will of necessity have to take the writings of St. Paul as a foundation. This eventuality will of course constitute a great advance for the Mystery nature and spiritual power of the Church, as well as highlighting the prophetic nature and all-embracing inclusiveness of the spirit of Sophia herself, the undoubted source of Paul's inspiration.

* * *

By the 3rd century the strategy which the Church was using to establish its orthodoxy, i.e. the seperating of faith from knowledge, produced its dividends. For a powerful new and fully-fledged religion had arrived on the scene! The Christians had managed to establish themselves in the world by rooting out what now came to be regarded with ever increasing venom as the 'Gnostic heresies'. And the Church was now busy with the serious work of evolving what amounted to an increasingly hate-filled theology of heresy.

This latter was in fact something which only revealed the full extent of its latent and awful demonic power with the inception of that most fearsome and vile of all male-dominated institutions ever conceived by human kind – the Holy Inquisition of the Middle Ages.

For in splitting off reason, knowledge, and wisdom as an ideal to be cultivated by all, and not just by a privileged priesthood, (and this at bottom is what the rejection of The Gnosis amount to!), the suppressed light of the benign spirit of Sophia could hardly work openly in the world at all any more. What was even worse however is that this spirit was manipulated, twisted and turned into its very opposite, the spectral or death-like shadow of a darkened spiritual power which finds its spiritual food deep in the baser instincts of the human soul.

For this is the selfsame negative power which in a spiritual sense has man's proneness to sin as its template and, even worse, has the very embodiment of evil as its goal. It is moreover a subtle and highly persuasive power, deceptive in the extreme, which lends itself very easily to those who, for whatever reason, are prepared to exploit it for their own dubious ends. And such exploitation, ultimately of course serving the purposes of evil, is always evident anywhere and everywhere goodness and wisdom are abandoned.

THE WESTERN CONSCIOUSNESS IS SPLIT

So it was in this way that the consciousness of Western man was painfully split and exploited spiritually. For the Inquisition may be truely regarded as nothing less than an inevitable, though blasphemous, outcome of a hate-filled trend within the Church, a trend which actually began once the pure spiritual light of the Holy Sophia was denied access to the dark and often blood-letting faiths of primitive or tribal man. And it must be remembered that this latter type constituted, by and large, the chief demographic characteristic of the place where Christianity was gaining its firmest footing in the world, i.e. continental Europe. This category of individual, i.e. the tribal man, thus supplied not only the obedient spirits that every faith needs to give it some kind of legitimate power, but it also supplied the necessary 'cannon-fodder' for the increasingly aggressive *realpolitik* that the Church was ever more tightly embracing. Needless to say none of this should be allowed to detract from the great amount of good that the Church also has been the inspirer of since its inception! It is very significant however that this good is often traceable to single or outstanding *individuals* whose insight into Christianity could go beyond the limits fixed by the doctrinal norms of orthodoxy, and could penetrate into a direct knowledge of the spiritual world and its angelic inhabitants. The case of St. Francis is perhaps one of the best known examples of those few individuals who somehow always managed to slip through the orthodox net of their time, however rigid or fine-meshed it may have been, and in so doing could bring the light of the pure spirit to bare upon the often materialistically clouded vision of their contemporaries.

It is obvious however from any spiritually informed appraisal of the history of the Church that the divine light which poured into the world through the advent of the Incarnation was never meant to be either fugitive in its appearance, or in any way restricted or selective in its application. The forces of temporalism and materialism however, powerful as they always are in the influencing of man's all too human nature, early opposed the entry into this nature of the divine spiritual element, this miraculous phenomenon uniquely enacted by, and poured into the world through the Incarnation.

For the mortal body of flesh and blood, transformed by Christ's Deed into a shining living temple of God, an etherial body freely given through Christ's supreme sacrifice as a gift to the world in which every man could have a share through his being membered into it through the Church – this began, after the initial flood of the glorious light of the Resurrection had receeded, to give way to the outmoded forces of decay once more. Mere tablets of Law began to replace those pure draughts of angelic enlightenment which gave to the very first Christians the power to discern in the Incarnation the *fact* of spiritual resurrection or rebirth, and the Church soon had far more to do with cold stones, chapels and their attendance, priviliged priests and so on, than it had with the living and immanent Presence of the Spirit of the etherial Sophia-Christ.

PAGAN SUN WORSHIP

Now the early Church, despite the fact that the troublesome Gnostics had been got out of the way more or less by the 3rd century, nevertheless could not avoid remaining tinged, to so some degree at least, with what from then on would be disparragingly labelled as paganism.[20] However it was this colouring, this delicate tint of the ancient Mystery wisdom that lingered on within the Church which made it attractive to followers of the many pagan cults operating in the Roman Empire at this time, cults whose potential for satisfying ambitions, spiritual or otherwise, was fast diminishing compared to the exciting, new, and modern Christians.

Let us look therefore at the psycho/spiritual dynamics at the back of all of this, for they are truely intriguing.

Pagan sun worship had been undoubtedly thrown into great confusion once the more sensitive, spiritually minded, and influential souls who adhered to it began to realize what in effect the Incarnation really meant. For they had slowly come to realize that this sun which they saw moving in the sky, rising in the east or setting in the west, could no longer be regarded as merely some object out there beyond them which they could only know or worship in an indirect, abstract or some other symbolic way. Something extraordinary and incredible, something almost indeed beyond belief, was now beginning to enter their consciousness and their spiritual life. For now in very truth the spiritual Being of this sun was felt to have entered into the dying temporal world, and by virtue of this miraculous fact they could, through an initiation experience, actually feel that it was somehow not outside them anymore, but was now to be truely found rising inside their very own spiritually enlivened bodies!

For the combined focus of the entire ancient wisdom had pointed to the fact that the sun God, the Solar Logos, was drawing nearer and nearer to the Earth as the aeons had passed, and then most wondrously, in the Incarnation it was perceived that this event had actually occurred! The God, the divinity, was now conceived to have not only entered into the Earth, but also into the very body and soul of man himself. It was a revelation with the most shattering and far-reaching of consequences imaginable for the individual who came to it.

It was also however a revelation which, once fully absorbed, begged the huge question as to the proper method and manner to be adopted if the dissemination of this knowledge was to take correct effect in the world. It was therefore a time of great soul searching, a time for the deepest thinking, and of course a time especially for the most careful of utterances and word-formulas.

So with this sublime knowledge lying at the very heart of Christianity, however encrusted over it may have gradually become by dogma and theology, the Christians could not but eventually have become a powerful religious force in the world over and above the claims of their pagan contemporaries. For the Incarnation had effected something in the world which was not merely cultic, mythic, or even psychic in its implications. But through it the very substance of the Earth itself was deemed to have been altered for the good. For it was felt that into the very composting matter of the Earth planet, a divine injection had been made. Through Christ's sacrifice a mysterious sun-like something was, in short, conceived to have fallen to the Earth and entered into the very bloodstream of mankind! And by virtue of this miracle a new evolutionary impulse was seen to have entered the world, giving to human and merely earth-born faculties a powerful new visionary and even divine possibility.

Now it can be seen from all of this that the forces at work in the making of our human history are often of the very essence of what is most fascinating and indeed almost even imponderable! And in the light of the little understanding that we can glean from the events in Palestine in the centuries immediately after the Incarnation, we should not be surprised at the fact that Christianity, after being initially subjected to much suspicion, repression, and persecution, was eventually legitimized.

CONSTANTINE THE GREAT

It was the Emperor Constantine the Great (born c. 274 A.D.) who was largely the one responsible for this move towards legitimacy for the Christians. But there was at the same time a certain amount of inevitability attached to Constantine's action. For he was deeply aware of the soul and spirit power inherent in the sun. He was indeed (it is now known) an initiate of one of the pagan sun cults of the time[21]. He was also of course a man of the world *par excellence*, nothing less than an Emperor in fact.

Thus as well as having spiritual, he undoubtedly also had very temporal matters always weighing heavily upon his mind, and no doubt figured deeply as to how he could put his spiritual knowledge into the service of his purely temporal needs and designs! In this way his sun initiation was to become a powerful and a highly useful weapon for regulating and ordering the turbulent and often unconscious impulses at work within his all too human realm. And the Christians, he gradually became aware, held the trump card in this respect! Furthermore by Constantine's time the new Church was perceived as being a force that simply now *had* to be reckoned with in the world, one way or the other. So better use it to the best advantage!

Now, while hardly a Christian, it is true of course that Constantine was able to relate to the Christ Being in a certain way. But the manner in which this relationship was expressed is actually very revealing indeed about how far the fabulous vision, which was so alive and so actively cultivated by the very early Christians, had fallen away from its original grandure and pristine purity. This vision of course was the tremendous one which represented to the followers of the new Way that the body of the new Church[22] was nothing less than identical with the body of the risen Christ. For certainly by Constantine's time this primary initiatory vision had faded, and had even undergone a process of decay from one which had originally upheld the incarnational reality of the human body of flesh and blood as being a living temple of the Christ Being himself.

This wonderful pristine vision of the Church had gradually turned back into one far more concerned with cold stone than with living flesh. It was in a sense a looking backwards to the old pillars of a religion based on dead letters written on tablets of granite or marble, something which had in fact been totally fulfilled, superseded, and rendered outmoded by the Event of the Incarnation. For stones, no matter how beautiful a form which may have been given them by skilled artisans or artists, could never, from the first Easter Sunday morning onwards, when the stone was rolled away from the empty tomb, be anything other than a backward-looking or empty symbol for the new free spiritual reality released into the world through the Incarnation.

This was however a reality which was being feared and shunned for many reasons by the emerging types within the new Church, suspect reasons all, not the least of which would seem to be that the Incarnation was reckoned in fact to be far too good to be true at all in the first place!

Or if not too good to be true then certainly it was a truth which could only be profitably dealt with by turning it into a mere object of faith, in the process of which however it became banished into the dark depths of the unconscious mind and there left to accrue its doubtful interest. For to aspire to a clear-headed, purposeful, and practical knowledge of the Incarnation seemed to mean nothing less than risking one's sanity within a maze of competing angelologies, intellectual wranglings and hair-splitting definitions, into which no amount of mere words was deemed capable of bringing order.

Faith, dogma, law and order; it was these therefore, and the mentality which they bred, that now, by the 4th century, had become the chief determinants of the Church's emerging and consolidating constitution. The spirit behind the letter and the law, that subtle discerning ability which had been the quintessential characteristic of the very early Church and which had promised, and often given, initiatory understanding and knowledge of Christ to all who came under its influence; this was now rapidly drying up in the heat of the theological warfare which came to a head in Constantine's time.

The issues in this warfare were subtle, complex, and often highly charged emotionally. And given the dogmatic nature of the disputes generally, the principle one was, needless to say, centered upon the correct definition of God himself. For quite understandably, from *its* viewpoint, the growing Roman style of orthodoxy wished to establish the fact the Jesus Christ was God once and for all, and shut up all the (for them) divisive chatter about it!

THE CASE OF GENTLE ARIUS

Gnosticism as such of course had been quite left behind by this stage. But these kinds of troubles were far from over for the emerging orthodoxy. And one of the biggest threats to this orthodoxy was that way of approaching the Mystery of the Incarnation which became associated with the theologian Arius. This style of exegesis thus acquired the name of Arianism. Basically what Arius was saying was that you just can't dogmatically assert, as the orthodox theologians were doing, that there are three persons in the One God and then turn this into a hell-binding article of faith, without expecting ordinary people to believe in something which was, quite simply, incomprehensible. For it was in point of fact incomprehensible, even to philosophers and theologians themselves! So while never denying Christ's divinity, he maintained that Christ himself must be distinguished or distinguishable from God the Father. But his manner of apprehending and teaching this distinction undoubtedly leaned far too heavily, for orthodoxy's liking, towards a Gnostic approach to the Trinity. For Arius could never hammer his knowledge or image of God into the straight-jacketed or sterile Trinity of this emerging orthodoxy. And he and his followers were thus not tolerated by the hard-heads in any way, though he himself tried heroically to please them.

And so the sweet-tempered and saintly Arius, this father of the emerging orthodoxy's most hated so-called heresy, was by some accounts poisoned just before he was prepared to make a grand gesture of reconciliation in Constantinople in 336. And we may say that such an eventuality for him, if true, fits the emerging picture of, and practises within, the new Church very well! For in truth Arianism had to be got rid of completely, once and for all, smelling as it did of the increasingly despised Gnosticism, the last traces of which the dogmatic Church was now violently in the process of eliminating.

Though this elimination of Arius was drastic, he, his knowledge and his teaching, nevertheless had a huge following, and Arianism lingered on as a threat to the Roman Church's authority for many centuries afterwards.

JESUS, THE ANGRY MAN!

We have hitherto been indicating the manner in which the new Church was gradually turning away from the early and truely spiritual vision of its mission and purpose in the world. The original inspiration was that via the Incarnation, the old temple wisdom was seen to have taken on a completely new form. Thus, in a totally real sense, the temple and its wisdom had actually *become man* through the spiritual power of the Incarnation. This was the very essence of the first Christian's understanding of the real meaning of their Church. Even the word 'Church' itself indicates this very well, for it is from a Greek word meaning 'Lord'. This wisdom-knowledge however, and the vision it engendered, began to be actively suppressed from very early on, for various reasons.

Now the fact that this crucial, central, and pure understanding of the Incarnation would be denied to most men and women soon after the completion of the Incarnation Event, was something that was prophetically foreseen by Christ himself. This fact is clearly indicated in the Gospel as we shall presently see. And it was the prophetic foreknowledge of this calamity which gave rise to one of Christ's most significant actions in the whole of the Gospel.

For it quite simply made him angry!

There is no greater wrath than a divine one (as even a cursory glance at the history of Europe or of our Western civilization generally will show). Of course it can be argued that even Christ himself said (in the Gospel of Matthew, IO:34) that he came not to bring peace, but a sword! Be that as it may, when anger and violence are used for the wrong reasons, they undoubtedly corrupt far more than they cure. For it is how and why anger is used that is the crucial factor. Used in ignorance it is in fact one of the most terrible and destructive of all human emotions.

We do not normally of course associate anger or violence with the person or temperament of Jesus Christ in any way. The overriding tone of the whole of the Gospel is in fact one of a yielding forgiveness, a simplicity of faith and virtue, a message of meekness, even of passivity and pacifism. Anger has virtually no place in it at all.

There is one scene however in the Gospels which is totally at variance with this general tone, and it is perhaps the only instance known in the whole of the Incarnation drama in which Jesus actually displays anger as such[23]. And significantly this has much to do with the Temple. For when he enters into the Temple in Jerusalem just after he began his three year ministry, he is angered to the point of violence by what he sees taking place there, supposedly in the name of God. Then astonishingly he makes a whip of cords and proceeds to drive out the money-changers and the dealers in sacrificial birds who were congregated and trading there, as was their custom and practise. And with his whip he scatters them and their money in every possible direction in a scene of unparalleled wrath!

What a scene this is! And immediately afterwards of course he is severely questioned about his beheavour here. By what authority can he do such astounding things? And how can he give a sign to explain such unbelievable beheavour? For in truth, given the way the Temple was regarded in the Jewish faith, his action here could be construed as nothing less than one of supreme and total blasphemy. His answers to his critics and questioners was twofold: The Temple, he said, is supposed to be the house of God, but you have made of it a den of thieves! And as for signs he said to them: 'Pull this Temple down and I will rebuild it in three days'[24].

Now undoubtedly in this important incident in the life of Jesus something archetypal is being alluded to. And it is this: In the most pointed and dramatic of all possible terms, the deepest and truest nature of the Christ's being and his mission to the Earth are being emphasised. The Gospel is here very graphically illustrating the fact that a true divining of the nature of Christ Jesus reveals him to have entered the world primarily in order to destroy the old way of life, the outdated modes of culture, the dried up practises in religion and initiation, all of which of course placed the temple at the very centre! This old hard and secret way of the stone temple, he was saying in the most emphatic of all possible terms, was now outlived, outworn and only capable, if perpetuated, of breeding confusion, division and corruption. And in referring to the destruction of the Temple and its rebuilding in three days, he was indicating allegorically the way in which his mission on Earth was to be miraculously fulfilled. For he was soon, he knew, to die physically, only to arise again three days afterwards from the tomb in a new etheric or spiritual body, the beauty and magnificence of which Paul and many others were soon after the event to fully behold.

We would be claiming no high ground at all therefore if, given the subsequent development of his Church, we were to cultivate a mood of moral empathy with this action of Christ as he hunts away the money changers from the Temple! For though he completed his appointed mission and fulfilled all the highest prophesies appertaining to him and the divine plan for man and the world, nevertheless the Church he came to inaugurate, i.e. the temple of stone turned into one of spirit-flesh and blood, quickly got overtaken by the 'money-changers' again. Worldly forces in other words, matters far more to do with temporal expediency than with true spiritual enlightenment, soon began to gain momentum within the body of the emerging and physically strengthening Church. Thus in driving away the money changers he was in fact expressing nothing less than a prophetic wrath, a divine anger directed against not only those present in the Temple at that particular time, but also symbolically against those forces which he knew only too well would soon raise their ugly head again and build stone temples in his name, (and moreover use them for selling far more suspect merchandise than these bird dealers in Jerusalem ever did!).

He *knew* this would happen once his own physical presence on the Earth had ceased. And he knew also that this temple-building was something which would be fundamentally in opposition to his Gospel.

AND THE TEMPLE BECOMES MAN

For the deepest truth of his Gospel lay in the fact that the old temple was never to be raised up again, except in the flesh. And no matter how magnificent a church or a cathedral may have been, the fact was that by cultivating such a church or temple-building trend, God would be once more locked up inside temples of stone.[25]

It made Christ angry to perceive this eventuality. For what he could foresee was that the inner voice of the pure, bright, and free spirit, which was meant, through the power of his incarnational Gospel, to infuse and transform the very flesh and blood of Everyman via his being membered into the living body of the new Church; this was in danger of being replaced by the strong, stone-hard, and often dark power of the pulpit, something indeed which eventually came about. The 'reason' for this was that the spirit itself was eventually deemed to be far too dangerous a thing for the ordinary man in the street to know or possess and it therefore had in effect to be put under 'house arrest'!

And the truth of all of this is well borne out by what started to happen in the Church as soon as it became officially sanctioned within the Empire, something which was due to the Emperor Constantine's initiative.

Thus once the Sophia Spirit which permeated the very early Church had finally been put away and the Church was about to take a big worldly leap forward, what do we find? Stone church-building on a grand scale! For emboldened if not truely spiritually inspired by Christ, Constantine soon sets about a church-building programme which by the time he died apparently amounted to no less than 21 in total. Though one of these, the church of St. George, soon afterwards became the site of one of the most beautiful churches in Christendom, (still is), and was renamed (significantly) the Church of Sophia in Constantinople, nevertheless the trend was well and truely started. The living God was being locked up once more inside temples of stone!

Thus with the legitimizing of Christianity in the Roman Empire during the reign of Constantine the Great, we have clearly marked the ending of the first phase of the Church's development in which the light of The Gnosis is well and truely quenched and the Church now embarks on a phase of development which is largely temporal, as well of course, it must be said, as being evangelical. And in tandem with this, the wisdom-eschewing, albeit faith-espousing orthodoxy is becoming fully established. However, even from this time of Constantine, the interminable hair-splitting debates that were taking place in the Church, debates and controversies which, though they may seem to us at our remove like a lot of hot, albiet theological, air, nevertheless eventually caused a major crack to appear even within this orthodoxy itself. And it is fairly obvious when studying these debates that no real solution, in fact no real understanding of them at all is even possible, while the banished Sophia wisdom is not available to shed its light upon them. It was also because of this that these ostensibly religious debates often appear to descend into nothing more than the pedantics of mere political manoeuvring. And it is from this latter angle only that their apparent absurdity may be somewhat excused.

THE GREAT SCISM

For given the turmoil that was now generally brewing throughout the whole of the Empire, political manouvering was becoming a very desirable and a veritable art in itself, and one moreover which involved very high political stakes; indeed the stakes could hardly have been higher, for they were nothing less than the very unity of the Empire itself! Though the final official split in the Church between East and West (the Great Scism) did not formally take place until 1054, such an eventuality was actually a long time in the brewing.

Now the machinations and horse-trading which led to this split in the Church are, needless to say, subtle and complex in the extreme. But one pertinent observation must be made here regarding it. And that is that the Scism represented the total cutting off of the Western Church from perhaps its deepest source of inspiration, a separation the consequences of which the Eastern Church itself was only too well aware. For it is the case, as we shall presently show, that it was from the Eastern portion of the Church's temporal body that the pressure, right up to the 9th century, was being exerted to keep a line of contact open with the very early Church and the ancient wisdom, however tenuous and progressively weaker this link may have been becoming as the centuries with their wranglings progressed. But the Roman orthodoxy would have none of it! We shall later see (chapter 10) much more clearly what actually happened here. But the final result was the triumph of the Roman militant orthodoxy in the West and the eventual decline of its culture into the unabashed materialism it now extolls, while in the East, in the Church and in its culture generally, at least a flavour of the true spirit of Sophia was, and still is, kept alive.

Chapter Seven

THE HOLY LAND OF ERIN COMES TO THE RESCUE

In our introduction we called attention to the fact that Christianity had from the very outset two distinct 'flavours', an Eastern and a Western one. Now these differences in the manner of apprehending the Incarnation and the cultic and civilizing influences which flowed from it, obviously became more pronounced as the centuries passed. But a clear recognition of the fact that they were actually there from the very beginning, as well as some understanding of the nuances which constituted these differences, will inevitably help towards an appreciation of just what the Sophia Spirit was perceived and conceived to be in these ancient times.

That there are very distinct differences in the spirituality generally, Christian or otherwise, of East and West is probably too obvious an observation to elaborate on here. For this is something which is very apparent to anyone who has any interest in, or knowledge of, the subject of spirituality at all. And this difference comes perhaps to its most obvious manifestation in what may be regarded as the robust or masculine 'practicality' of the Western, as opposed to the more effeminate or the 'etheriality' of the Eastern way. And these two, at bottom opposing cultural tendencies, undoubtedly played deeply into the development and eventual split of the Church into Eastern and Western blocks.

In the very far West however, that is in Ireland, the manner in which Christianity took root reveals something of its truely universal nature. For here it seems that there came about a happy blend of these two erstwhile opposing facets, so that the Mystery or etherial side of the Incarnation did not come into such conflict with the more historical or down-to-earth aspects, as it obviously did in other places. In other words, in this wierd and wonderful land of Erin, a cultural as well as a religious unity could be maintained with regard to the Gospel and its dissemination, which would in time become the very model of a true and practical, yet fully spiritual, Christianity. In Ireland in fact, the Gospel had found perhaps the most fertile soil in the world in which to grow in its truely esoteric or most inward manner. And long after this inwardness or freedom of its spirit had been more or less spent or banished, both in the field of its first genesis, (the near East generally), as well as in its later development on continental

Europe, it remained green and alive in Ireland.

And thus it was here that it came to its full flowering in the 5th – 8th centuries, a period which is known to history as that of the Celtic Church. This was a short but Golden Age of Christianity which is becoming increasingly recognised as having been nothing less than the source of that light which kept the lamp of civilization aglow in an increasingly darkened world.

THE CELTIC CHURCH

This phenomenon of the Celtic Church and its background we will now look at quite closely, for in doing so we will be able all the more readily to gain a practical understanding of the inherent spiritual/religious power of the Incarnation itself, as well as some working knowledge as to the manner in which this spiritual power was effectively depotenitized or destroyed. In other words we will learn to understand that what should have been a primary factor in the later development of mainstream, exoteric, and especially Western culture, was banished underground to become esoteric instead.

Even long before Christianity was ever heard of anywhere in the world, the ancient land of Hibernia was held in the highest esteem by wise men, for it was considered by them as a dwelling place fit even for the very gods themselves! All ancient lands of course inevitably have their own particular air of mystery attached to them. It has always been recognised however that Ireland lays claim to a kind of special magic all of its own. And even a little knowledge of the modern country can convince one fairly easily as to why this should be the case. For there just seems to be something in the very air, especially as one goes farther south of the island! The elements combine and work together here in the atmosphere of Ireland to create a landscape of such soft and virginal beauty that one may yet, especially in the spring and early summer, get a sense of how and why the ancients regarded this place truely as a piece of Paradise.

The sun divinity too, the Solar Logos Spirit, had an ancient mystic and mythical attachment to Ireland. For long before this Spirit ever came into an historical association with the Earth through the Incarnation, the very oldest books in the world, those written in Sanscrit, had referred to Ireland as 'Hiranya' which means the 'Island of the Sun'. Furthermore, Ireland was also known as the very 'Garden of Phoebus'. (Phoebus is one of the oldest names in the world for the god of the sun, Apollo). Even the Gaelic word for sun, 'graine', was, according to the first century B.C. writer and esotericist, Virgil, another name for Apollo!

Now given the perennial nature of the cloudy and often misty weather in Ireland, it may seem a bit strange at first why this place should actually be the home of such a pure and cultic sun-worship for it to be regarded as the very home of Apollo himself. This however is nothing at all to be really puzzled about once we begin to realize something of the depth, profundity, and spiritual sophistication of the culture and civilization which existed in Ireland in prehistoric times. For at the head of this culture, nurturing, guiding, and instructing it in every aspect of its needs and development, were a special class of people whose wisdom, knowledge, and craft, ranked equally as high, if not indeed higher, than the priest-king initiates of the ancient Egyptian civilization at the height of *its* achievements. These were none other than the famous Druids, a clear and pure image of whom we need to have if we are to properly evaluate the sun-inspired nature of the ancient culture of Hibernia. For these were people whose highly trained spiritual and magical powers passed easily through the atmospheric vapours of the merely physical world and its clouds, and in the process were able to behold the majesty of the Sun-Being in all his spiritual beauty, glory, and divine power.

THE QUESTION OF ATLANTIS

We are talking here of course of a time long prior to the arrival of the Celts in Ireland, of a civilization that stretches in fact so far back into the mists of time that some say (and the great Greek philosopher Plato was one of these!) that it can only be truely accounted for by seeking its origin in a totally lost civilization which had its geographical location centered somewhere out in what is now the Atlantic ocean. We speak of course of the legendary Atlantis, the possible existence of which can still excite the imaginatively inquiring and philosophical mind quite as much now as it did in Plato's time, for the simple reason that the time scales involved are so great that the only true measuring instrument for them can be none other than the human mind or the imaginative power of the soul itself!

The ancient wisdom tells how this continent of Atlantis, as well as virtually its entire culture and civilization, was submerged in the rising waters of the ocean. And esoteric literature sometimes states that the reason for this catastrophy was that the Atlantean initiates became, over time, very decadent and eventually abused and misused their very great magical powers. In doing this they also triggered atmospheric and climactic changes which caused (obviously over very long periods of time) the Earth's oceans to rise. Eventually this led to the alteration of the entire physiognomy of the Globe itself.

Now whatever one's attitude to this may be, it has however to be accepted that what is generally referred to as The Flood or The Deluge is an indisputable event in the prehistory of the world, traces of which can be found in the mythology of peoples virtually everywhere. And of course in the more specific terms of the history of Western spirituality, this event is recorded in the Bible as marking the beginning of a new epoch in man's relationship (covenant) with God.

Regarding Atlantis however, it was Solon the Wise (6th century B.C.) who told Plato that the Egyptian Initiates had told him that it had disappeared 9000 years before their own (the Egyptians) time! This partly is the reason of course why Ireland would have been held in such high esteem by the ancients of the East. For for them Ireland may very well have been a tiny remnant of that fabulous though almost forgotten land in the far, far west, a land full of mystery and magic which had been all but submerged in the Deluge. And this would also certainly explain why Hibernia was known to the ancients as the Garden of Phoebus, a last little bit of a lost paradisial civilization remaining on the Earth, a wondrous place certainly, and one where the almost forgotten gods of the Atlanteans actually still lived and were known to its people, the Hibernians.

THE HIBERNIAN MYSTERIES

Indeed when one considers the very special case of the Hibernian Mysteries[26] one can hardly doubt but that in the minds of the ancients Ireland represented a vital link with a virtually unknown or forgotten pre-history of the Earth, of its civilizations and its gods. For knowledge of the Hibernian Mysteries reveals that they had the possibility to evoke or create a synthesis of the combined wisdom of all of the other extant Mysteries. The ancients would have been acutely aware of this and it would undoubtedly have deeply coloured their attitude to Hibernia, its people and its wise initiates. For within the sanctums of these Hibernian Mysteries there seemed to the ancients to be contained the possibility for mankind of a great refinement of his cultural, religious and social life, indeed even his very consciousness itself. The Hibernian Mysteries in other words seemed to constitute a great advance on not only what the other Mysteries actually taught, but also on what they could ever hope to achieve in the future.

As we have mentioned earlier, the Mystery religions in different parts of the world had always, from the most ancient of times, venerated the divine as it came to expression in Nature around them and in the Cosmos above them. This the different races and nations cultivated in various ways, and in the process and over great expances of time, evolved their own rituals, religious practises, initiations and so on, all of which were based on their own particular images or understanding of the gods. However, knowledge of the universe and the gods was such a vast thing that it was surely also understood by the initiates generally that no *one* particular type of initiation could ever be expected to cover every aspect of this magnificence.

In the Hibernian Mysteries however this was not entirely the case. For here there was an initiation available into the greatest and most profound secrets of the universe that exist, secrets pertaining not only to the divine ordering of the world and man, but also secrets revealing the divine plan for mankind's future, a future so profound and grand that even angels could not tell of it.[27] And yet these secrets were revealed here to the Hibernian Initiates!

Though there were sun cults and sun religions all over the ancient world, it was in Ireland however that the sun divinity revealed to the druid initiate the most universal, profound, and at the same time purely Earthly aspect of his relationship to man. And this of course was something which was intimately connected to the coming event which was to change the entire course of our world's history, the Incarnation. For long before this event actually took place on the Earth itself, the Initiates of the Hibernian Mysteries had been aware of its approach and had prepared for it through the rites of their initiation practises in a manner which was simply not possible for others elsewhere. The result of this was that the whole culture of the island of Ireland was ready to receive the news of the Incarnation in a totally pure and profoundly spiritual way. To these people therefore the Incarnation was not some strange or unlikely event to be debated and philosophized about *ad nauseum*. Quite the contrary! For it was an event that was actually expected in a wholly matter-of-fact manner. And when it did eventually happen, it was something to be wholeheartedly participated in.

For ...'when in Palestine those remarkable occurrences took place which we describe when speaking of Christ Jesus on Golgotha and of His environment, – at that very time solemn Festivals were celebrated within the Hibernian Mysteries themselves and the community associated with them, that is to say by the people who belonged in some way to the Mysteries.(...............) The events that took place in Palestine at the beginning of our era and were visible there to the physical eyes, were beheld spiritually in Hibernia. (There) men experienced the Mystery of Golgotha in the spirit. And this was the basis of the greatness inherent in everything that subsequently went out from Hibernia into the rest of the civilized world but disappeared as time went on'.[28]

That Christianity took hold in Ireland in a somewhat mysterious way is actually well known to scholars generally. It is a mystery however which will only be really solved via the foregoing insight. For in Ireland the whole phenomenon of Christianity was a totally 'organic' process.

The real facts about the Christianization of the Irish is actually very far removed from the 'churched' version of the truth! For it is really only a sort of (Roman!) Church-inspired 'myth' to assume that it was St. Patrick who brought Christianity to Ireland. In recent years however this 'myth' about Ireland (and many others too hopefully!) is gradually being dismantled.

For it is quite well established by now that Christianity was cultivated here long before Patrick came in 432. Which is not to say either of course that Patrick did not do powerful missionary work in Ireland. But he did not 'convert' Ireland.

Indeed if we wish to look at this phenomenon from another angle there is an old story, even still very much alive in the folk memory of the Irish, which throws some very revealing light on how the Gospel came to them, and it would be worthwhile here to recount it in its essence, for apart from anything else it illustrates very well the way in which stories and legends generally, if backed up by proper insights, can give truely accurate and historical information about hitherto little known facts.

THE STORY OF KING CONOR AND THE DRUID

The story goes as follows: "King Conor MacNessa was the King of Ulster. One day a battle took place in which his ally, the King of Leinster, lost his life. However, the king's brains were taken from his head by a warrior, and a very precious sling-stone was made out of them. This treasure was then placed in King Conor's headquarters at Emain Macha. However one day the Connaught champion, whose name was Ket, stole it. Now eventually at a place called Ardnurchar (The Fort of the Sling-Cast) a battle was fought between the Connaughtmen and the Ultonian (Ulster) warriors. King Conor was there too and when he saw the great array of beautiful Connaught ladies present he rose to the occasion and proceeded to exhibit his ferocious skills much to the jealous disapproval of the Connaughtman Ket. Ket, at a loss what to do, eventually took out his precious stolen brain-ball, put it in his sling and aimed straight at Conor. King Conor was struck right between the eyes and the ball lodged firmly in his forehead. When the Ulster warriors eventually got back home with their wounded King, the Druid physician declared: 'If I take out that ball King Conor will die!' And so it was agreed to leave the ball in Conor's head. King Conor then had his forehead sewen up with golden thread and was ordered not to do anything excitable or passionate anymore.

Now one Friday afternoon, seven years later, King Conor was out riding. Suddenly he saw the sun grow mysteriously dark. He summoned one of his Druids immediately and asked him what was the meaning of this? The Druid in a magic trance soon proceeded to tell King Conor of a hill in Palestine on which he saw three crosses. To one of these crosses was nailed, he said, a figure like one of the Immortals. King Conor was astonished!

'Has he done wrong?', he enquired.

'No', the Druid answered. 'This is the Son of the living God'. The Druid then went on to tell King Conor the whole story of the Passion and Death of Christ.

Conor lost his temper when he heard of this terrible outrage. He suddenly whipped his sword out from its scabbard and ran wildly into a sacred grove of oak trees hacking in every possible direction.

'This is what I would do to his accusers', he cried. However, in his great anger the brain-ball burst from his head and he dropped dead".[29]

(One can see from this story that the Irish reserve their greatest passion for their gods!).
What is indicated quite clearly in it of course is that the Druids, from within

the sacred sanctums of their Mystery groves and temples in Ireland, were able to behold with their clairvoyant faculties what was actually happening in Palestine! And the 'brainball' alluded to here clearly indicates one of the most widely known aspects of esoteric knowledge, the subtle body's inner or 'third eye', the primary organ of clairvoyant vision which is known to be approximately located in the area of the physical body's forehead.[30]

Now the initiates of the Mysteries could undoubtedly themselves communicate with one another through their extrasensory powers in much the same way as modern clairvoyants can transcend physical boundaries in their work (though it has to be said that we must be careful of making too close comparisons here). It is therefore not in the least unreasonable to assume that, given that the Hibernian Druids were able to 'watch' the Incarnation drama as it unfolded in Palestine, the fact of this astonishing ability would have been known to the initiates of the Eastern or other Mystery rites. And these (Eastern) people, who would obviously have had much more physically orientated contact with the events in Palestine, would undoubtedly have been eager to make physical contact with the Irish in order to boost their own (these Eastern Christians) particular knowledge and understanding of the Gospel.

And so it is not in the least surprising that we find from the very beginning of Christianity evidence of contact between the Eastern Church and the Irish. There is in fact a growing body of external knowledge regarding this phenomenon. The Desert Monks of Egypt and Palestine seem like the most fruitful conduit of communication. And the Egyptian Tau cross on Tory Island off the north coast of Ireland is perhaps the most solid monument to this early traffic between Hibernia and the Eastern Church generally. It would of course be missing the point to regard this Egyptian influence as evidence relating to the mystery of how the early evangelization of Ireland actually took place. It would in fact be much more in keeping with the reality of the situation to assume the reverse, i.e. that *they* came to Ireland to develop and expand their own spiritual and initiatory awareness of the Christian Mystery.

For given the parched deserts of the land from which they came, with its tradition of hard and ascetic contemplation, these monks would surely have found the soft and misty land of Erin, where Christ was regarded with such loving warmth, a very special place. Indeed, driven by a holy thirst for Christ as they were, something which seemed often to border on the fanatical, the natural and virginal beauty of the Irish landscape must have seemed to them like little short of Paradise itself.

SUN AND CROSS

There was no fear here, they must have instinctively felt, of the new wonderfully free God of love being locked up anymore inside stuffy old pyramids of stone, forgotten secret temples, or even modern exquisite churches! No! For they would have been moved to the very quick of their being by the freedom of the Holy Sophia Spirit and how here she wrought Christ from out of the very soil itself and into the new and consciously Christian soul of Ireland.

For in Hibernia it was Nature herself in all her grandure, grace, and ineffable beauty which was the temple. This is not to say of course that the 'hard stuff', the 'spirit of stone' as it were, would have no place in the Irish consciousness as it learned and developed its new relationship with Christ. Quite the contrary! For here stone was to become the matter of a profound artistic/religious impulse stemming directly from the Incarnation, but one which nevertheless would express the free spirit of the Celtic soul. Here therefore stone was not to be the cause of shutting up the spirit of God inside church and temple buildings, but rather the occasion for chiselling its hardness into a musicality of expression unsurpassable in its spiritual dignity. We refer here of course to the famous and beautiful decorated high stone crosses of the Irish Celtic Church. And in this ancient Irish art of the high stone sun-crosses of Christ we have evidence of a stone-craft, megalitic in its depth and span of knowledge, which, when combined with the incarnational impulse, was brought to a lofty and spiritual perfection.

Furthermore these old Irish Celtic crosses actually are excellent examples of an art which mark, and through which we may wondrously observe, the unique transition from one epoch in the descending and Earthward history of man, ancient and cosmic beyond all imagining, to a new, light-filled era of free ascension to an ever higher form of consciousness and creative being.

On these crosses the decorative images are always of course scenes taken from the Gospel story as well as from the Old Testament. But the formal motif, the cross or crossbars projecting outwards from the central sun-disk, was a form and an image used in the cultic life of the people of the land for millennia previously to the making of these crosses. (Wonderful examples of these cosmic sun-cross discs, finely wrought in pure gold and said to date back to 2,500 B.C. can be seen in the National Museum in Dublin).

Christ himself is of course invariably placed at the centre of the cosmic sun-disk of the stone crosses. And often his arms and hands are outstretched indicating the manner, as much as the inevitability of his death in or upon the physical planet of the Earth itself, which the bars of the cross represents. All of which draws our attention in a highly artistic yet profoundly simple fashion, to the initiatory knowledge known to the ancients and passed on orally from generation to generation, of how Christ, as the divine Solar Logos Being, was the One who had decended from the cosmic sun heights and had incarnated, even unto the death, as one of *us* here on Earth.

THE TUATHA DE DANANN

The prehistory of Ireland, as well indeed as its 'real' history is full of accounts of invasions and conquests. In fact one of the best known sources of Irish mythological stories is actually called The Book of Invasions! And perhaps the most famous of these mythical invaders were the Tuatha De Danann, a name which when translated from the Gaelic means The People of the Goddess Dana. Now Dana is identical with the Goddess Brigit, a very ancient 'mother' deity who was widely worshipped in Europe. Significantly however in Irish mythology she is recognised as having given birth to Ecne (pronounced Ec-nay) who is identified principally with 'poetry' (in its aspect as the spiritual embodiment of a divine art, of course[31]).Thus in conformity with the definitive principles that are to be found underlying the mythologies of every race, where quite naturally the mother goddess comes before her son, in Ireland we have Dana, or Brigit, as the mother of the first or the highest god as well. But here in ancient Ireland we can see how this son or sun-god is revealed in his most spiritually sophisticated aspect as being none other than the sun-Logos or the divine Word. For here the god, Ecne, actually becomes poetry itself to the spiritual consciousness of these people, thus also highlighting how this art of poetry is regarded as the highest form of spiritual expression that the word can receive or be given.

Later when the Celts begin to 'invade' Ireland in approximately the 5th century B.C. they easily absorbed into their own culture the existing deities of this ancient Druidic civilization. (Indeed this receptivity and spiritual flexibility on the part of the Celts was the hallmark or secret of their successful expansions everywhere in Europe around this time).

The Celts in other words had a very marked spiritual magnanimity which allowed them to meet other cultures always with an openness and a gesture of welcoming, especially if they felt these influences to be good and in accord with the betterment of their people generally.

When they came to Ireland they thus had no difficulty in absorbing into their own ways the mythic, cultural and spiritual influences at work there. And so it was that later when Christianity actually began to take root in Celtic Ireland the ancient mother goddess Brigit or Dana, who still lived vividly in the mythic consciousness and spiritual awareness of the people, found her way easily into the new consciousness being wrought through Christianity. Thus eventually via this incarnational consciousness she came even to be identified with a real flesh and blood woman. No ordinary woman this of course, but a quite extraordinary one. And she came from Co. Kildare in the midlands of the island.

ST. BRIGID OF KILDARE

Now given the still very rich mythic consciousness of the time and place in which she lived and grew up, it is not easy to say very much for certain (from an historical point of view) about this 'real' Brigid, apart from the approximate year of her death which was between 523 and 525 A.D.

For the cronic myth-making appetite of the Irish has left us little regarding Brigid in the way of those much (perhaps too much!) valued commodities of our own day – hard facts. However, the abundance of stories and legends about this early Christian saint does more than make up for this lack. Moreover it is a situation which actually stimulates us into using our imagination and in this way perhaps forming an even more appropriate picture of Brigid than one built merely out of hard and dry prosaic facts. And thus we can picture a woman inspired to the hilt with the fiercely independent spirit of the new Christian path, a woman deeply empowered certainly, so as to enable her to work many marvels and wonders in the name of the great new God, as she went about the country baptising and preaching the Good News in her own extraordinary and richly feminine way. And in all of this, what she was surely most anxious to do was to try to wean her (especially male) contemporaries away from their all too war-loving way of life, while at the same time remaining, because of her ancestral background, deeply sympathetic to, and understanding of, their own pagan spiritual orientation. Unlike the Romanised Britishman, Patrick, who was actually her contemporary in this great missionary work, Brigid's background was purely Hiberno-Celtic and her upbringing, as we can deduce from the medieval hagiographic 'Life of Brigid' in the Book of Lismore, was actually given over to one of the initiates (druids) of the old pagan religion, a caste which was still very much flourishing during her lifetime. And to these Druids, a class of individuals whom, as we have seen, were capable of a clairvoyant perception of the Incarnation, this spiritually fired virgin of Christ must indeed have been quite a force to be reckoned with! Furthermore, they as a body must have understood clearly her destiny and have taken great care to stimulate, nourish, and to so refine her spiritual faculties for her to become a primary vechicle through which the Christian purification of the very soul of the nation could take place.

So, as her fame and renown grew, and stories of her miracle-workings spread far and wide throughout the land, this woman, in the simple minds of her people, soon became the live focus of a new type of consciousness that was being forced, precisely because of the implications of the Incarnation, to shift away from its age-old functioning through symbol and myth, and towards one concerned principally with the tangible and the actual. Thus memories, thoughts, and feelings, and all of those psychic and psychological faculties that were formerly only or mainly directed towards myths, the gods and so on, were now beginning to be given over to historical realities, so that this Brigid, once her great virtues and deeds became well known, not surprisingly grew in stature to such a degree that she became, with the passing of time, a semi-divine figure. Eventually she actually acquired the status in the imagination of the people of nothing less than the foster-mother of God, i.e. of Christ himself![32] Indeed in the 'Life of Brigid' she is referred to as none other than the 'Mary of the Gael'. However, from the point of view of our investigations here in this book, it would be more instructive to now regard her in the light of Sophia or the Sophia Mystery as such.

For it is only this Sophia aspect of Brigid which will fully and clearly reveal, if properly investigated and understood, the mystery of the incarnational Spirit and the way it worked (or works!) in Ireland, which was, or is, fundamentally an inward, free, and essentially esoteric way. In Ireland however this inwardness was, paradoxically, as much to be found and cultivated in the beauty and expance of nature at large as much as in the free-soaring spirit of the individual man or woman as he or she built up his or her new Christian relationship with the angels and the angelic world. And it is in this sense that it can be said that Nature herself, seen through this Christianized and angelic spirit-vision, was here regarded as the very temple of God. The Mystery temple-wisdom of the ancients however, always gave the feminine Sophia aspect of their trinitarian Godhead equal status with the Father and Son aspects, and this wisdom too was fully at work in the old pre-Celtic Irish religion.

In this way we can come perhaps a little nearer to understanding how the esoteric Mystery spirit of Christianity worked its way so profoundly into the soul and spirit-religion of the Irish through the Druids and their disciples, one of whom was Brigid. And so of this revered 'Mary of the Gael', we very revealingly read in her devotional biographic Life of Brigid "... her name among created things is Dove...", the dove being, as we have earlier pointed out, the most ancient of all symbols for the Sophia spirit.

THE CELTIC TRINITY

In trying to give expression to what is most essential to an understanding of Esoteric Christianity we have by now hopefully established quite clearly its trinitarian foundation. For it is this more than any other aspect regarding the divinity which holds the key to penetrating the deepest mysteries of God, man and the universe. Now this 'secret' was well known also to the Celts long before they arrived in Ireland where they found it to be a well established foundation of the much more ancient druidic culture and religion there. For the mythology of these continental Celts is actually full of references to a triune god. Indeed there is in Klagenfurt in Austria (an ancient Celtic stronghold) a statue of a triune god, one component of which is pointedly feminine in gender, as it has breasts. And this symbiotic relationship between the Celts own and the existing druidic culture which they found flourishing when they arrived in Ireland in around the 5th or 6th century B.C., undoubtedly contributed much to the harmonious atmosphere which prevailed there some centuries later during the vital transitional period of Christianization.

It is therefore not surprising that, deeply associated with the legendary stories about how St. Patrick 'converted' the Irish, we have the symbol of the trefoil, or the tiny, almost esoterically (!) difficult to find clover-type plant called the shamrock.

This trinitarian foundation of consciousness, though lost to, or actually banished from, formal Christian teaching and learning for a long time now, has nevertheless maintained at least an outward presence in modern Ireland. For the shamrock has, quite significantly, since become the famous national lucky emblem of the country. And furthermore, the three colours of the Irish flag (the tricolour) may be regarded as being related to the three types or grades of initiation into the Christian Mystery which the early Irish saints cultivated through a consciously sought martyrdom.[33]

Now in trying to characterize the most revealing tenets particular to this early Irish Christianity, one, more than all other aspects, is most apparent. And that is how these two ancient historical figures of Patrick and Brigid stand out at the head of it almost like a father and mother stands at the head of a large family. It is also quite pertinent to note that these two complimentary figures, as archetypes, are still very much alive in the psyches of the Irish. And in many ways they can be looked upon as Celtic representatives of that necessary gender balance which must be sought for and achieved in the human soul if it aspires to a genuine and a strong faith. This latter of course is something that the Irish have always been noted for.

And this is still undoubtedly the case, though it is a faith that will of necessity take on a different form as time passes.

SAINT PATRICK

Now Patrick and Brigid were, roughly speaking, contemporaries. Of the two however it was St. Brigid who struck deepest into the soul of the nation, partly due no doubt to her mythic associations with the ancient goddess, but also of course very much to do with the spiritual/religious jurisdiction she gained in the country because of her inspired missionary activity. In fact there is evidence in the records of early Irish Church history indicating how at this time there were two quite distinct 'sees' in the country, one under the control of Brigid and her successors, and another stemming from Patrick. The ancient Book of Armagh for instance records in a missive to her that her 'own province will be left completely under your sway' while outside of there, to the east and west, it was deemed to be Patrick's domain.

In this controversy in the early Irish Church we can see at work the polarisation of two very distinct tendencies, in the manner in which evangelization was actually taking place in Ireland. On the one had there was the ancient druidic wisdom culture, the christianization of which was embodied in Brigid, a development which may be termed *sophiacal*.[34] On the other hand there was also the Roman type influence, essentially ecclesiastical in character, embodied in the work of Patrick, and which may be called (conveniently), patristic. And it was in the careful marrying of these two complementary, but potentially opposing powers, that the strength of the early Irish Church lay. Furthermore, the benign and pacifying manner in which the resolution of these potentially conflicting tendencies was effected, given the depth of power which they actually possess to stir the human soul – this is testimony enough to the presence of the Spirit of the Holy Sophia in this early Irish Celtic Church.

Patrick of course is a much more historical figure than Brigid. There are many reasons for this. But perhaps the main one is that some of his own writings have actually survived. Moreover they have managed to survive unsullied through all the burnings, pillagings and literary forgings that are so characteristic of our Western spiritual history. Perhaps their 'simple' unlearned and unpretentious nature helped in this escape! In any event they are there for us now, and are actually in very wide circulation, allowing us to easily examine them with much profit regarding just who this Patrick was and what he was about. We are enabled to look at him, in other words, stripped of all the somewhat artificial legends and myths that were put out about him by the Roman Church for its own restricted purposes.

For nothing, after all, contributes more to giving a man real flesh and blood than his own very word!

Now by far the most interesting and revealing of these writings is the one known as the Confession, an extended letter undisputedly attributed by scholars to Patrick's own hand. Whereas a lot of what was later written by 'churched' scribes and hagiographers about Patrick (and the saints generally) tends to be clouded by varying (albiet usually well meaning!) degrees of myth, mist, muddy mysticism and so on, in Patrick's own Confession the real man of flesh and blood, in all his human weaknesses, as well of course as in his undeniable virtue, piety and saintliness, comes very clearly across. Moreover we can also gain for ourselves in reading his Confession some of those much sought-after items indispensable in the pursuit of any discipline, spiritual or otherwise, i.e. precise and concrete facts.

Thus we know for certain that as a boy Patrick was abducted from his home in Britain during one of the on-going slave and cattle raids that the Irish made upon her big neighbouring island in those far-off days. He was sixteen at the time. He was subsequently sold to one who (legend has it) was a Druid. So here at this impressionable age we have a young man who was suddenly and violently wrenched from the (comparatively speaking) highly civilized and cultured life of his Roman Christian upbringing, one where his father held the priviliged position of a deacon in the Church of the period. And in this providential way our Patrick is thrust deep into that misty and forbidden land to the west, a land so brimfull of myth, magic and wonder that no boy like him could possibly have been there for any length of time without becoming deeply and permanently touched by the experience. And so Patrick was in Ireland, he tells us, for six long years, all of this time with the one man whom he served as a slave and a shepherd.

Though Patrick does not say it explicitly, we can easily imagine this wise master of his becoming very aware of his boy's simple and developing sanctity, and in this would have undoubtedly wished to encourage him. Furthermore, though not necessarily Christian, this Druid master w o u l d surely have taught and shown Patrick many things through which he could learn to stimulate his intuition, strengthen his imagintion, and thus spiritually nourish his tender and growing Christian soul. And though it was certainly a hard life for the young Patrick as he clearly indicates, it was also one that was full of mystery and enchantment as the manner and content of his Confession also very convincingly reveals.

And so having thus become well acquainted with this strange land, its sophisticated religion, its seasonal customs, and its deeply spiritual people, Patrick had been able, in this atmosphere, to thoroughly cultivate the Christian virtues he had heard about in his boyhood schooling. Especially he practised those virtues of modesty and piety, and he became also very accomplished, he tells us, in the valuable and subtle arts of prayer and meditation. In this way he was gradually awakened to the wonderful reality of God and by virtue of this, also to his own higher and guardian angelic being. Not surprisingly he was therefore led eventually, he tells us, by the medium of a prophetic dream, to a ship in which he would, with great joy and excitement, escape his slavery.

PATRICK'S DREAM

Now what happens next provides us with a very deep insight indeed into the manner of Patrick's full initiation into, or confirmation of, his Christian baptism. And this also took the form of a kind of visionary dream. For in his recounting of this episode we see very clearly at work in the young man's psyche the influence of the ancient sun-wisdom, so vitally and vibrantly cultivated within the druidic and gradually christianizing traditions of Hibernia, much of which Patrick had absorbed during his six years of slavery.

For on the ship taking him away from Ireland Patrick tells us '....I was sleeping and Satan tempted me powerfully, which will be a memory as long as I am in this body, and he fell on me like a great rock (while) nothing in my limbs had any strength. But how did it occur to me in my ignorance to call upon Helias? And meanwhile I saw the sun rise in the sky, and while I shouted Helia! Helia! with all my might, lo and behold the splendour of that sun fell down on me and at once smashed off all the weight from me: and I believe I was helped by Christ my Lord'[135].

Now Helios is of course another name for the ancient sun god, Apollo or Phoebus.* (The slightly different spelling can easily be put down to Patrick's own use of the Latin which is widely recognised by modern scholars, and especially by Patrick himself, as being of a low standard).

And later on in his Confession Patrick reaffirms his deep awareness of this sun-nature of the Christ Being when he says 'we shall rise in the brightness of the sun, that is, in the glory of Christ Jesus our Redeemer'.

Furthermore in a vision he had a number of years after he left Ireland he indicates even more clearly how deeply his soul had become infused with the Sun-Spirit as it manifested itself so powerfully in its solar Logos or Word aspect in Hibernia: 'And there I saw in the night the vision of a man whose name was Victoricus, coming as it were from Ireland with countless letters. And he gave me one of them and I read the opening words of the letter which were: 'The voice of the Irish'; and as I read the beginning of the letter I thought at the same moment I heard their voice – they were those beside the Wood of Volclut, which is near the western sea – and thus did they cry out as with one mouth: 'We ask thee, boy, come walk among

* See Page 26 and note 13

us once more'.

Immediately after this account of his vision Patrick says that in another dream the Irish spoke to him as if they were the very mouth of Christ himself!

We can be left with no doubt at all therefore of how deeply connected Patrick felt the Sun Logos and the island and people of Ireland to be.[36]

So through his dreams, his visions and his intuitions, as well as in many other ways, Patrick's enchantment with Hibernia gradually matured into a religious and spiritual conviction of the very highest order, and so he promised Christ he would return to the Irish to establish more firmly the Word of God there. And after overcoming great obstacles placed in his path by some of his Church contemporaries, who doubtless envied or were suspicious of his humble yet great and willful spiritual strength and energy, he was eventually made Bishop and came to Ireland with the authority of the established orthodox Roman Church. His mission was to bring some kind of ecclessiastical order to the Christians in Ireland which he duely did, as well as extending the paramiters of the Gospel's influence greatly by penetrating with it, through unceasing toil and effort, into every nook and cranny of the (often very difficult to negotiate) terrain.

PELAGIUS AND THE ANCIENT WISDOM

Patrick did astounding and marvellous work for the Gospel in Ireland. There is no doubt whatever about this. But in attempting to make a true assessment of his place, not only in the history of the Irish Church, but also in the whole strange development of the spirit within the wider Church itself, we must now consider the life and work of another man, one who was Patrick's contemporary, and one in fact who can be regarded in many ways as much more complementary to Brigid than Patrick himself actually was. This was the monk-philosopher Pelagius.

This individual, Pelagius, shot like a bolt of spiritual lightening out of the far western twilit world and into the limelight of busy and important Church affairs in Rome and elsewhere towards the very end of the 4th century. This big, strong, rough featured Celtic holy man must surely have cut a strange figure in the dying and shabby grandure of the decadent Roman culture of the period. For he was proffering a brand of Christianity, fully matured, light-filled, at once freely, eloquently and convincingly expressed, yet also totally at odds with the centralist and theocratic designs of the increasingly Roman-influenced orthodoxy. Pelagius' free Celtic expression of the incarnational spirit was in fact far too pure and strong for the dogmatic type of theologians emerging in the Roman Church at this time, of whom St. Augustine is probably still the best known.

They called him Pelagius because this name was a Greek rendering of the Celtic appellative 'morgan' meaning 'sea-born', or 'from over the sea', and without any deliberate intention of creating a school or encouraging an organised following of his beliefs and practises as such, this man soon began to attract a growing number of followers.

For Pelagius was a product of that period of pre-patristic Irish Christianity about which, apart from Pelagius himself, very little at all is actually known. However from this one highly influential and colourful exponent of it we can nevertheless gain a good appreciation and understanding of the spiritual depth and richness of the transitional and increasingly christianized culture of this time in Ireland.

And that Pelagius was from Ireland need hardly be doubted. For although he was nicknamed 'Brito' by his prime opponent St. Augustine, this need hardly be taken as a true indication of his origin, which it often has been. A 'Brito' may indeed have been one from 'over the sea' (i.e. from Britain), but in those far-off days the whole of the British Isles were lumped together in the minds of most people, even educated ones. However, St. Jerome, perhaps *the* most learned of all of the Latin Church Fathers, plainly calls Pelagius 'of Irish race, from the region of Britain'.

Now, by the time Pelagius had arrived on the scene, the western Roman Church was becoming ever more hierarchical in its style, and freedom-denying in its spirit. The light of The Gnosis had by this time been well and truely put out, and more recently the defeat of that other great 'heresy' of the early Church, Arianism, had been more or less defeated too. And the hardening and expanding triumphalism resulting from these victories within the Church had of course to have its 'theorizers' and, even more importantly, its 'theologizers'. And in St. Augustine of Hippo (354 - 430) we have the most eloquent, prolific, and convincing protagonist of this emerging trend in the early Church. But it is a trend nevertheless that can hardly be truely seen in any other light than that of a gathering of the forces of darkness, for it was something essentially to do with the denying of the individual freedom of the human spirit. It was thus also and inevitably a trend that was death- far more than resurrection-centered in it's psychology and theology. In fact Augustine's troubled life and the negative brand of theology that it produced was so thoroughly shaped by, and steeped in sensual remorse, the darkness of sin, and the burden of guilt, that he would probably have needed another re-birth extra to the one he speaks about, if he were to truely see the light of the sun-spirit that was shining so purely through this holy and freedom-loving Celtic sage, Pelagius.

St. Augustine however was rightly very highly regarded for the eloquent manner in which he could define and articulate a basis for a real and solid faith in Christ, something moreover the Church simply had to learn to do if it was going to succeed in a world where many gods vie for the people's simple faith. One can thus say in a sense that the Church was adopting a policy of 'faith at any price'. For the price in fact was one which demanded a relinquishing of the true soaring spirit of knowledge and wisdom in order to gain this depth of faith.

Pelagius' theology of the free spirit had no place at all in such a half-baked scheme, and it is not surprising that this free ambassador of the Christianized Mystery-wisdom of the spirit would get branded quickly as a despised 'heretic'.

In fact the whole furore in the early Church surrounding this Irishman and his great wisdom, i.e. the Pelagian heresy, and the manner in which Pelagius himself became anathematized through it, was one upon which the Church of Rome, as distinct from the still broadly unified universal Church of Christ, thoroughly sharpened its dogmatic and power-hungry teeth. For up to this point there was as yet no clear division between the Eastern, Western, or indeed any other 'see' of the Church. The one and only 'Holy See' as such had not yet been evoked. When the controversy between Augustine and Pelagius reached its climax however (and this significantly came only *after* the Eastern bishops *in collegium* had refused to anathematize Pelagius!) the highly influential Augustine took the decisive step of honouring the Bishop of Rome with a request to him to personally, officially, and finally adjudicate in the entire matter, once and for all! Innocent I, needless to say, jumped at the opportunity to strengthen his own hand regarding his authorative ambitions for Rome, sided with Augustine, and quickly denounced Pelagius. It was a very decisive moment in the history of the Western Church! For from then on the Bishop of Rome gradually established and strengthened his centralist power structure and gradually became known and duely recognized as the Pope of this Petrine Church.

And so in this manner this great early Irish exponent of a free logosophical or Johannine Christianity, Pelagius, vanishes from the scene even more suddenly than he arrived, for no trace whatsoever of him has come to light after this time. The only legitimate picture one can form of this sorry episode in the Church is that of yet another bright-shining and living spirit-light being simply snuffed out! Needless to say however, Pelagius' influence, like that of Arius and other 'heretics' and free spirit-lovers before him, undoubtedly continued for a long time afterwards.

We can thus see that already by Patrick's time the Celtic Church had reached a very high degree of cultural and free spiritual/religious sophistication. Pelagius himself is a fine testimony to this reality. We can tell that his wisdom and learning was at once ancient, forward looking and eclectic. For we know that his consciousness would have been infused and informed with the Mystery and mythic wisdom of his druidic/Celtic forebares. He had this ancient cosmic awareness and would by dint of it have cultivated a most profound feeling for the moral/spiritual being and beings of the planets and the stars, i.e. for the gods as such. However, Pelagius achieved his high status because he was also highly learned in the progressive and civilizing disciplines of his own day. He would not have been able to go to Rome or elsewhere as a missionary if he did not have these qualifications. Thus he spoke Greek and Latin (an probably even Hebrew) fluently, and though none of his written works survived intact the inevitable book-burnings which followed in the wake of his branding as a heretic, numerous books by him are known to have existed. Ironically much of what we know of his thought actually comes through St. Augustine, who obligingly (for us!) quoted his broad concepts at length in order to refute them in his (Augustine's) own narrow way. We know also that Pelagius wrote no less than three works on the sublime subject of the Trinity.

Now in any informed and genuine history of the logosophical Spirit as it manifested itself within the body of the Christian Church generally, something which we are of course here attempting, the part played in this overall development by the early Hiberno-Celtic Church is pivotal. For by understanding both the nature and the manifestation of this Spirit here in Ireland, and by clearly recognising it as both the foundation stone and the driving force at the heart of this unique Christo-Celtic culture, we are enabled to see it fully, vitally, and productively at work in the world as it was, or indeed is generally intended to be. Not only that, but we are also enabled to see, by learning something of the manner in which this high spiritual culture was purposely and ignorantly terminated, how the spirit itself thereby actually failed to penetrate the Western Church to any significant degree at all after this dismal termination. For this failure was an eventuality which was, or is, directly linked to the successful incorporation of the unorthodox but spiritually imbued free Celtic Church into the dry Roman orthodoxy and its largely temporal, dogmatic, and law-ridden agenda.

The sending of Patrick to Ireland was the first step in this direction. Patrick however was very much his own man, and his influence, despite his Roman background, can only be regarded as positive to the overall development of the Celtic Church. The manner therefore in which the Roman orthodoxy managed eventually to kill off the Celtic spirit came about in a different way, and to this we shall now turn our attention.

Chapter Eight

ROME RULES...OR ELSE!

In order to fully understand and appreciate how the demise of the Celtic Church spelled the virtual end of a true and genuine spirituality within the Western Church generally, we must know that the chief characteristic of the spirit of this Celtic Church, was the essential freedom of its expression, something which was in total opposition to the Roman outlook.

So in effect what did this mean? In a nutshell it meant that the Celtic Church affirmed with the deepest possible trust, faith in, and love of Christ and his Mother, that each man or woman can come to know God, overcome sin and so on through the power of his or her own unique and spiritually imbued free will. The pure and esoteric inwardness of the working of the spirit in man himself was therefore fully and unambiguously upheld. Thus the whole edifice, structure, and culture of the Celtic Church, all of that which naturally and organically followed upon this prime realization and its implications, was totally different from, and completely at odds with, the orthodox position upheld by Rome. For conventional Roman theology was now busily inculcating the doctrine into the minds and hearts of its flock that a man or a woman can only come to God by being told how to do so by someone else! And in effect this meant of course *us* in Rome! Blind faith for the masses, yes! Inspired knowledge, no! Simply put, this was the foundation-stone of Rome's theocracy. If there is to be any dispute at all about knowledge from now on, we in Rome will decide about it, full stop! This was the whole idea! The divine, faithful, trusting, and inwardly renewing grace of the individual's own higher angelic being, i.e. his true and deepest spirit Self, was quite simply not, or hardly at all recognised (comparatively speaking) by the outward looking and temporally influenced soul of the Roman Church. The outer disputes which took place at this time between the Celtic Church and Rome about the true dates of Easter, about how to cut your hair properly (the tonsure) and all the rest of it, were merely spurious or political 'red herrings' designed to bring the Irish into a Roman line of thinking. (They can hardly appear as anything else from our advantageous and retrospectively enlightened viewpoint. See page 96). And it was merely a matter of time, of course, given the sort of political backing which Rome had, and which it was busily consolidating, before it had its way fully.

For even in the old pre-Christian Roman world there was virtually no feeling for, or understanding of, the ancient Mystery wisdom upon which most of the religions, cultures and civic societies of antiquity had in fact been built. This of course would have been most especially true for the Romans regarding that mystery-filled and strange land far away to the twilit west, Hibernia. Rome in fact was probably unique in the respect of its being the only city and culture of antiquity which was not founded upon, born out of, or inspired in some way by the initiatory insights of the ancient Mystery temple-wisdom. In fact quite the reverse was the case. For the impulse for this Roman civilization arose fundamentally out of an exploitation of those very vacuous psychic forces which, having been lost to the tight, ordered, and mostly benign control of the initiates and their disciples as the Mysteries gradually fell into disuse, then spread out loosely all over the world in the wake of this spiritual decline in pre-Christian times.

Let us digress here a little and look at this matter briefly, for it is important to an understanding of the brutish and hard nature of this Roman consciousness.

ROME AND THE BEAST

The city of Rome was founded in the year traditionally 753B.C. and from her very beginnings she set her face resolutely against the prophetic, the spiritual and the cosmic, against all those forces in fact inherent in the truely human form, and the cultivation of which had been of the very essence of the Mystery temples, of their work, and teaching. Even worse, this Roman creation proceeded to twist whatever baser spiritual power she could derive from what was left of these Mysteries into serving her very imperialistic, militaristic and materialistic ends. The Roman culture was thus highly synthetic and artificial in nature, and thoroughly unoriginal in character, having no natural or indigenous spiritual nourishment which, as a matter of course, sustained former cultures out of the richness of their own temples and its initiates. All of which helps of course to account for the hideous demonstrations of institutionalized cruelty and butchery which lay at Rome's very centre, and which were the focus of its chief ceremonial and civic trappings.

In fact if we wish to try to gain some understanding of just where all such bestiality could possibly have originated from, the situation is really very well illustrated by the fact that the only truely or purely Roman god, i.e. a god who does not have a counterpart or a precursor in any other pantheon, is the one they named Janus, who apart from being their *one supreme god* was also a god with *two* heads (the apotheosis, you could say, of confusion, divisiveness and even of psychosis!). And he was also always very revealingly placed at the doorway of their temples, looking both ways. Hence the significant and defiant gesture of looking away from the temple as much as into it!

Rome and its culture in other words epitomizes this turning away from the ancient starry wisdom of the gods in the heavens, and sets her narrow eyes greedily and angrily upon the hard earth itself. She represented essentially a denial of the cosmic warmth of the Sophia spirit in man, and brazenly and ignorantly tries to twist this spirit around by turning man himself, in his purely materialistic aspect, into a god. We have here, in all of this, a sort of deification of the material, something which in fact is nothing less than a perversion of the truth of the ancient wisdom. It was inevitable therefore that the embodiment of a spirit such as this i.e. Caesar, would in the end arrogantly declare himself to be a god!

We can thus see that Rome was founded upon, and built up out of those dubious forces and strengths inherent in man's lower nature, those angers, passions, desires and turbulent emotions, all of which it is the business of true spirituality and religion generally to subdue and tame, but certainly not to indulge in and cultivate for political, or indeed any other purpose. Edouard Schure, who had an encyclopaedic knowledge of the ancient wisdom and ancient cultures generally, characterized the situation thus: "What is Rome's origin? The conjuration of a greedy oligarchy in the name of brute force; the oppression of human intellect, of religion, science and art through deified political power; in other words the opposite of truth according to which a government draws its power only from the supreme principles of science, justice and economy. All Roman history is but the outgrowth of this pact of iniquity by which the Roman senators declared war first on Italy and then on the human race. They chose their symbol well! The brass She-Wolf, raising her wild hair and moving her hyena-head on the Capitoline, is the reflection of the government, the demon which will possess the Roman soul to the very last".[37]

Now given this background, when the light of the Mystery wisdom, which had been so powerfully renewed through the Incarnation, eventually reached and became consolidated to some degree in the Roman world, it was inevitable that it would not meet there with the same understanding and appreciation that it met with in other places, especially Ireland. The Christo-Celtic culture which flowered in Ireland was of course, as we have seen, a direct outcome of the Hibernian Mysteries. It was a remarkably pure, perhaps a unique spiritual culture, and this was probably due to the fact that unlike all of the other ancient Mysteries, these Hibernian Mysteries had not in fact been destroyed or corrupted at all. They had merely withdrawn and, taking note of the gathering darkness in the world, became even more careful, secretive and esoteric in their working than was normal for them.

The spiritual perceptions of the Christ Being thus available within the framework of this Irish culture was infinitely more inward, etherial, and profound than that which could be had in any other, especially Roman influenced, cultures. It was also of course in Ireland manifestly a simple and humble expression of this spirit which took place, (humility being, after all, the hallmark of all true and genuine spirituality). Inevitably therefore the outer cultic forms of the new religion also took on a relatively simple mode of expression. For instance, the physical churches themselves, if and when they were necessary to build at all, were nearly always small, simple, made of wood, and rarely of stone (and only then in places where wood would not withstand the harsh weather). The people regularly worshipped out of doors amidst the beauty of their natural surroundings and gathered devoutly around their exquisite high stone sun-crosses which were often erected in places known from time immemorial to have been receptive to the spiritual vibrations entering the atmosphere of the Earth from the cosmos.

An echo of the dignified, profound, etherial, yet simple Christ-consciousness of these early Irish followers of the new Way can be found in the prayers and blessings which they used and some of which have actually survived from this time. These prayers and blessings are full of a wondrous and heartfelt expression of the love and beauty that shines out from the Christ-imbued natural world and hint to us of the deep spiritual treasures of the Celtic Church.

THANKSGIVING[38]

Thanks to Thee, O God, that I have risen today,
To the rising of this life itself;
May it be to Thine own glory, O God of every gift,
And to the glory of my soul likewise.

O great God, aid Thou my soul
With the aiding of Thine own mercy;
Even as I clothe my body with wool,
Cover Thou my soul with the shadow of Thy wing.

Help me to avoid every sin,
And the source of every sin to forsake;
And as the mist scatters on the crest of the hills,
May each ill haze clear from my soul, O God.

Of course in an environment where a spiritually imbued consciousness is nurtured such as the one capable of producing hymns and prayers like this, structures and organization fall naturally into their proper place. There is no need here of dogmatic and rigidified codes of practises and structural methods stringently enforced. To the hard, narrow, and organizing worldly gaze of the Roman eye however, the simplicity and profound spirituality of the Celtic Church was nothing but backwardness, rusticity and paganism.

Worse still, it became ever more in their eyes a harbinger of that dreaded and demonized individual, the heretic.

ROME AND IRELAND

The Pelagian controversy undoubtedly had stirred the whole Roman Christian world into a deep suspicion of what was going on in Ireland. Patrick of course, because of his intimate knowledge of the Irish people, coupled with the perspective he had gained from his now wider worldly experience, knew deep in his heart what the Irish wanted and needed. And through this, in his own truely inspired way, he wished to help them awaken to an even larger sense of community in Christ than they already possessed. Rome however had a very different agenda than Patrick.

The Pelagian controversy had actually preceeded Patrick's arrival in Ireland by only a short number of years. And as such it must have had a strong baring upon the now pending question of Patrick's proposed mission. Certain reactionary forces were thus aroused within the Church against Patrick, for they feared he would not be able to forward Rome's agenda properly. For, as Patrick himself so painfully recalls in his Confession, the most insidious types of obstacles were placed upon his path of gaining the proper authorative blessings for his mission to the Irish, an authority he rightly required, he knew, if he was to properly execute his mission there.

Undoubtedly Patrick's whole demeanour, his background, his self-confessed 'rusticity', if not indeed his actual philosophical leanings, would all have very strongly smacked in the eyes of the emerging intellectual princes of the Roman Church, of what was to them wishy washy Pelagianism. Patrick therefore was both opposed and even villified in his efforts to gain episcopal recognition for his projected work. In this manner Patrick and his holy mission were sidelined, and Rome, in its ambitious plans to haul Ireland and the Celtic Church generally into the sphere of its ordered, ecclessiastical, but essentially temporal influence, sent someone else instead. He was someone whom they obviously felt could carry out their plans in a much more orthodox fashion. This man was called Palladius and he came to Ireland in the year 431.

Patrick was, needless to say, shattered to the very depths of his soul and spirit by this turn of events. For ever since he had left Ireland many years before, his whole life had been lived in a sort of preparation for going back to these beloved people. His rejection was thus undoubtedly his own particular 'harrowing of hell', his very own experience of the Passion, for he indicated most sorrowfully in his Confession that he came very near to losing his Christian soul during this time of his severest testing.

Providence however was secretly at work in all of this and Patrick came through his period of testing an even stronger and more willful servant of Christ than he had already been beforehand. For Palladius died unexpectedly very soon after commencing his work in Ireland. And this was a propitious and (for Patrick) a fortuitous event that enabled him very soon afterwards to obtain the vital seal of approval for his hopes and plans from his superiors. And so in the year 432 Patrick began his great work for Christ, for the Gospel, and for the universal and free Church of God in the holy island of Ireland.

* * *

As we have said earlier, Christianity, right from its very inception, began to work spiritually within the very receptive vessel of the Irish folk-soul in quite a unique way. Furthermore we have seen that this was essentially an inward or an esoteric working, a phenomenon no doubt of which Patrick would have been only too well aware, having spent the most absorptive years of his youth there. He knew therefore that no outward coercion or conversion to Christianity as such was needed here. His mission, he would have well known, was much more a question, or a process of *confirming*, or of actually harnessing the growing national Christ-consciousness into a greater or more conscious unity. And this Patrick set about doing in an ordered and thoroughly inspired way.

It has been authoritatively stated that Patrick brought Christianity to every corner of the island in the space of his 30 years work there. (He is reputed to have died in the year 461 and is buried together with Brigid and that other great early Irish saint, Columba, in Downpatrick, Co. Down. At least there is an ancient gravestone in the old graveyard there to this effect, though of course it is not easy to authenticate such things. Whether authentic or not, it nevertheless is very interesting to note how the trinitarian concept or knowledge yet again comes to the fore in this unusual burial arrangement).

Now the ordered Celtic Church, of which the thriving monastic settlement was the linchpin, a highly disciplined general society of closely interlinked spiritual *famalia* communities where every branch of learning was deeply cultivated, this was largely the outcome of Patrick's work in Ireland. And because such learning and spiritual activity penetrated and took hold of the country to such a large degree, the land eventually became known as the Island of Saints and Scholars. And at a time when the rest of Europe was yielding to the turmoil of the various barbarian invasions, Ireland, in its sea-bound seclusion was providentially in a position to profit from this turmoil. So that, in so far as they could at all manage to reach the island, Ireland provided a safe haven for many a Christian scholar on the run from his ignorant head-hunting and blood-letting heathen contemporaries. And thus into this slowly forming Christian vessel in old Hibernia was mixed, together with the rich residues of the ancient druidic wisdom already very much to the fore there, a steady flow of the new Christian-inspired learning which had been cultivated in the East and elsewhere.

94

All of which helped to produce the diverse and spiritually imbued art and learning which has come to be known as the Celtic Church. It was indeed here in Ireland that the light of the Christ Spirit in its truely Western configuration took hold fully. And here this Spirit was tended and nurtured so lovingly that it benefited and enriched not only the already deeply spiritual qualities of the Irish soul herself, but also in fact the whole of Europe.

For it was during these dark barbaric years of European history that the precious Christ-light streamed out of Celtic Ireland and into Europe with those bands of missionary saints who in this highly productive way elected for the privilige of a Christian martyrdom. In doing so these saints and scholars managed heroically to keep alive in an ever darkening world the great incarnational Mystery-spirit in its most essential characteristic, that of freedom.

THE ONE TRUE CHURCH?

We speak now of the 5th to the 8th centuries which is the approximate duration of what is generally referred to as the Celtic Church. This was also of course precisely the period when the Roman Church was busily attempting to consolidate in various ways its own peculiarly unilateral claim to be the 'one true Church'. In its limited vision however, Rome, on the continent, tended to lump the Irish in with everyone else who got in its way and who were always simply put down as the 'heathen'. This was a blatant error and one committed much to the ultimate detriment of the spirit of the truely universal Church!

In their work of the Christianizing of Europe at this time the Irish were of course far more tolerant of, and sympathetic to, the old customs and rites of the ancient worship which inevitably still lingered on within the migrating tribes, echoing their own diverse and particular Mystery religions and wisdom. Rome however had totally different, totally opposite methods to the Irish in the handling of these delicate areas of evangelical activity. And because of the tolerance of the Irish in this and other aspects of this missionary activity, they were very widely respected and much sought after by intelligent leaders and rulers as being capable of injecting a much needed civilizing, pacifying, and benign influence into the more robust practises and warlike psychology of many of these tribal groupings under their jurisdiction. The Irish however then became, because of their apparently 'soft' approach, an easy target for the Roman legalistic and conforming bias to focus upon. Thus in their religious politiking and spiritual propaganda they proceeded to anathematize the Irish right, left, and centre.

It is in the person of St. Boniface (675 - 754) who appears on the scene at this time, that the whole approach or Rome finds its most energetic, coercive and even fanatical expression. Although this English saint is widely recognised and eulogized in conventional and often biased accounts of European and Church history as the 'Apostle to the Germans', '....detailed knowledge of his work reveals that he was less a converter of the heathen than a commissioner with the task of bringing into the Roman Church those regions on the mainland (of Europe) which had been christianized by the Irish........."[39].

Now Boniface went about his work in very steadfast ways, many of which carry the hallmark of the true fanatic. For instance one of his chief methods of evangelization was the ruthless destroying and desecration of traditional places of worship! Brazenly daring the pagans and their gods by virtue of his zeal for Christ and his thirst for the power of Rome, this Boniface was Pope Gregory's prime emissary in the continuation of the Romanizing of the Church which his predecessor, the very strong first Pope Gregory (the Great) had, about a century before, so resolutely put into full steam ahead.

ROME ABHORS THE CELTIC SUN-WISDOM

And in the conflict between Boniface and the Irishman Virgilius (Fergil) who was made Bishop of Salzburg around this time, we have a good example of both the spiritual shallowness of the Roman Church and its methods, and the fanaticism which this inevitably bred. Thus because Virgilius was an exponent of the Christo-Celtic Mystery wisdom of Ireland, he was privy to much astronomical/astrological information of which the Romans not only knew nothing, but actually cared about even less. For the fabulous sun wisdom of the Celts represented little more to the Romans than merely a confirmation of that catchall and criminalizing appellation which they were so wont to use to classify all those who did not toe the dogmatic line – pagans in other words. This Celtic wisdom was nevertheless something which, precisely because of its sun and star nature, was capable of producing true scientific knowledge and insights into the Earth and its relationship to the cosmos, and it could thus put forward ideas which were very advanced for their time. For it is evident from this conflict between Boniface and Fergil that the Irish already actually had at this early time very advanced astronomical concepts regarding the Earth and the Solar System generally.

Fergil could show for instance, even here in the 8th century, to the total bewilderment of the Romans, that the sun and the moon could exist not only above the Earth but actually below it also. The Romans however had no wish at all to look up to the sun, moon, planets and stars, and seek in them the spiritual/scientific language of the Celts. Moreover it was this very kind of thing that most galled them! For the Catholic doctrine makers wanted to know nothing whatsoever about the planets, the stars and the cosmos. And thus, understandably, Boniface was furious when this 'heathen' Fergil was made Bishop of Salzburg! And so he wanted to be rid of him as quickly as possible!

Now in setting about this important work of Romanization, Boniface solicited no less a personage than the Pope himself. He apparently had to go to this extreme, for Fergil was not to be so easily got rid of! Indeed Fergil obviously stood in very high esteem with many high-ranking people of the secular world at this time and had even secured the Bishopric of Salzburg on foot of the Frankish King's (Peppin the Short) high recommendation. Notwithstanding this, Pope Zacharias threw his full support in behind Boniface, for he was full of admiration of him and in total agreement with his methods of Romanization. He thus wrote to Boniface saying: 'This Virgilius (Fergil) was found guilty by you of deviating from Catholic doctrine. .....If it is established that in his opinion there is yet another world and other human beings under the Earth, and (there is) another sun and moon, you are to hold a Church assembly and drive him out of the Church after you have stripped him of his priestly status'.[40]

Zacharias went on to say that Fergil then should be arrested and brought to Rome and charged there with heresy!

Apart from anything else this episode is indicative of the strength and depth of the Irish spiritual wisdom by the very fact of Virgilius' surviving this systematic programme of villification. For survive he did! And moreover he 'remained until his death in 784 a brilliant embodiment of the free Irish school of thought'.[41]

Boniface alas met with perhaps a more predictable end! For in 754 he and a band of his converts were set upon and unceremoniously massacred by an army of deeply slighted 'heathens' in the region of West Friesland.

THE DECLINE OF THE CELTIC CHURCH

What has been called the Golden Age of the Celtic Church was in fact quite a short period, approximately the duration only of the 6th century. It is indeed an Age so short that, when one evaluates its contribution to the overall and long-term civilizing of the life of Europe generally, is evidence enough of the quality, depth, and intensity of that Age's spirituality.

But already by the latter part of the 7th century Rome saw fit to call a general Synod in England, the chief objective of which was to curb the activities of the Irish monks there, and undoubtedly also to indirectly begin what it surely considered its much more important work, that of the complete Romanization of the Island of Saints and Scholars herself. The Church assembly we here speak of is the famous Synod of Whitby which was held in the year 664, an event which historically marks the beginning of the end of the free Celtic Church. For it was from this event onwards that Rome, by cleverly manipulating its existing claims to authority, obtained substantive and broad agreement, despite Irish objections, regarding the correct method of fixing Easter Sunday in the Church calender. So by virtue of gaining victory in this as well as in other even more minor matters at the Synod, Rome was able to gradually suppress the esoteric spirit at work within the Celtic soul and subsequently imposed more and more its authorative, centralist and dogmatic kind of ecclesiastical control over the evolving Church in Ireland.

But if this Synod and its repercussions can be seen as the sounding of the death-knell of the free Celtic spirit, there was yet another crucial and apparently quite seperate factor in Irish history which can be seen as the veritable making of this spirit's coffin! And this was the factor of the Viking invasions. For although Ireland and the Irish had escaped the stamp of Roman imperialism in much earlier times, and had also subsequently escaped (primarily because of her isolated situation) the cultural and civic upheavals resulting from the barbarian invasions during the break-up of the Empire, Ireland's time of safe seclusion eventually came to an end. And this began in the year 795 with the arrival of the first black shiploads of hard fighting-men from Scandanavia. These men, who were in truth the real terrorists of their time, were out to impose their crude will upon whomsoever provided them with the most lucrative spoils. And the island of Saints and Scholars was indeed a paradise of rich pickings for their appetites. These were the Vikings.

Thus over a period of a few centuries this crowd of wild foreigners terrorized the quiet, deeply spiritual and pastoral land of Erin, killing, pillaging, looting and ransacking everything and everywhere they went. This especially applied to the monasteries of course which by this time housed all or most of the wealth and valuables worth talking about in the country. Throngs of the holy monks and saints were also, needless to say, massacred into the bargain, and it was in this bloody and tragic manner that one of the greatest periods of Christian culture the world has yet known soon came to an end.

A spirit as strong as that which built and sustained this Celtic culture is however not one to be easily or, one hopes, ever entirely beaten! It is true of course that by the time of the Viking invasions the great missionary activity of the Celtic Church to Europe was well and truely over anyway. But despite this decline, Ireland continued to be a place where knowledge of the true spirit of Sophia was capable of being systematically cultivated. And though we can have but little idea of the actual spiritual perceptions available to the people at large in such far-off times as these, it is obvious from what we *can* glean from an historical overview, that the' soul of the people of Ireland remained rich in spiritual content for a long time after the Roman Church began to tighten its dogmatic grip and squeeze out the Celtic Mystery spirit. And it is obvious also that something of this spirit survived the systematic destruction by the Vikings. And though from the rich tapestry of Gaelic story, legend and folklore we can get some idea of the depth of the soul and spiritual life of the people at this time, perhaps the best evidence we have for the continued cultivation of this spirit-imbued Celtic wisdom in Ireland emerges in the personality of one whose influence has reached far beyond the boundaries of his native land. This is the 9th century Irish scholar John Scotus Erigena, who is rightly generally regarded as one of the key figures capable of unlocking the whole confused history of our Western spirituality. For at this vital time of his appearance, when the last rich and colourful remnants of the ancient cosmic wisdom was being flattened into the dark uniformity of Roman authoritarianism, this great individual emerged like a thunderbolt out of Ireland onto the European scene as a sort of philosophical saviour.

JOHN SCOTUS ERIGENA: SHAPER OF THE MIDDLE AGES

John Scotus Erigena acquired such a high status precisely because he was expounding in his teachings and writings the selfsame wisdom of the ancients, but a teaching and a wisdom that was now vitally renewed through the powerful spiritual Event of the Incarnation. Moreover he was doing so at a time when Europe generally was in the very thick of its own darkest age and desperately in need of one such as him.

We arrive now at a time in Europe when its destiny can be seen in terms of a crucible wherein the Church, at whatever the cost, was going to assert herself and carve out her place in the world amidst an ever increasing awareness of the power of darkness and evil. It was however a time which in retrospect can also be seen to have a seed or womblike quality to it. For within it preparations were being made for the great cultural and spiritual rennaissance soon to emerge and which would culminate in the achievements of the Middle Ages.

Now John Scotus Erigena was actually a key figure in this cultural and spiritual rennaissance. For his philosophical work can be viewed as fundamental to the foundations upon which this great period of our recent Western history and culture was laid, and which had as its central concept the remarkable one of 'Christendom'.

Needless to say the web of political, spiritual and psychological circumstances which played into the creation of this Age are complex in the extreme. We will therefore have to content ourselves here with merely highlighting some of the more salient features involved, and in so doing hopefully appreciate all the more readily the significance of Erigena's contribution. We should thus recognise clearly that we are now entering a time in Europe when the Church was penetrating ever more fully and thoroughly into the lives of each and every individual and, more to the point, was doing so with a spiritual power which was based squarely on a blind and a forcibly imposed acceptance of an incarnational faith in Jesus Christ. Now in such a circumstance it was only to be expected that reasons for all the Church's strange actions in this regard (and we need not bother to recount any of these right here) had to be ever more carefully teased out and defined. For it must be remembered we are also entering a period of history when individual consciousness was very much on the rise, and out of this, their very *self-recognition*, human beings were beginning to question themselves and the world in a way they had never done before.[42] Thus an intellectual backdrop was gradually emerging within this growing Medieval culture which had the primary function of supplying the 'proofs of reason' for (especially) the Church's confusing, often irrational, and regularly immoral conduct. And this is the movement we have come to know as Scholasticism!

Now although he could not by any means be regarded as being in sympathy with Scholasticism as such, nevertheless in so far as the Church saw fit to cultivate a pure philosophy which it understandably regarded as being ultimately the only way in which it could manage to survive in the long-term as a cohesive religious entity in the world, John Scotus can be seen as the father of this philosophical movement. The fact that he was later branded as a heretic is evidence enough of the growing strength of the opposition within the orthodox Church to the logosophical (or, to put it more conventionally, the Johannine) spirit still lingering within it, something due chiefly of course to the Irish dimension, of which Erigena was the latest and perhaps the greatest spokesman.

For Erigena's wisdom was of the very essence of the spirit of the divine Logos to which his most celebrated work is the perfect witness. Let us therefore briefly consider it.

This short work is called 'The Voice Of The Eagle'[43] and in it Erigena expounds upon the Prologue to the Gospel of St. John. Erigena takes these verses of the Gospel and uses them to articulate the depths of his own knowledge and wisdom because it is in these verses, he was only too well aware, that the Gospel is proclaimed in all its deepest, purest, and most philosophically rich spirituality. For in the profundity of its utterances, the opening of St. John's Gospel brings the 'Good News' into full accord and alignment with the most exalted and ancient of all wisdom teachings, those concerning the Sun Logos.

It is here in the Prologue to his Gospel that St. John proclaims the Divine Word or the Solar Logos Being as having incarnated into a flesh and blood human body through Jesus Christ.

Of course the mainstream Church was opposed to the cultivation of this vein of wisdom, especially in its complementary sophiacal or feminine emphasis, precisely because it worked so much against the centralist

101

designs of the Roman theocracy. For this latter type of consciousness always managed to smell, in the great Johannine wisdom, traces of the despised pagans and their often anarchic love of nature. Nevertheless this suppressive urge has not stopped this esoteric wisdom totally from being cultivated. And undoubtedly John Scotus Erigena is one of the chief figures who managed to keep it from drying up altogether. For he was totally aware of the triune God in its full sophiacal, as well as its Logos, revelation. There was, or is, indeed no greater champion of this trinitarianism, in its initiatory capacity to resuscitate the power of the ancient wisdom within the body of the Church, than John Scotus Erigena.

Erigena thus holds a somewhat paradoxical position in the Chruch's history. For on the one hand he can be looked upon as the father of that movement which gave to the Church its much needed philosophical underpinning, i.e. Scholasticism. On the other hand he and his philosophy may be regarded as that vechicle through which the despised ancient wisdom was actually kept alive to some degree. It is therefore not difficult to understand how it came about that he was eventaully branded a heretic by the orthodox Church.

Apart from his written works however (copies of which happily somehow managed to survive the flames of the heretic-hunters!) the course of Erigena's life itself is actually a very good indicator of just how deeply the resistance to the sophiacal spirit ran (or runs) within the soul of the Church.

TO HELL OR TO ROME!

John Scotus Erigena first came to prominence during a religious controversy in the 9th century regarding the so-called Augustinian doctrine of 'double predestination'. It was thus during Erigena's lifetime that this particularly dark piece of Augustine's thought was being actively promoted by the Church. The reasons for this, we can justifiably assume, were that the doctrine quite simply gave to the more aggressive elements, now very active within the Church, the power to preach Hell to those who opposed the Church's authority.

The doctrine in other words was a vechicle via which the ultimate power over the now largely superstitious minds of the ordinary people could be fully enforced, i.e. it was the doctrine of damnation. Basically it stated that *inside* the Church you went to Heaven, while *outside* of it you quite simply went to Hell; i.e. every individual was predestined to one end or the other (double predestination), the only possible hope of salvation being of course within the (Catholic!) Church. Erigena opposed this dualist doctrine vehemently! He called it in fact 'a most cruel and stupid madness', for he could clearly see that evil does not emanate from God, but from man himself, and that furthermore all of man's sin had been redeemed through the miraculous power of the Incarnation. Thus if Hell existed at all, a man did not go there because of God but because of the evil in man himself,[44] and the Church most certainly did not exist as the agent of a divine and everlasting punishment. Quite the contrary; it existed as a harbour of perpetual spiritual renewal and of divine forgiveness!

None of these types of free-spirited ideas however washed down very well within the mainstream Church, anxious as the majority of its dignitaries were to ever increase their arsenal of weaponry by which their Church could impose its authority upon the unruly masses. And thus it was at the Synod of Valence in 855 that John Scotus was condemned for his writing and teaching. And his sublime wisdom, so alien to the ears and hearts of the hard-headed dogmatists surrounding him, was pronounced there to be nothing more than a mess of 'Scots porridge' (*pultes scottorum*).[45]

Nevertheless Erigena, thankfully, despite all this villification, had his patrons and admirers, one of whom was no less a personage than the powerful French King of the time, Charles I, more commonly known as Charles the Bald. Erigena had actually been invited by this enlightened and pragmatic King, long before his anathematization, to take up residence in his Court School (in 845), and there Erigena remained for very many years, teaching, studying, writing and lecturing, even long after his official condemnation.

The heresy-hunters however were, as always, never very far away, and it appears that eventually after King Charles' death, Erigena had to seek refuge once more. This time he found it in England, under the patronage of the English King, Alfred the Great. It is said that Erigena actually became the Abbot of Malmesbury. In any event, the hatred continued to be stirred up against him, his professed and highly articulated freedom of spirit being his only sin. And the erudite medieval historian William of Malmesbury gives us a sordid account of what this hatred led to in the end. For he claims that Erigena was eventually stabbed to death by some of his so-called students with the nibs of their sharp pens! Thus in this tragic fashion yet another brilliant light, heralding the free spirit of the ancient wisdom in all its wonderful incarnational renewal, was violently and cruelly snuffed out!

* * *

There is something of an esoteric irony attached to the curious fact that the face of this great man, John Scotus Erigena, is known to virtually every adult person in Ireland today, without hardly anyone knowing who he really was or is! For up to fairly recently he had the dubious privilige of being in the widest possible visual circulation in the country by appearing on one of the old low value currency bank notes. Though such a phenomenon could hardly of course be seen as being conducive of a deep appreciation of Erigena's philosophy or spirituality as such, nevertheless it can be tentatively taken as grounds at least for an initial preparatory or general interest in the man, in his life, and his work.

Now such a general or popular revival of interest in Erigena would be most apposite in our time! For he lays claim in fact to a much more important place in European history than is as yet generally recognised. Such a recognition will of course only become widespread when Erigena's esoteric influence as a fighter for the true logosophical spirit is fully recognised. For he was a great champion of this spirit amidst the unfolding and increasing suppression of it during his lifetime, a suppression that was up to very recently the blind and chief driving force within the mainstream Church.

This is not to say of course that formerly the Church itself did not deeply strive to understand the nature of the true Spirit. It surely did! But the very fact that someone like Erigena could be branded as a heretic by the Church speaks volumes about how handicapped it was in this respect. For the Church had quite simply shot itself in the foot way back in the early centuries when it eschewed absolutely the ancient wisdom, without which it could, or can, get nowhere regarding the true nature of the spirit!

Chapter Nine

THE SPIRITUAL FLOWER OF CHRIST
VERSUS
THE 'DOGMA MACHINE'

John Scotus Erigena represents a vital link in the chain of survival of the esoteric knowledge of Christ and Christianity generally, a knowledge and a wisdom which has for a very long time been the focus of a concerted programme of suppression by the mainstream Church. However the healing effects of this wisdom are very much needed again in our own day and moreover it is very obvious that this wisdom struggles to re-emerge once more. For ours is a time of the very deepest longing in the hearts of so many ordinary people for the ways of true virtue, for the keys to real meaning and wholesome values, in work, and play, and in life generally. Esoteric Christianity has the possibility to fill this vacuum in the spiritual life of modern men and women because it draws upon the richest veins of wisdom the world has ever known but which it has nevertheless tragically almost forgotten in the technological jungle of the modern world. But Esoteric Christianity has the real possibility to resurface again, now that the days of the heresies and the attendant witch-hunts are hopefully over and done with for good, (in the Western democracies at any rate!).

However, such a revival can only effectively come about if some clear understanding of the causes and the manner of this suppression are understood. It would be wise therefore to look a little more closely now at Erigena and this epoch of his in particular. For it was a time which was so formative in its influence regarding the overall and subsequent development of our European history that we are still very much involved with unravelling its ramifications. And from the point of view of our own particular study here, we have to say that this period of our recent history was one in which matters concerning the spirit were to play an overriding and very vital part.

Now it is true that if one looks close enough one will always in the end be able to discern that ultimately at the heart of all movements on the stage of the world's history there lies the human spirit itself. Especially regarding the development of the Medieval culture however, one discerns that it was how this spirit in its deepest and truest relationship to Christ, and how such a relationship was defined – *this* was the paramount question. Moreover it was in fact a question which also underlay virtually all of the period's exoteric, outer, or purely historical developments. It must be remembered that this time was, or is, generally known as the Age of Faith, albiet a dark faith and one which, as we have seen, rested squarely upon a blind belief in dogma and the like. But it was especially 9th century Europe that seems to us now a most strange, dark and confused period. Moreover it was a time in which the Church strove hard in any and every way it knew how, to keep alive and promote this faith in the truth of the Incarnation, while at the same time knowing full well it had to be able to 'explain' this truth to all and sundry. This it undeniably did with varying degrees of erudition and sincerity. However, the finest bequests from mankind's purely philosophical heritage, the arts of logic and reason, these certainly did not constitute part of the Church's strength at this time, having from very early on in its institutionalized life cut itself off from true knowing or reason i.e. from 'gnosis' *per se*, as we have seen. Rethorically and dogmatically asserted articles of faith, doctrinal formulas, papal bulls and carefully crafted ecclesiastical missives; it was all these and more which represented the Church's growing points during these hard and difficult times. Logic and reason as such only began to have a real impact much later when Scholasticism came into its own and especially when it reached maturity in the person of Thomas Aquinas (1226 -1274).

But with the disappearance of the old Roman imperial order, and with it the quality and stability of life and manners that were part of this order, all of which here by the 9th century were hardly more than a vague folk memory; and with the great mass movements of the tribes still unfinished in its repercussions, Europe was, at this time a ripe place for an attempt at a form of government that would be both trans-national and in tune with the ordered discipline of the Roman Church. And in its body as well as its soul, Europe thirsted deeply for the arrival of such a secure state of affairs.

DIONYSIUS THE AREOPAGITE

The hierarchical system of government which was to emerge, feudalism, was of course one with which the Church could easily identify, as well as indeed actively encourage. And under the perceptive influence of Charles the Bald, feudalism took hold in France and soon began to spread out from there.

Furthermore at this time when both the Church and the state needed to find ways to bolster their respective positions from the point of view of a recognised purely spiritual or incarnational authority, it is not very surprising that they should look to great or heroic Church figures of the past for inspiration. And in this way another figure soon begins to come into view in the unfolding tapestry of this Medieval order. Though he is one who was long dead, his spiritual teachings nevertheless survived and were still cultivated to some degree, especially in the Eastern Church. Moreover this individual was recognised as the traditional Apostle of France. We speak of St. Denis who was the first Bishop of Paris and who subsequently suffered martyrdom for his faith at the hands of the Roman governor there. What is more pertinent to our investigation however is that this was the same Denis whom the Greeks identified as Dionysius the Areopagite. It will be remembered that Dionysius was the one who had become the intimate pupil of St. Paul when he (Dionysius) converted to Christianity from the old pagan or Gnostic wisdom which he cultivated in the School of Athens (see page 49).

We shall return in a moment to this 'French connection'. But first a few general words about Denis or Dionysius, for his place in the history of Esoteric Christianity is absolutely crucial.

It is a fact that Dionysius eventually became (still is!) a very controversial figure in the mainstream Church, something that is of course entirely bound up with, on the one hand his direct link with the ancient Mystery wisdom, and on the other with the Church's active suppression of the sophiacal spirit inherent in this wisdom. This suppression may be demonstrated historically in many ways, but from the standpoint of this focus on Dionysius it is most clearly illustrated by the fact that no sooner had Christianity itself been made into a state religion of the Roman Empire than the Emperor (Justinian) ordered closed this ancient School of Philosophy in Athens where Dionysius had studied and taught! The great tragedy of this act of utter ignorance, from the point of view of the general spiritual welfare of the world, is of course that this was by then the only remaining place in the civilized world where people still, after the defeat of The Gnosis, could freely occupy themselves with the task of bringing the ancient star-wisdom of the human race into harmony with the great new incarnational religion of Christianity. But this was a work to which Rome was vehemently opposed from the beginning as we have already seen. This closure by Justinian happened in the year 529, thus bringing to an end for a very long time to come all possible hope of a spiritual harmonization between the ancient wisdom and Christianity. Moreover this was only the most blatant of a number of acts of suppression carried out by this Emperor in his misguided and grandiose plan to bring the newly confessed 'christianity' of his empire into full line with Rome's age-old patristic and militaristic origins, a regime which wanted nothing whatsoever to do with the ancient Temple wisdom. And the irony is that this strange man, Justinian, proceeded with his egotistical plan, despite, perhaps indeed because of, the fact that his empire was rapidly falling apart!

And if this suppression was really going to go as deep as it possibly could, something which this resolute personality obviously wished for it to do, it had of necessity to apply itself not only to the outer or political aspects of censure, law, order, and so on. But even more importantly this suppression must extend to the very core esoteric teachings of the Church itself which, as far as the Mystery spirit of its purely Eastern manifestation was concerned, was contained in and continued to be taught through the work of Dionysius the Areopagite. And so around this very same time these teachings of Dionysius became the subject of a 'doctoring' and of a subterfuge, the primary intention of which was of course to discredit as much as possible the ancient wisdom. Notwithstanding the fact that it would obviously fail in the end to achieve such a goal (for the ancient wisdom is also we must remember the *perennial* wisdom), this doctoring has over the centuries resulted in a spiritual confusion unending in its capacity for provoking intellectual controversies.

Intellectual controversy aside however, even in the diluted form in which the writings and teachings of Dionysius the Areopagite have come down to us, nothing is more obvious in reading them than that they appertain to a form of knowledge and a depth of wisdom which, though this constituted the very foundation of the early Church's teachings (1st to 4th centuries approx.), the modern Christian knows virtually nothing whatsoever of them. This of course came about precisely because of the (hopefully short-lived) success of Justinian's efforts! Justinian and others like him were successful because their opposition to, and suppression of, the true Spirit has led to modern man's almost complete alienation from any kind of clear or sustaining relationship to the esoteric or divine reality that underlies our sense-perceptible world, i.e. true spirituality.

For, broadly speaking, modern man's knowledge of or feeling for the true Spirit is only capable of expression, when or if experienced at all, through a cloud of mysticism, of mystic or highly personal jargon. And this kind of thing more often than not does nothing more than make spiritual matters even more confused than they already are.

Now any return to a full, true and clear understanding of the spiritual nature of man and the cosmos, within the context of the incarnational body of the Church, must on the one hand eschew any irrational mysticism and yet on the other must of course be able to maintain the apostolic link with the Gospel of Christ and its obvious Mystery nature. The great significance of Dionysius the Areopagite is precisely that he provides us with this latter link! And this at least is something we can be quite clear about. Over the centuries of course this process of the elimination of the ancient wisdom from the Church has progressed to a very great degree and the vital work of healing the psycho-spiritual split within the individual human soul which this suppression has inevitably caused, as well as the broader work of Church (spiritual) unification itself, is a huge task for mankind now and into the future. It must nevertheless be done!

DIONYSIUS DEFINES THE ANGELIC WORLD

Even however way back in the 9th century, there was, one could say, an instinctive and acute alertness to the spiritual danger inherent in this process of the Romanization of the Church. And this was something that was most keenly felt perhaps by the French more than any other nation on the continent at the time. It was after all the Frankish tribes who, through their independence of spirit had earlier constituted a prime factor in the eventual cessation of the Roman Empire as an effective political entity. Charles the Bald however, shrewdly alert to the deeper forces at work within his realm, as well as being fully in tune with the spiritual psychology of the Church of this time, showed his capacity to act in accordance with a higher wisdom than the merely conventional one when he crowned his patronage of John Scotus Erigena by allocating to him the great task of translating the work of Dionysius the Areopagite from the Greek into Latin. This was in the year 858. And through this enlightened initiative it became possible for the sophiacal spirit to at least maintain some sort of a presence within the conventional Western Church, however esoteric, fugitive or controversial it may have had to become by dint of the forces of opposition upon which it continually came. For although these teachings and writings by Dionysius had been well known in the Greek-speaking Church and culture (i.e. in Byzantium), their injection into the dead letter of the Latin language at least gave the wisdom of the Areopagite an intellectual currency in the West which it would not otherwise have had. Indeed it is nowadays quite well recognised by independent scholars that it was primarily the availability of these, more than any other writings, that constituted the core substance of whatever may be called the spirituality of the Western Church from the time of their translation by Erigena onwards. Without them, it can be confidently argued, that even the barest semblance of the mighty spirit of the Incarnation may have become totally and irretrievably lost to the (especially Western) Church!

For what Erigena, through Dionysius, essentially had done was to take the ancient temple wisdom of the Initiates and the knowledge they cultivated therein from time immemorial of the powers and potentates residing in the heavenly bodies and the constellations of the stars (in other words, the gods), and translate it all into a context that would be in harmony with the fact of the Incarnation. Thus the most important book of Dionysius, the one on the trinity of the spiritual hierarchies (*The Celestial Hierarchy*) gives Christian names, and what we may call an incarnational order, to all the gods of the ancient Mystery religions. So in the language of Dionysius, the god Mars and his hosts came under the heading of Mights, those of Saturn under Thrones, those of the Moon under the Angels and so on. These correlations can in fact be confidently made through a spiritually informed understanding of the work of Dionysius.

This latter fact also of course constitutes the core reason why they have had such an aura of suspicion woven around them!

However, once we begin to orientate ourselves correctly regarding the supernatural or Mystery nature of the Incarnation and how in its most sublime expression in the Gospel of St. John this event is seen and described as the descent of the ancient Solar God, the Logos, into a human being, we can have little difficulty with Dionysius.

Quite the contrary! For then he emerges as our best available witness from the early Church in all these difficult matters, allowing us through his wisdom to focus on Christianity in its deepest essence which is actually, when properly expressed, a continuation or culmination of the perennial wisdom. Moreover his writings are an underlining of the fact that Christianity will only be fully understood when it is seen as a thoroughly modern renewal of the most ancient secrets of God the world has ever known, secrets the wisest men and women have always studied and strove to share with their followers.

One need not enter into the technical, astronomical, philological, or indeed any other kind of the disputations which revolve around the figure of Dionysius in order to appreciate the obviousness of this latter fact. For one need only read say his letter (no. 7) to Polycarp[46] to realize how deeply imbued Dionysius was, and also how technically conversant he was with, the finest points of the ancient solar Mystery wisdom, a wisdom which he knew found its culmination in the powerful Event of the Incarnation. For instance to take just one point: the solar impact of the Earthly death of the Sun God on the outward or physical heavenly body or bodies themselves. Regarding this the Gospels merely say that at the time of the Crucifixion the sun went dark. Dionysius however, who was a witness to this astronomical event, here in his letter to Polycarp describes its miraculous nature and does so in fascinating detail and, in an effort to refute a disbeliever, who was nevertheless a very wise man (the sophist Apollophanes) he places this marvel within the context of a much more elaborate and ancient solar astrology, or star wisdom.

✳ ✳ ✳

Something of the working of a benign Providence can certainly be seen therefore in the timing of the translation of these extraordinary sun-filled writings of Dioysius for the Western world in the dark 9th century. Being instigated by a secular ruler however, this work of translation by Erigena inevitably had for Charles the Bald an element of astute political practicality in it also. Thus Charles could undoubtedly have appreciated that the essentially hierarchical but purely divine wisdom of the Areopagite would accord well with the more down-to-earth temporal and ecclesiastical designs of the growing Church. He would also of course have had an eye to the fact that they would be capable of giving a sort of spiritual back-up to the newly emerging structures of the (also hierarchical) medieval feudal order, an order he was moreover actively encouraging .

Now this hand-in-glove relationship of Church and state, a situation which has in fact a fine expression in the figure of Charles the Bald and which was the very hallmark of the whole Medieval culture, was entirely dependent on the notion of a terrestrial hierarchy (as the still current usage of the word 'hierarchy' to donate the Catholic Church's authority well illustrates). We may easily understand therefore that it was due principally to the fact that Dionysius could speak, out of his initiation wisdom, of a similar hierarchical structure in the spiritual world, and perhaps this alone, which prevented his writings from getting the decisive chop like so many other wisdom writings which various Christian sages produced over the centuries. For it is evident that here, regarding Dionysius, the heretic-hunters were content merely to fiddle with his writings rather than burn them, something which they could easily have done, for they are a veritable compendium of the ancient wisdom put into a purely Christological framework. Moreover it is evident that they arise out of a true initiation knowledge (Dionysius refers explicitly to this), and were the products of a highly developed 'gnosis', all of which of course spelled anathema to orthodoxy from the 3rd century onwards. They should therefore have been high on the hit-list of the sophiacal spirit-hunters. However, like the original writings of Erigena himself, which also somewhat miraculously managed to survive the thorough-going burnings of them; by the skin of their teeth, for the wrong reasons, but nevertheless intact, these writings of the Areopagite have thankfully been preserved for us and as such can stand as a valuable testimony to a reality at work within the spirit of the true but esoteric Church which points to a knowledge more sublime than few dare to contemplate. It is a testimony moreover to a magical spirit which will obviously not be defeated however great the opposition to it may have been in the past or indeed may yet become in the future. And thanks to Dionysius (and others) in our very own time this wisdom has a greater possibility to blossom than it has had for many a long day. For though we live in a time of great religious confusion and moral uncertainty, it is also a time of great spiritual freedom. In former days it was the Church itself which defined the paramiters of this freedom for the individual. Nowadays however individuals themselves, especially if they live in one of the Western democracies, are in a position to act almost entirely out of their own personal choice in matters of spirituality. And this is so because we can live now (if we so choose!) without the death-sting of excommunication and so forth hanging like swords of Damocles above our heads, (although it has to be said that remnants of such rusty legal weaponry still exist in the religious arsenals).

It is however out of a sense of the spiritual freedom tangible in our own time that a book such as this one you are now reading could actually be written at all. For even up to quite recently, the criticisms levelled against the Church, especially the Roman Church, which the book contains, would hardly have been possible (especially in Ireland), or even if they were, they would undoubtedly have been met with the greatest of intolerance. For highlighting as the book does the very core of that which constitutes a true and genuine spirituality, as well as trying to trace historically the vissisitudes of this true, esoteric, and sophiacal spirit, it depicts how the Church has largely been the agent of a spiritual repression rather than what it is truely meant to be, i.e. a conscientious upholder of the deepest power of the Incarnation.

Chapter Ten

A TRAGIC DENIAL

In our historical survey of the spirit of Esoteric Christianity we are passing the point of the 9th century. But before moving into the Medieval period proper and then farther into the more recent or even current times, we shall have to look at certain events towards the end of this 9th century which, though little is known about them to historians generally, they are nevertheless hugely significant and revealing as far as the history of the West and especially of Western spirituality is concerned. Moreover they are events which in a very real sense are an inevitable outcome of all that had gone before. For the consistent drive, right from the 4th century onwards, to suppress all direct knowledge of the logosophical spirit within the body of the Church, led in fact one can say directly to those events we will now look at.

Now the 9th century always puzzles historians quite a lot! If the centuries previous to it may be truely regarded as dark, then the 9th may be best described quite simply as murky. We cannot say a lot for certain about it at all. But what we can say however is that much was afoot deep in the soul of Europe at this time. For the cultural blossoming which was to come to the fore somewhat later, beginning in the 11th century, was surely brewing in the strange stew of this 9th century.

We do know of course that the Church was, as it were, 'jockeying' at this time for the best possible position as the 'straight' of the Middle Ages began to unfold before its deliberating eyes. And the manner in which it now begins to set the tone of its authority in readiness for this can be judged by certain crucial events which we will now describe.

The crux of the whole matter of the Middle Ages, as every historian well knows of course, had to do fundamentally with the whole problem of *authority* as such, and its proper exercise. Where does authority originate from? And who is entitled to it in an absolute sense? Pope or Emperor? Which is the same as: Is it temporal or spiritual in origin? These were the key questions on the minds of most thinking people at this time. And we have seen just how difficult such questions always in fact were for the Church, especially since it could never truely get to grips with the deeply spiritual aspects involved because of its early and wanton abandonment of the Mystery wisdom.

THE SPIRIT IS DENIED BY THE CHURCH

By the 9th century however things had hotted up generally to such a degree in this regard that the Church sorely wished to sort it all out once and for all! It had to in any event, if it was to gain a clear-cut power in the temporal world! So whatever else it was doing at this important time it must not be seen to be diddering with regard to this crucial question of spiritual authority. The Church in other words had reached a point where any talk of spirit at all within the confines of its orthodoxy and its teachings, became nothing more than a cause of confusion, embarrassment, and conflict. Nobody had any idea of what spirit meant any more anyway. And so in the latter half of the 9th century this whole process reached its ultimate climax. For it was precisely in the year 869, at the Church Council of Constantinople, that a formal declaration actually *abolishing the spirit* for good was finally and shamefacedly made!

And this tragic fact was something of course which followed almost automatically upon the course the Church had taken from the time of the defeat of The Gnosis onwards. For quite simply the keys to a true knowledge of the spirit were by this time virtually or completely lost! And in a sense the only honest thing to do was to make a formal and binding declaration that there was in effect no such thing as spirit anyway – a sort of dogmatic denial of the spirit, one may justly say. And this in effect is what one of the Cannons of the Council of Constantinople[47] does when it declares to be heretical the Mystery teaching that the human soul is not one, but two, one part of which is entirely of a divine essence, and therefore may be regarded as being *purely spiritual*, unlike the soul proper.

This is the correct interpretation of this particular Cannon from the point of view of the ancient wisdom, and an Initiate[48] of this wisdom is specifically referred to in the Cannon and singled out there for anathematization by dint of his Mystery teaching regarding this trinitarian spiritual knowledge, a knowledge which knows, and has always known, man as consisting of body, soul *and spirit*.

Before proceeding further therefore we will recap briefly now as to how such a diabolical situation could have arisen in which a crucial declaration by a Church Council actually abolishing the spirit could not only have come about in the first place, but that such an abhorrent denial was actually felt to have been in need of a formal and dogmatic cannonization. This recap or digression is necessary in order that the fullest possible picture emerge as to how this incredible denial by the Church could have occurred. And following upon this recap we will give the precise details of this denial by the Church.

∗ ∗ ∗

Ever since the defeat of the Gnostic Church in which the ancient Mystery temple wisdom had mixed freely with the new incarnational wisdom, knowledge of the spirit as such had been placed in jeprody. For what this defeat had at bottom amounted to was the complete abandonment of the very Mystery through which the Incarnation was made comprehensible in the first place, i.e. the Mystery of Sophia or of Love incarnate. For, as we have earlier shown, at the heart of all the ancient wisdom lay the trinitarian knowledge of man's relationship to and with God, or the gods as such. And precisely one-third part of this Trinity was that represented by Sophia or the Mother Goddess. The early Church Fathers rejected her and later tried vainly to put the purely Earthly mother of Jesus in her place, in a feeble effort to compensate for this most basic of errors regarding the sublime Mystery wisdom. It couldn't work! For the Church was in fact, by rejecting Sophia, also rejecting the crucial and precise focus of its origins, which lay within the sanctums of the Mystery temples and their initiation wisdom.

Sophia, as the Mother Goddess had always represented the divine Wisdom. She was known and revered by the initiates from the time man first became aware of himself, his world, and his Creator. She represents in fact the feminine or wisdom side of a divine wisdom/knowledge, feminine/masculine polarity. With the development of the Greek philosophy however, which began in approximately in the 6th century B.C., this wisdom/knowledge, and with it knowledge of Sophia herself, began to emerge as it were, out from the secret 'holy of holies' of the temples and onto the wider stage of human affairs. It came in fact to be taught much more openly than was ever hitherto allowed or even thought of as being possible. And so, especially in the figure of Pytagoras (see page 19ff), during his time we have the Mystery wisdom being put forth in a manner now more suitable to man's evolving self-consciousness. (Prior to this man's consciousness was far more tribal or ancestral, as opposed to purely self-consciousness, which only fully emerged in the Middle Ages). In other words the whole vast edifice of the mono-theosophical wisdom (mono-theo-sophy = the wisdom of the One God) which had been cultivated and taught in the temples of initiation from the most ancient of days only to carefully selected and very strong individuals – this was all now being brought much more down to Earth and made accessible to purely individual human thought as such and was thus made ever more widely available. Individual human thinking-power in other words, as opposed to the relative inflexibility of the gods' cosmic or nature power, was now beginning to flex its own great and free spiritual muscle! Thus, what was formerly taught mainly through god-images, myths, symbols and so on, now began to be put into the framework of purely human concepts and ideas. And after the perceived revolution in the life of the human being brought about by the Incarnation, in which this whole free spiritual trend received a huge new Sophia-inspired impulse, men inevitably began hotly to debate about the divine v human nature of the Christ. The whole direction of this Gnostic debate however worked very much against the sophiacal or feminine manifestation of the incarnational spirit, a spirit which was moreover the very kernel of the Mystery knowledge. This latter therefore found less and less a voice within the mainstream Church, eventually coming to constitute only a tiny part, in what may rightly be called the Esoteric Church. But, in the East initially, and later in the West also, this true spiritual wisdom retained a fructifying presence, something which was due chiefly (though not entirely) to the teachings of Dionysius the Areopagite.

THE EASTERN CHURCH V ROME

It was Dionysius however who proved a most difficult nut to crack for the heretic-hunters! For especially during the reign of the Emperor Justinian, when the imperialistic mentality began to exert itself most strongly in the Church, great efforts were made to banish all the Mystery-knowledge from the See of the Church. Significantly however it was around this same time that the teachings of Dionysius then appeared in written form. Up to then of course they, or at least the essential and deepest core of them, like all esoteric and wisdom teachings, had been transmitted mainly orally. So while it probably proved impossible to suppress these teachings, representing as they did a core knowledge relating to the deepest truths of the Gospel, (as well as being largely irrefutable in their own spiritual nature), these writings of Dionysius were placed under suspicion on a variety of counts. And because of this they failed to gain universal cannonical, or authorative recognition. This was not however before the

Eastern Church tried to win this recognition for them as an antidote to the repressive or more worldly noises that were always emanating from the direction of Rome and its gradually developing claim to be the 'one true and universal Church'.

Thus at the general Synod of the Church held in Nicaea in 787 A.D. the 2nd Cannon declares that study of the Gospels should be amplified by the Dionysian teachings. This cannonical declaration was made precisely because certain enlightened influences emanating from the East knew very well that if these writings were not made cannonical the Church stood every chance of losing all contact with its rich spiritual Mystery source, and would simply dry up as a truely Christian/religious movement, no matter how theologically refined the dogmas it promulgated regarding Christ may be. Moreover a subsequent Church assembly held in 867 in the East declared the previous 'Dionysian' one of 787 to be the '7th 'Ecumenical Council', Ecumenical meaning that its decrees were binding on the whole or universal Church of Christ. Now, needless to say this Eastern exercise of authority did not go down very well with Rome! And the result was that political intrigue hotted up fiercely immediately after this significant event, with among other things the Byzantine Emperor (Michael) himself being murdered, and this probably with the Roman party's connivance. For the new usurping and murdering Emperor who replaced him, Basil by name, soon became the Pope's obvious puppet in the emerging struggle for supremacy in Christendom between East and West. So Pope Hadrian who had been thoroughly baulked in his ambition for his Roman Church by the action of the Eastern Synod of 867 could now decide freely on what do next. And true to the Roman spirit he went for the jugular and decided on the most resolute and bellicose form of protest. He could afford to do so for he had in effect the new Emperor eating out of his hand! Thus he (the Pope) immediately convened a Synod in Rome (in 868) and the Cannons of the 867 Council were thereby deemed to be null and void. And to make the point most aggressively, the documents pertaining to these Eastern cannons were then all publicly burned! In this manner the scene and tone was set for the crucial and highly controversial Council of Constantinople which took place in the following year, 869 A.D.

It can thus be seen that the whole push from the Western, or Roman, side was for the total abandonment of the ancient Mystery wisdom which they saw as nothing more than a threat to their great plan for a single worldwide Church dictated from Rome, and Rome alone. For Rome did, was indeed always doing its utmost to prevent this knowledge from gaining any kind of official sanction within the orthodox Church. It seems moreover that it reserved its most bellicose and resolute of actions for the prosecution of this more than any other of its causes. For the freedom of will and of action which the cultivation of the ancient wisdom necessarily promoted ran totally against all that Rome had ever stood for.

Thus the trinitarian nature of this wisdom, a wisdom which knew man in his reflected image of God to be *tripartite* in his spiritual essence, this whole idea was, at the Council of 869 finally to be scotched for good, and man was there declared to be of a *dual* nature only, a being merely of body and soul, nothing more. This dualist nature of the Church's teaching has remained with it ever since and to therefore regard Catholicism as a truely monotheistic religion anymore, something which it claims to be, is in fact nowadays quite without a philosophical foundation. For from 869 onwards any further talk of pure spirit as a fully distinct part of man's total constitution, as distinct that is in essence from the soul as the soul itself is from the body – this true spirit and divine knowledge of man was thenceforth to be considered heretical and those who 'pay any regard or obedience to the decrees of the author of this impiety, let (him) be anathema, and outcast from the faith and fellowship of Christianity' [49].

Now this is the sorry spiritual state the Church had finally reached by the year 869. Significantly of course this Council also spelled the beginning of the end of Christendom as a power for the brotherly unification of all the peoples of the world, a practical ideal which, as well as laying at its own heart, also of course represents the esoteric core of all true religion. Moreover the promotion of this practical ideal, so very much needed in our modern world, is intimately bound up with a revival of the Mystery wisdom and of Esoteric Christianity, both of which have so much to gain from, are indeed rooted in, the soul of the East.

THE CHURCH DIVIDES INTO EAST AND WEST

From 869 onwards however the East and West begin to go their own quite seperate ways. A global axis of Christianity, which had been created to some degree at least in the first millennium, through the alignment of the ancient Eastern Mystery wisdom with the Western Celtic Church, this now began to fall rapidly apart. For the Roman dominated Western consciousness subsequently became ever more worldly orientated in its 'spirituality', something of course which was an inevitability since it had now set its face resolutely and 'Janus-like' against the divine Spirit of God, and began to look for it in worldly matter instead! And as the universal Church itself became more and more entangled in 'spiritual politics', East and West finally broke up into two totally seperate spiritual and cultural entities in the 11th century, 1054 being the formal date the history books generally give for this Great Scism of the unified Church. So what was formerly and ideally meant to be universal, now took on the highly ambiguous and fearful presence of a spectral, dark, and split spirit in the consciousness of mankind!

And as far as Christianity was then concerned, mainland Europe now became the principle theatre of the world's spiritual wars and battles.

And left to itself as it were, without the 'mothering' influence of the sophiacal Eastern wisdom, the now fully despiritualized Western Church could 'carry on regardless' with its worldly ambitions, and this it surely did in an ever more militant way. In time its Scholastic philosophy would develop to such a degree that, especially through the gigantic influence of the great St. Thomas Aquinas, one could justify doing almost anything in the name of Christ. Even the supremely unchristian travesty of all-out war was deemed to be O.K. in certain circumstances. For the mighty and growing power of human thought, which the Scholastics developed to an extreme degree through their over-use of Aristotlian logic, this was now entirely on their side. Thus it mattered far less with what this thinking should concern itself than that it should 'prove' its point. Certainly from our perspective this can sometimes look like nothing more than the triumph of absurdity often at the very expence of logic itself. (We are reminded here of the famous medieval dispute carried on with the greatest of earnestness and sincerity among theologians and philosophers as to precisely how many angels it was possible to balance on the point of a pin!!).

Thus although the medieval mind was entirely engrossed in the meaning and purpose of the Incarnation as such, to this mind's purely intellectual configuration logical proof was in the end all that mattered. Nothing more. Thought itself therefore was the Church's latest and greatest addition to its arsenals of weaponry as the great war-games of Europe, initially of words, progressed.

The outcome of it all was that now anything became possible with thinking so long as you logically made with it the basic division which was the linchpin of all Scholastic philosophy, i.e. the division between God and man, and asserted axiomatically that you could know nothing at all about God, the spirit, or the world it or God inhabits. All this was stated to be entirely a matter of faith, the content of which was to be determined fully and exclusively by the Church's divine teachings and must therefore have nothing whatever to do with ordinary human thought or feelings. It is interesting on this score to observe therefore how Thomas Aquinas was in due course given an almost divine status, becoming known as a sort of 'angelic doctor' whose bag of words contained all possible cures the Church could ever conceivably want. He duely spawned a whole new generation of theologians, and is capable even to this day of inspiring a subtlety of argument meeting the Catholic needs of even the most complex issues concerning spirituality. It has to be stated however that thought alone, or mere words as such, as far as the Mystery wisdom is concerned anyway, is never final. Feelings must be allowed to play their part in the overall picture also, and this latter is part of the 'problem', if you like, of Thomism; its intellectual sharpness is gained precisely at the expence of pure feeling. There is a great danger lurking here. And until this is fully understood by the Church in general, it will always have difficulties here.

A certain dualism is thus seen to emerge regarding the Christian religion. And it was this very dualism which was the root cause of the intellectual pride and even arrogance of the now totally de-spiritualized Western Church which was gaining ground in the Middle Ages.

Thus 'Give me the dogmas', St. Thomas could boldly assert, 'and I'll supply the proofs!' And so in all of this we can observe how the arrogant 'Church Militant' was beginning to get into its full stride.

THE ISLAMIC THREAT

Now it will be clear to anyone who looks into these matters thoroughly that the eventual triumph of Thomism was entirely bound up with the defeat of something which the Church at this time perceived as a great threat to its well being. It can thus be said that the Church had in effect no choice but to sharpen up its act at this time. For the threat that was now asserting itself was of a very fundamental order, even archetypal in character. It was, or is, called Islam.

On the one hand this was seen as a temporal threat in so far as Islam was an aggressive militaristic movement encroaching into the territory of Christendom. On the other hand however it was also perceived as a spiritual threat in so far as at the back of Islam stood a highly sophisticated culture and philosophy informed and embellished by some of the finest minds the world has ever known.[50] The Church was right therefore to feel threatened, aggrieved and fearful of its standing, in the face of this latest onslaught.

Thus it was that Arabism, or more specifically Islam, now took on the face of 'the enemy' for the Church! A great new heresy, perhaps the greatest ever, had arrived on its very doorstep. And with it a whole new negative focus entered the consciousness of the Christian Church.

With the spiritual wall between Eastern and Western Christianity becoming ever more impenetrable however, and with both sides of the Christian divide increasingly going about their own seperate business, the colours of heresy as such now had of necessity to take on somewhat different shades. And thus it was that Rome came to find in 'the infidel' a powerful new target for its heresy-hunting, something which had become almost instinctual to it by this stage. The temporal advance of the Arab empire provided this focus on a basic level of course. On a higher or more spiritual level however, in the Arab's denial of the divinity of Christ, Rome could hardly have found a better target. And with this as its backdrop the stage was now set for a whole new phase in the Church's overall development.

PART TWO

THE SECOND MILLENNIUM:
A LEGACY OF CONFLICT

A GOOD MAN,
THROUGH OBSCUREST ASPIRATION,
HAS STILL AN INSTINCT OF THE ONE TRUE WAY.

Goethe's *FAUST*

Chapter One

THE HOLY GRAIL AND ESOTERIC CHRISTIANITY

Many subsequent events in the history of Europe illustrate very well the sort of sclerosis the Church underwent after it had finally and formally seperated itself from all knowledge of the spirit. We shall look at some of these events in detail a little later.

Now however we will attempt to show the general way in which the sophiacal spirit managed to survive in the Church at all, albiet and necessarily in an ever more concealed, symbolic, or hidden manner. And in illustrating this phase of the history of the esoteric spirit in the Church we shall therefore have to consider most carefully something which, ever since it made its first appearance in the literature of the West, has proven to be an endless source of mystery, speculation, as well as scholarly investigation.

Its route into the spiritual and folk consciousness of the West is not an easy one to discern. But it certainly owes a lot to Arabism and orientalism generally in that it is an object of great magical and mystic significance. The whole idea of magic is, of course, in the Western consciousness at any rate, very much bound up with the mysterious Orient.

And what we speak of is also a vessel symbolic of this ancient Oriental wisdom in its deepest and purest sense. This is none other than the Holy Grail.

We shall now examine this question in some detail. But before doing so we should first say a few words about the Incarnation itself, something with which of course the Holy Grail is intimately connected.

Without entering into any detailed theological or other discussion about it, we have so far, it will be noticed, placed the Event of the Incarnation at the very centre of our discussion of the history of Esoteric Christianity. This has been done by assuming a certain amount of common knowledge regarding the Incarnation on behalf of the reader. Furthermore the nature of our study precludes the detailed appraisal of any purely theological nuances in this regard. In any event theological discussion can, for the general reader, often serve more than anything else to blurr or dull the spiritual importance of the Incarnation! Such discussions may of course be fine for the intellectually minded. This book however was not written for the intellectually minded only, but for everyone possessed of a healthy sense for the questing nature of human life generally. One need not be an intellectual to have questions regarding the true meaning of life! Likewise neither must one be an intellectual to answer them!

Thus it may be said that what is most important of all regarding the Incarnation for people generally, is that it is food not just for thought alone or even for the spirit alone for that matter. For the phenomenal nature of the Event of the Incarnation is such that it is food for the *soul* as well, i.e. for the whole life of feeling as well as ultimately being food for the very flesh and blood of the earthly body itself.

Now, that the Incarnation is somehow tied up with the health of our physical bodies may of course seem like a pretty startling statement at first sight! It nevertheless may be fully understood if approached without prejudice in a certain way: Thus in so far as part of our soul-nature plays downwards into our physical organism (as well of course as upwards into our purely spiritual being); and furthermore in so far as our soul understandably responds holistically when we are able to contemplate the Goodness, Truth, and Beauty to be found in the Incarnation; in this manner the truth of the foregoing statement may be approached. There is food in other words for the body, but there is also another different kind of food for the soul. And in so far as the health of the soul effects the health of the body, the soul too must be nourished. This nourishment comes fundamentally from a contemplation of Goodness, Truth and Beauty. And, spiritually speaking, the Incarnation can be looked upon as the very embodiment of this trinity of virtues. Thus the Incarnation is, one can say, an Event which in its essence represents the very apotheosis of the word 'holistic'. (It is after this kind of thinking also that Christ is often regarded as the archetypal Healer or Physician of man).

FOOD FOR BODY AND SOUL

The proper contemplation of the Incarnation must of course take the archetypal Christian Meal, the Last Supper, fully into account. And it was here Christ, as it were, poured his entire Being into the Cup or the Chalice. The Cup then became the proper Christian symbol of the soul's nourishment, that by which the soul would in time be fully healed, even to the point of overcoming death itself. It is for this and similar reasons that the Holy Grail found the place it once had, (or indeed still has, though unconsciously) in the soul of Western man. For it encompasses in an holistic way the full reality or overwhelming importance of the healing power of the Incarnation. That is to say it appeals not just to our sense of logic, reason, or our historical sense alone, but to the imagination also, and thus to our whole subconscious life out of which our will impulses are born. It may be said therefore that the image of the Grail proved or proves to be so enduring by dint of its ability to stimulate the imagination in an artistic, holistic and therapeutic way.

Such an idea of course raises a host of other thoughts and questions regarding the Grail. It is however the very answering of all these questions that actually represents what has always been called the Grail Quest. This questioning may indeed be regarded as the very lifeblood of the legend of the Holy Grail itself. Imagination is paramount to it. And any who take up the Quest dilligently will find that it is a Quest full of magic and mystery just, like our dreams. It is entirely to do with the healing power of the imagination. Furthermore it is a Quest which can be taken up by anyone regardless of intellectual ability, and can be pursued on a greatly varying number of levels.[51]

Unlike the Incarnation itself however, we must speak of the Holy Grail in terms firstly of legend rather than historically. For if nothing else, logic alone, that is the correct and precise use of our means of communication here, our terminology, demands of us that when we talk of the Incarnation at all we mean (among other things of course) the *actual*, the real deification of the flesh (the 'word made flesh' of the Gospel). The Incarnation *by definition* therefore cannot be regarded as a legend as such!

Now the fact that the Holy Grail has come to embody so much of what we may term 'incarnational lore and legend' has a lot to do with the fact that the mainstream Church has not been able to accommodate, within the boundaries of its narrow theological and dogmatic framework, the Mystery and mythic element which the Incarnation justifiably engenders in the soul-life of man. The mainstream Church cannot do this of course since it denies to the Incarnation in the first place the essential Mystery continuum around which all such poetic, imaginative, and even subsconscious, activity would naturally coalesce! And this of course is just another example or reason why the Holy Grail has proved to be such a fascinating object for so long, especially among poets and sensitives alike who, by their very nature, will always be the first to suffer the ill-effects of spiritual repression. To the poets in fact we owe our real knowledge of the Holy Grail.

THE HOLY GRAIL ~ FACT V FANCY

One could fill a library by this stage with the books written about the Holy Grail. Many of them however are spurious, like a lot of esoteric or spiritual literature generally. And one can get happily (or indeed very unhappily!) lost groping around in the subconscious murkiness which an undisciplined approach to this fascinating, albiet often confusing, subject can engender.

We will not hopefully add to the confusion during the few pages we will now allot to this subject which is however, despite all the irrrelevancies, fundamental and very central to the study in hand. Indeed one can go so far as to say that in the Holy Grail we have in fact the very symbol of Esoteric Christianity itself. Esoteric Christianity may thus also be called Grail Christianity. For as we shall presently show, the Grail can be most easily and instructively seen, from a purely spiritual point of view, as that object which best signifies the transition from the ancient and esoteric temple Mysteries to the new incarnational Mystery of Christ himself. The Holy Grail did not ever achieve any such recognition in the mainstream Church of course, precisely because of this Mystery connection. Quite the contrary! For due primarily to the Church's repression in this regard, the consequence was that the Holy Grail then became that object around which coalesced, in an imaginative way, all the disparate threads of the extant ancient wisdom which were by now well scattered upon the winds by the Church's relentless hostility. The Grail thus became the individual soul's focus through which the greater psyche of Europe could continue to legitimately harbour vestiges of the sophiacal Mystery wisdom, and could do so in an imaginative and deeply meaningful way.

Traces of the ancient Mystery wisdom continued of course to exist in many of the magical but by now (Middle Ages) largely superstitious practises of the folk cultures. In this milue, during the Dark and Middle Ages however, the Holy Grail became an object which had the effect and intention of Christianizing this Mystery or magical element. And in this dynamic lay its appeal, its efficacy, and its rise as a symbol in the consciousness of Western man.

For although the Grail legend is woven from many different threads including pre-Christian and pagan ones, in the West it came to be identified pre-eminently with the Cup of the Last Supper. And this was the same Cup which Joseph of Arimathea was said to have caught some of Christ's blood in as he was dying on the Cross, and which he (Joseph) subsequently brought to England.

Thus during the centuries of the Church's sustained stamping out of the ancient wisdom, the Grail symbol gradually arose within the Western folk consciousness as representing that great depth of Eastern, or of oriental wisdom generally, which had culminated in the Incarnation. And it had filtered into the Western consciousness in many ways, not the least of which was through the now fully established and thriving Islamic culture. For during the otherwise Dark Ages, Islam had become a great and thriving force for the enlightened pursuit of knowledge and wisdom in many places within its realms, but most importantly perhaps for Europe, in nearby Spain. For here, apart from more orthodox pursuits, Islamic mysticism, magic, and the whole hermetic and temple wisdom generally had taken a very strong root. Islam itself of course did not see anything particularly special in the Event of the Incarnation, did not indeed admit even to its occurrence. Islam had however risen to prominence partly because it had been able to pick up on those aspects of the Mystery wisdom which the Church had left behind in its dogmatic drive to 'spell out' the uniqueness of the Incarnation. As a result Arab culture became one in which a rich magic played a vital, fructifying, and central part.

THE POETIC IMAGINATION AND SPIRITUAL REALITY

Stories about magic cups and cauldrons were quite familiar of course within the oral folk culture generally at this time, and as the Christian culture of the West gradually developed, with its poets no doubt looking longingly beyond the Pyrenees and towards the Islamic and Oriental world generally and the magic being worked there, the stories about the Holy Grail seemed to them the best possible way of transmitting their inspirations regarding their Christian conception of the spirit and the spiritual world. (The question of the validity of the spirit or the spiritual world was not a problem of course for these poets, just as it never is a problem for true poets anywhere. For this is something which, like the saints themselves, they never have very much need or reason to dispute or doubt).

So in this way the Grail stories eventually came to be written down and thus put into those literary forms through which our exoteric knowledge of the Holy Grail has been transmitted to us. But this did not happen until much later – the end of the 12th and the beginning of the 13th century to be precise. In fact virtually the entire corpus of the original Grail literature was composed within a short span of about 50 years at this time. All the rest of what we know exoterically about the Grail stems from these works and all other and subsequent artistic and poetic work is based on them also. From the point of view of our present study this in itself is quite significant for it implies almost a 'rush into print' before it was too late! For very soon afterwards, the great upsurge of Grail Christianity known as the Cathar movement, was to be annihilated by the Church with a frenzy of hatred and fanatical violence that has never quite been equalled in any other human endeavour before or after.

We shall come back to this catastrophy a little later (see next chapter), but here it should be noted that the Grail stories reached the highest point of their development in the work of the great medieval German poet, Wolfram von Eschenbach who in his extraordinary and epic poem, *Parzival*, raised the Quest for the Holy Grail to a level of the highest possible art.

Wolfram indeed is said by some to have been a member of the aforementioned Cathar movement himself. In any event he tells us in his poem that his knowledge of the Grail was transmitted to him through a Spanish wizard called Flegetanis.

THE STONE FROM HEAVEN

Now although Wolfram von Eschenbach does not speak about the Grail explicitly as the Chalice of the Last Supper, the manner in which he does refer to the Grail implies his deep knowledge of it as that object by which the great Mystery wisdom of the Orient is connected intimately with Christianity. Wolfram calls the Grail in fact the *lapsit exellis*, an appellation which has puzzled scholars ever since he first put it in writing, for its meaning is several. Apart from the obvious fact however that it is the poet's perogative to be manifold in his meaning and use of words anyway, it is commonly agreed that *lapsit exellis* can easily mean the 'stone that fell from heaven' or something very similar. And in the New Testament of course Christ is on a number of occasions deemed to be a Stone: 'So come to him, our living Stone', (I Peter 2:4, etc.). This is the obvious sense in which Wolfram means the 'heavenly stone', especially when it is coupled with the Oriental legend wherein it is related how a jewel from God's crown once fell from heaven to the Earth and was thereby fashioned by angels into a precious cup.[52]

Now the cup as an image or symbol which signifies the passing of the ancient Mystery temple-wisdom of the East, through Judaic/Christian influences eventually to the West, is best illustrated initially by recalling an incident in the Old Testament where it is pretty obvious that what is being spoken about is precisely this great and very important transitional moment in the spiritual history of the world. It does this by presenting to the reader a figure straight out almost it seems from another world. He appears from out of a background of which we know hardly anything definite but of which we nevertheless can feel or suspect great depths: the Mystery temple-culture of the very ancient Oriental world in other words. This is the figure of Melchizedek who can perhaps lay claim to be *the* most mysterious of all the early Old Testament personalities. The twilit nature of his significance however is lit up once we become aware of the fact that he actually represents a vital link between the ancient secret temple-wisdom of the very remotest antiquity, stemming from the Orient, and the newly emerging and more outgoing form of this wisdom which the gathering nation of the Israelites represented. For in the Book of Genesis Melchizedek appears, as it were 'out of the blue' as an extremely exalted figure, and confers on the greatest Patriarch of the Jewish nation, Abraham, a blessing in the name of the 'God Most High '. This, together with other references to Melchlzedek in the New Testament letter to the Hebrews, clearly indicates that Melchizedek was a highly exalted Initiate of the Mystery temple-wisdom, those individuals who almost invariably, as we have already seen, worshipped the One God, i.e. were monotheistic in their religion. And the writer of this letter to the Hebrews, it must be remembered, would most likely have been privy to much oral, esoteric and Cabbalistic knowledge in this regard, knowledge which was not of course ever rendered into writing as such. Thus he can speak to the Hebrews in a very authoritative and revealing fashion about Melchizedek saying that he is a representative of 'the first principles of the oracles of God', and in another place that he enters 'through the veil'. The veil in Jewish thought and in the temple rituals represented of course that which divided the mundane or secular world from the divine or spiritual world, the 'Holies of Holies'.[53] Melchizedek is thus seen to confer upon Abraham an initiation into the most ancient of the wisdom-teachings stemming from the mysterious and farthest depths of the Orient. These were the same monotheistic and perennial wisdom-teachings of course that were going to become in time the very bedrock upon which Moses would eventually forge the Hebrew tribes into a cohesive nation, for they represented an initiation ultimately into a knowledge of the Supreme Creator of all mankind. Melchizedek is for this reason also likened in the *Letter To The Hebrews* to Christ himself who now performs, the writer says, the same kind of initiation to all who turn to him, and does so moreover in a direct line of succession from the ancient temple wisdom. But in a manner that is nevertheless totally new and free from the yolk of the Law. [54]

What is even more to the point however in relation to our consideration here of the Holy Grail specifically, is that Melchizedek bestows his initiation on Abraham by giving him *bread and wine*, (Genesis14:18),[55] an act of the deepest symbolic significance. For what the bread and wine emphasizes most clearly is the continuity between, firstly, the very ancient Mystery wisdom, then the Judaic Mysteries, and on into the new Mystery of Christ. It indicates in other words the direct link between the central ritual sacrifice of the temple Mysteries of which Melchizedek was a representative, the subsequent Passover Meal of the Hebrews, and on into the later Mass of the Christians. Thus the central ritual of the very first Christians, that gathering which was later to evolve into the Mass, has its origin in the ancient temple Mystery-rites of initiation. This is very clearly indicated by the figure of Melchizedek.

THE LAST SUPPER

Christ is also of course referred to as the Lamb of God in the Gospels, the Lamb in this case representing more the purely Hebrew Mysteries, for at the Passover meal the Pascal Lamb was always eaten also. At the Last Supper however (which was also the last ritual meal of the old covenantal order as well as the first one of the new spiritual Mystery of Christ) a fulfillment of the Jewish blood-rites are achieved and a return to a more pure and spiritual form now becomes possible and is hereby inaugurated. Thus it is over the purely vegetarian species of bread and wine that Christ utters the ultimate words of the incarnational miracle. And from that point onwards the Cup, as the Holy Grail, becomes the barer of the new sophiacal and incarnational Mystery Deed of Christ, as well as being the absolute symbol for his continued presence in the world.

Herein lies the real meaning of the Holy Grail, for in the lives, the minds, and the imaginations of those Christians most intuitively alert to the true spiritual nature and origin of man, a knowledge which was nevertheless being systematically snuffed out, the Holy Grail in the Middle Ages became the vessel into which was poured from many different sources the now

Christianized modes of this perennial but increasingly esoteric wisdom. And it is with this in mind that we must appraise Wolfram's hero Parzival who, as the Grail winner, has been justly called the blueprint or archetypal forerunner of the truely and fully enlightened Christian personality.

The Quest for the Holy Grail can of course be pursued in a variety of ways. To place too much emphasis on its claim to reality as a purely physical object in this search is however to very much miss the point, just as much as it is to miss it in placing too much emphasis on the purely historical side of the Incarnation itself, and not enough on the Mystery aspect. Like all other pursuits in life, balance here is the key to success also! In any event, when once we become at all aware of the reality of the spirit and the spiritual world, we need have no more difficulty in ascribing to it the power to materialize and dematerialize objects, than we have in ascribing to air-temperature the power to materialize and dematerialize ice out of water! And it is after this way of thinking that we may make sense of that part of the Grail legend which tells of how the Grail, having been brought to 'England' by Joseph of Arimathea was eventually, because of greedy eyes, 'dematerialized' by a choir or angels, and will only now be seen on the Earth by those suitably or properly initiated into its mysteries.

Be that as it may, it is not unreasonable to assume that in the very first years after the full and final completion of the historical Incarnation, the same Chalice as was used in the Last Supper would have continued to be used in the first 'love-feasts'[56] or communal meals of Christ's followers. From very early on however we must note how this communion or community meal was divided into two parts, an inner and an outer gathering. This fact is very well known to students of the Liturgy. For just as Christ himself (as well as, it should be noted, his later Grail-inspired folk prototype, King Arthur) had his inner circle of twelve, similarly did the very first Christians divide themselves into groups ordered into a hierarchical relationship with the cosmic wisdom (see Acts 19:1-7)[57]. Thus at the communal meal there always came a point when the initiates, i.e. those who had acquired the capacity to behold the reality of the spiritual presence of Christ manifesting in or through matter or material substances, (the bread and wine) were seperated off from those who were under instruction in this regard (these were known as the *catechumens*). It was thus, we can safely assume, at these inner gatherings that the real spiritual and mysterious power of the Gnostic Church was generated, and the Cup, quite obviously, would in this setting have been the primary meditational focus for the whole of the magical and miraculous happenings which took place in the souls of all those individuals present.

TWO WAYS OF SEEING: THE INNER AND THE OUTER

And in all of this we can therefore discern what may legitimately be called an 'inner' as well as an 'outer' Grail. There were those present in other words who in attending the 'love- feast' would have had some knowledge of the Gospel, and in beholding the Cup would as yet have seen or felt no more than was in accord with their degree of understanding and spiritual development. These of course would have been aware only of the outer Grail. On the other hand those whose faculties had developed spiritually to a sufficient degree were capable of beholding the inner or mystical facts pertaining to the Grail or Cup. In so far as they could do this they became aware of the inner Grail.

Now all of this is actually very nicely summed up in the word Grail itself, for it means 'gradual', (from the Latin) implying that the path to initiation-wisdom is a slow and gradual one as indeed the exploits of Parzival, before he finally wins the Grail in Wolfram's poem, so well illustrates. But we must note here that this same principle, which is given an individual emphasis in *Parzival*, is seen also to be operative in the first Christian congregations. In other words the method of evangelization employed by the Christian initiates was that the Gentile or pagan peoples were initially told all the basic facts relating to Christ, the Gospel, and the Incarnation, etc., and then afterwards were asked to change their ways, taking all of this knowledge into account. Depending then of course upon the individual convert concerned, it would take a longer or a shorter period of time for him or her to arrive at a point where he or she could be led carefully into the deeper secrets. Those initiated into this more inward nature of the divine Presence thus constituted an inner grouping within these first congregations. And though we must not presume to know exactly or precisely what happened at the inner gatherings of these first Christians, we can state that there was obviously an initiatory awareness of the Holy sophiacal Spirit cultivated there, and moreover that through this cultivation a spiritual strength was thereby generated and developed which subsequently allowed these previously somewhat timid disciples of Christ to go confidently and bravely out into the wider world to disseminate this knowledge of him, through what they called the Gospel or the Good News.

136

So though it is true that we may not know very much about them, we can nevertheless make some fairly general comments on these secret 'inner Grail' gatherings of the first Christians, based on certain aspects of the ancient temple wisdom generally and the knowledge cultivated therein of the purely spiritual make-up of man's being.

Now the Mystery wisdom had always spoken of not just the physical body as such, but of a spiritual body (or 'subtle bodies') also. So what precisely therefore was being referred to here. What did this mean? How are we to understand in practical, or down-to-earth terms what is meant by a spiritual body? For if we can gain some conception of what this might mean we can also come a little closer perhaps to understanding how the body of the first congregations or communion of the Christians was inwardly beheld.

And so to answer this complex question in a practical way we must call attention to something which may be described as a network of bio-etheric vortexes of energy situated in various parts of the human body and which may be regarded in fact as the spiritual blueprints of the purely physical body itself.

THE CHAKRAS

So let us now look carefully at this very esoteric aspect of the overall situation, for here we approach the heart of the matter of the Holy Grail.

Knowledge of these centres of the body has been cultivated, especially in the Eastern spiritual wisdom, from time immemorial, and they are nowadays quite well known in the West too and are referred to usually as the chakras.[58] And it is these centres which are activated and strengthened in any deeply spiritual discipline, thereby allowing the student to eventually acquire a capacity for a kind of intuitional awareness that is not based either on the rational faculty or even on the senses themselves. It is nevertheless a form of consciousness entirely valid in its own right. Moreover it is an awareness which points to another world that exists behind the physical world as such, a world which is as real, if not indeed more real, than the purely physical world itself. In other words it is a spiritual world proper. So eventually with time, study and effort, the student acquires, in very varying degrees according to his or her predisposition, a truely clairvoyant insight into the world in general. And out of this clairvoyance, a spiritual certainty, as well as a certain feeling of invincibility regarding the world and the universe, duely emerges.

All of this is quite well known to serious students of the spirit, and we draw attention to it here because it is a type of development similar to that which has always been cultivated within the Mystery wisdom generally.

Now this whole spiritual developmental process would undoubtedly have been very highly charged at these first Christian gatherings, given the fact that a harmonious and systematic development of the chakras, under the guidance of Christ, would have been taking place.

We can do no more here therefore than merely vaguely imagine what occurred at those inner communion meals. Undoubtedly individual egos would have been able to fade entirely into the background within the radient Presence of the Christ-light, a sort of blending together of the various individuals present into a truely unified and higher Presence, brought about through the ritual and the pure white magical work, a sort of communal meditative exercise focussing of course on the Cup itself. In this manner the division between the inner and outer was consciously and in reality overcome through the spiritual fact of the true communion.

How this particular ritual differed from many preceeding forms of pagan or other Mystery rites was of course entirely connected with the fact that it was no longer an animal that was being sacrificed (for sacrifice the ritual surely was!) but the very God himself. One was, through the Incarnation no longer dealing with the thought of merely animal blood being purified; but human blood, through transformed earthly substances, (the bread and wine) was now raised up to God by virtue of God's (Christ's) blood being mixed into the human through the God actually becoming human and shedding his blood himself! This latter point being of course one of the primary incarnational thoughts. (See Appendix 2).

THE PURIFICATION OF THE BLOOD OF MAN

Now modern clairvoyant insight can come to our rescue if needs be here, in case of difficulties of interpretation or understanding arising out of these delicate and problematic matters relating to the deepest aspects of the Christian life. For it is principally by this faculty of clairvoyance that one can apprehend the essence of the ongoing and great Christian miracle. For clairvoyant observation, trained in the correct way, allows one to observe the adding into the Earth, via the Incarnation 2000 years ago, of a purely divine substance (i.e. Christ's blood through his bodily sacrifice). So that merely human blood *now* has the possibility to become purified, spiritualized, or, to designate the process more precisely, etherized.[59] Moreover, such a clairvoyant capacity enables one to understand how this etherization process takes place via a charkra-related centre in the human brain whereby the spiritually developing individual is able as it were to 'distill' all his life's experiences to such a degree that he now receives back from this brain-centre a new, purified, and divine blood into his ordinary blood, thus giving to even his physical life a totally new power and possibility, a possibility which moreover points clearly to what we may truely call a resurrection![60]

In speaking about the Grail therefore it can be seen from these briefest of indications relating to the heart of Esoteric Christianity, that we are here not dealing with something wholly or ever partly 'mystical' as such, but on the contrary with something very precise and down-to-earth indeed. For this chakra-related part of the brain is none other than what we may undoubtedly regard as being intimately related to, if not actually the 'inner Grail'. And it is along these lines of thought and through this type of knowledge, a knowledge moreover that may be cultivated by anyone wishing to do so, that true clarity and vital spiritual meaning may be attached to the Grail Quest, as much now in our own day as it did in olden times.

The Grail Quest is in fact the spiritual challenge *par excellence*, demanding of us in speaking of it the greatest subtlety of verbal or oral expression because of its deeply esoteric nature. Thus we can understand the difficulty that the first Christians had in bringing this kind of deeply spiritual inner knowledge out into the open world in a form that would be accessible to ordinary folk. For at the end of the day the Mystery of Christ was something which really had to be truely experienced before it was fully understood, and it was out of *this* realization (or *real*-ization) more than anything else that the Gnostic Church had in fact emerged.

Herein also lay the great spiritual strength of the first Christians, a strength born of the knowledge of Christ's Presence and his work in the world, a work which was in essence the purifying, through the Communion, of the blood of man; it was from this that the early Church and the first saints derived their great capacities of fortitude and endurance in the face of consistent persecution. The Persecutions arose mostly out of mistrust and ignorance, for the Mystery was something which was obviously not easily understood, or if it was, was not easily evangelized. And because of this it began to be discredited.

So with the defeat of the Gnostic Church the inner gatherings were soon depotentized spiritually and with this loss the Cup inevitably faded in its sublime power also. In time the magical inner gatherings at the 'love-feasts' gradually merged into a single outer gathering,[61] and very set forms of liturgy began to take the place of what was initially a very special and great event of rememberance, of free thanksgiving and spiritual transformation for all concerned. And the ultimate and final death-blow, as far as the spiritual manifestation of Christ in the lives of the ordinary people was concerned, was dealt when the Cup itself was withdrawn from them and thus became the coveted privilege of those selected few who were in turn appointed merely out of a theocratic and ecclesiastic, and often no doubt even a purely political necessity only.

Denied access to this object which for the people represented, indeed in fact was the very source of their greatest joy and delight in the reality of Christ's nearness to them, is it any wonder that this Cup, the very centrepoint of those wonderful early gatherings of Christians, became in time for the ordinary folk such an object of magic, mystery, and adventure, especially in the spirit-starved life of Western man? In the light of the foregoing considerations, could indeed the spiritual goal of the West be captured or symbolized in any other way *except* through what gradually evolved in the imaginative life of the Western soul as that greatest of all adventures, the spiritual one of the Quest for the Holy Grail? Hardly! And this is the reason also why this elusive object has become in our own day the very touchstone and keyword of virtually all human endeavour, finding its way even into the most common and materialistic of language, thus betraying in the hardened soul of modern man echoes of the buried core of his deepest spiritual desires.

THE HOLY GRAIL ~ SPEAK FROM THE SPIRIT ONLY!

Much can be said about the Holy Grail. Indeed too much is very often said about it! We have in the foregoing endeavoured however to bring to light *the essence* of the matter of the Grail, for truely it is only in the light of the kinds of considerations mentioned above that the blood Mystery of Christ and the Holy Grail can ever be truely and fully evaluated. Without these insights, talk about the Holy Grail can too easily (and often does!) take on the guise of mere fantasy, wild speculation, and even downright nonsense. And it is precisely because of the deep symbolic and archetypal attraction of the object itself that such literature can in fact seduce the undisciplined into false feelings, assumptions, and beliefs regarding the Holy Grail. We shall always however keep our perspectives true regarding the Holy Grail if we endeavour to keep in mind that it has these two fundamental aspects of the inner and the outer. The Holy Grail is the perfect symbol in other words, for the famous 'double truth' of medieval theology, a concept moreover which is also the very centrepiece of all the Dionysian, or Mystery wisdom generally. Furthermore we must always keep in mind that when talking about the Holy Grail we are talking about the evolution of the very soul and consciousness of man himself, something about which we can hardly be definitive in the abstract terminology of the merely written or printed word. We can however, via our more imaginative kinds of endeavours, learn to empathise with earlier (and by virtue of this, differing) forms of consciousness to our own, and thereby learn to appreciate the vital place the Grail can play in our overall understanding of the essentially magical (as opposed to mechanical) nature of the wonderful world we live in.

We are therefore from a purely spiritual point of view better off saying less, rather than more, about the Holy Grail, being content merely to point out its most essential aspects. Anyone who takes up the matter of the spirit in a truely serious way is, in any event, actually searching for the Holy Grail, and will no doubt find it according to his or her own lights, in the end. For the awakening of the spirit is, as the name of the object itself implies, 'gradual', and each one is awakened in their own very individual way. This is, always has been in fact, the very essence of the Christian initiation, right from the very beginning, from Paul onwards. And it will always remain so. But it is however precisely this individual and free aspect of the awakening that called up such hatred against the spirit in the past by those forces bent on acquiring and exercising a merely temporal, hierarchical and centralist power.

Chapter Two

THE ALBIGENSIAN HOLOCOUST

The rise of the ecclesiastical Roman power in the West, determined as it was to stamp out all traces of true spirituality, was accompanied there, as we have seen, by a concomitant rise of the Grail legend in the folk consciousness. This development actually took place throughout the Dark and early Middle Ages. It represented one could say a sort of a soul and imaginative fermentation, coalescing around the sophiacal and Mystery spirit of the Incarnation. The pagan and magical elements which clung to these folk cultures, despite all the antagonism directed towards them by the Church, actually survived in many ways because they found a focus in the Holy Grail. And this was something the Church was highly suspicious of, precisely because it smacked of nothing but 'paganism'. The Grail or Chalice thus very significantly never achieved any status or recognition within the offical Church, unlike many other of Christ's 'relics'. And the 'pagan thorn' in the side of the Church was duely either banished altogether or absorbed into the mainstream, in which case it quickly lost its Grail, Mystery, or magical significance. To give credence to any kind of Grail or esoteric spirituality in other words, would have meant risking supporting something which went totally against the grain of Rome's authority. For what the Church was most determined about was that there was going to be no challenge to its supreme authority as the guardian and sole directors of the religious and spiritual life of Europe. However, the Church, having become by the 12th century a major political power, this fact coupled with the inevitable ill-effects resulting from its complete rejection of the spirit earlier, meant also that by this time parts of the Church had fallen into utter decadence. Many of its dignitaries and clerics were now in fact openly living totally profligate and immoral lives.

Now in southern France this overall situation added momentum to a religious movement which although it was Christian in essence, was nevertheless evolving in a manner that was totally independent of Rome, just as the Celtic Church had similarly done many centuries previously. Moreover it was a movement which, although it cultivated an unorthodox form of Christianity, was nevertheless far nearer in spirit to the roots or origins of Christianity proper than was now the case with the conventional Church.

The movement we speak of is the Albigensian or Cathar movement which spread rapidly in Europe during the 12th century.

We shall now look fairly closely at this movement, for by doing so we will be able all the more easily to appreciate the fact that ever since the abandonment of the sophiacal Mystery spirit by the conventional Church, this spirit had nevertheless continued to, as it were, bubble beneath the surface in all manner of ways. And we shall see that it was all of this undercurrent of psychic and spiritual activity in the soul of Europe which came in effect to a head in the historical Cathar movement.[62] Furthermore by the time the conventional Church really began to take notice of it, the Cathar movement had evolved into an elaborate and fully fledged mystery/spiritual organism. For this in essence is what the Cathar movement amounted to. It was a sort of spontaneous expression of a spirit which had for far too long been forced into an underground existence, and eventually surfaced here in twelfth century southern France into the full view of history as an organized religious movement. Thus we can say that the Cathar movement was a bona-fide expression of the Mystery spirit within the paramiters of Christendom itself.

THE HOLY INQUISITION

Nevertheless in order to fully illustrate and appraise this fact we shall have to resort to ways that cannot by the nature of the task be simply academic or satisfy the strict demands of orthodoxy. For it is a fact that most of what we know regarding these medieval Christians comes from the records of the Inquisition which, it is very important to keep in mind, was initially set up to eliminate them! Thus in relying, as we have to, upon the records of the Inquisition for information regarding the Cathars, this actually bares the very same relationship to a situation in which we were forced to rely only on Nazi records to get reliable information about who the Jews were, or what they stood for!

One thing of course that we can see very clearly from all of this is that the Cathar movement was hugely significant, one way or another, in the eyes of the Church, given the fact that it had to resort to such vile methods as the Inquisition to deal with them. But following on from this we may also realize that precisely because of this situation we have the greatest of difficulty in accessing the truth about the Cathars. And moreover as a result of this there is often very much misinformation passed on about them, especially in encyclopaedias etcetra, where they are mostly dismissed simply as 'heretics' with a few bits of relevant information (extracted no doubt from torture-induced confessions) to back up the claim. Recently however, as the modern European soul wakes up, and as we learn to confess to the many horrors inflicted by our so-called Christian forebares upon our fellow men in the name of Christ, a more truthful picture is emerging about these pious and truely Christian people. Here however all we need to do is to give this medieval spiritual movement its correct perspective from the point of view from which this present book is written, i.e. to place this movement correctly within the overall history of Esoteric Christianity. We may therefore now confidently state that the Cathars constituted perhaps one of the most significant movements yet to appear in the history of the Church in relation to both the latter's denial of the spirit and the inevitable backlash that such a denial engendered. So though we must be cautious about what we say regarding the Cathars, given the relatively little reliable information that is as yet available about them especially in the English language, what we can nevertheless say for certain is that they cultivated a kind of Christianity which arose essentially out of the esoteric spirit, a spirit which of course had its roots in the ancient Mysteries. We know for instance that the Cathars taught a type of metempsychosis to their members, a teaching which had always in fact formed an essential, if not *the* most essential part of the ancient spiritual wisdom generally, especially in the East. The deeper aspects however of this reincarnational wisdom were usually only revealed to the initiates themselves because of its highly complex nature. The masses' knowledge of it tended merely towards superstition, as is still the case mostly where reincarnation is believed in. In the Western Mystery and religious traditions however this knowledge was deemed to be far too potent spiritually to be revealed even in any from, and was thus, like the Mystery of Sophia itself, kept entirely away from the masses, even long before the advent of Christianity. For virtually nothing of it is taught exoterically in the Judaic religion either, although it is perhaps hinted at, as it is in the Christian scriptures also.[63]

THE CATHARS AND THE ANCIENT WISDOM

In the Cathar movement however this was not the case, for as is obvious to anyone who investigates the movement with any degree of Mystery/spiritual insight, it was the purpose of this movement to bring the Mystery knowledge generally more out into the open and make it available to ordinary folk, after the long centuries of its repression during the emergence and consolidation of Christian orthodoxy. One can thus realistically assert that the Cathars were in many ways an inevitability.

The rise of the Cathar movement in southern France in the 12th century is nevertheless quite a puzzle for scholars generally who invariably approach the problem with an academic or materialistic frame of mind only. There is great uncertainty therefore as to where the Cathars actually came from or who originated their ideas, beliefs, and practises etcetra. And merely labelling them as 'gnostic' or 'heretics', as is usually done, does not really get to the root of the matter either. However, when one views this phenomenon of the Cathars or the Albigenses in the light of all that had gone on previously within the Church, i.e. with regard to its ongoing suppression of the spirit and of true spiritual knowledge, the Cathar movement may be better understood. And from this point of view one of the most revealing and significant things one can say about them is that they were (or are) generally believed to have been in possession of some fabulous treasure or other. Now leaving aside the fact that to be in possession of deep spiritual insight is in a sense to be in possession too of the treasure of the 'Kingdom of Heaven', it is not difficult to see that even if they were in possession of lots of gold, silver and jewels etcetra, the spiritual possession of the 'keys to the Kingdom' could be easily mixed up by greedy minded materialistic people with mere gold or money.

However, the mistique which surrounded the Cathars in this regard went very much further than this. For the most significant aspect of this whole 'treasure' mistique is that it incorporated the idea that they were actually in possession of the Holy Grail itself![64] This is a persistent mistique which surrounds the entire and fascinating story of the Cathars and their spiritual movement. And if we review this knowledge about them in the light of how we have illustrated the inner nature of the Holy Grail in the preceeding pages (see page 138ff), we can gain a very good feeling of just what this movement really and truely represented.

We may further express this by drawing attention to the fact that though the Cathars constituted a variety of different groups or sects,[65] this was really of no consequence to them at all. Nevertheless this was an attitude which was in total opposition to the way that such a multiplicity or diversity of cultus was a cause of the greatest concern to the mainstream Church with its fanatical insistence on a centralist form of control. For the Cathars however, it was the symbol, or more importantly the inner *reality* of the Grail itself that was the only thing they needed to unify them in their vision, in their knowledge, and in their brotherly and sisterly love for one another. And this latter was something which they are widely known to have exercised in a deeply spiritual way, like the first Christians. Moreover it was this vision that lay at the heart of their movement, just as similarly a 'Grail- gnosis' had lain at the heart of the very early Church also. We can say all of this very confidently for we know for certain that the Cathars did genuinely cultivate a form of 'gnosis' in so far as the primary power of their teachings and their religious practises and organisation generally, relied fundamentally on a direct spiritual or individual experience of God. Thus the word Cathar itself, apart from its primary meaning (derived from the Greek word *katharoi*) as 'the pure one', also implies the initiation experience in the sense of its meaning as 'a catharsis'. For it is a fact that this related word implies in its original Greek meaning, the concept of becoming pure through a dramatic or an artistically/religiously inspired experience of some sort. And here we find yet another excellent clue as to the deepest impulses at work within the Cathar movement generally.

This 'gnostic link' was also of course the primary reason why such terrible hatred was stirred up against them, a hatred which led eventually on the part of the Catholic Church to nothing less than an all-out war against these pure ones, an atrocious genocidal war which, by the time it was over left a whole people slaughtered and a vast area of southern France, the Languedoc, totally devistated. This is the conveniently forgotten war of European history and which is known generally as the Albigensian Crusade.

THE CATHARS: THE PURE AND PERFECT ONES

There were other reasons too of course why the Church undertook this, perhaps the most demonic of all its acts of repression so far. For the fact was that the Cathars, though by the very nature of their beliefs and practises did not need a hierarchical or centralist structure to their movement, they were nevertheless by the time of the Crusade coalescing into a clearly defined Mystery-wisdom or esoteric movement within the confines of the Church itself. Though they did not have priests as such, they did have a structure whereby the 'gradual' process of initiation actually took place in an ordered way for all their members. Thus if one became a convert one could eventually progress from being an ordinary outer member to an inner one by becoming what they called a *parfait*.

This word actually means a 'perfected one' and incorporates within it some of the deepest aspects of the esoteric or perennial wisdom. For in its deepest essence the Christian Way is also the esoteric Way that can be found at the heart of all true religion and which is known universally as the Way of Perfection. Moreover because of the sophiacal nature of the Mystery wisdom which lay at the root of the Cathar movement, the *parfaits* could be either men or women. The ceremony or ritual in which this confirming of the *parfait* took place was known as the *Consolamentum*, the most significant of the Cathar's communal, ritual, or sacramental gatherings.

The Cathars were also, by the beginning of the 13th century, at a stage of their spiritual development as a single Church body, whereby they were organized territorially into areas of jurisdiction, something akin to the diocese of the Catholic Church. And by now they even had Bishops (or the Cathar equivalent) within their movement. By this time also, although their greatest stronghold was the Langudoc province of southern France, they were gaining a following in various other parts of Europe also, the most significant perhaps of which were some of the urban centres of Germany, Flanders and Champagne.

Now needless to say, no matter what their beliefs or practises might have been, all of this development was hugely threatening to both the temporal ambitions as well as the spiritual authority of the 'one true Church' (in Rome!). Indeed, by now the Cathars were beginning to look as if they were openly challenging the orthodox Church's authority itself, and moreover seemed even to possess the possibility of becoming a sort of rival 'catholic' Church in their own right throughout Europe. The Cathars were now in fact poised to do this! All of which was of course, nothing less than anathema to Rome. And how indeed in this kind of situation could the Cathars be considered by Rome to be anything other than 'heretics'? Inevitably therefore the dreaded demon heretic was once more pulled out of the Roman closet, this time dressed up in suitably despicable apparel and given the label 'Cathar'. And this monster was duely put to work in *the* most horrifying of ways yet conceived for him.

So this very briefly, one could say, was the more down-to-earth reason for the orthodox Church's brutal action against the Cathars. There had, no doubt, to be very good 'spiritual' reasons too, for at the end of the day a true heretic was, after all, far more a spiritual than a merely bodily entity!

And here we enter very tricky ground. For as stated previously, little or nothing has been transmitted to us of what the Cathars truely believed apart from what can be culled or patched together from the records left behind by their accusers and tortures, the highly orthodox and often extremely fanatical employees of the Inquisition. In this regard the Church was determined of course that nothing should be known about the Cathars except what it (the Church) wanted! And in this it actually succeeded, by and large. We can however infer quite a bit about the Cathars.[66]

So in trying to do this let us recall the meaning of the word, or for that matter the being, 'heretic'. He was, it will be remembered, originally conceived at a time when the orthodox Christian Church had unilaterally derogated unto itself the terrible power of being the sole representative of God's voice on Earth. We have also previously indicated how such a derogation was actually felt to have been necessary in the first place: for the Church felt it simply *had* to take this power unto itself in view of the very uniqueness of the Incarnation Mystery as it was fulfilled through Jesus Christ. For it was the view of the Church that to deny the Incarnation was in effect to damn oneself, full stop! The word heretic actually means 'to choose'. In other words, the heretic choose himself to be damned! It was in fact a totally black and white situation from the Church's point of view. And the trap was that the Church, as the sole voice of God on the Earth, defined the meaning of the Incarnation! Thus if you disagreed with it you automatically were a heretic! You had no freedom to choose in the matter as far as it (the Church) was concerned.

To actually choose for oneself therefore one's own unique and individual relationship or path to Christ, something which may, from the point of view of the ancient initiatory wisdom be said to be of the very essence of Christianity, this, quite disasterously, became the very means by which a heretic was to be defined! And most of the early heretical conflicts in the Church occurred precisely because, in denying the essentially gnostic or knowledge element inherent in the ancient Mystery tradition, the Church placed intolerable burdens on those who in fact, in faith, as well as in full knowledge, perceived the truth of the Incarnation *only* in so far as it was an historical fulfillment of the ancient mythic and Mystery traditions. But anything to do with the ancient Mysteries, as we have already seen clearly, was total anathema to the Church from very early on and especially when it became fully Romanized. And this became ever more the case in the Church as it went about the business of gradually defining and refining its role on the Earth, a role which became moreover, because of this very denial of the sophiacal Mystery spirit, ever more worldly orientated. And it was out of this black and white mentality that another anathema

148

subsequently arose within the early Church which was in fact almost as bad as 'heretic'. This was the accusation of 'dualist' or of dualism as such, a charge which at bottom was reserved for those who upheld a view of Christ's incarnational divinity which merely differed (usually verbally!) from the orthodox definition. It was nevertheless almost equally as powerful a sentence against someone as 'heretic', consigning him or her in effect to the pit in one fell swoop!

THE CHARGE OF DUALISM

Thus one of the things that can be constantly culled from the records of the Inquisition regarding the Cathars is that they were *dualists*, almost as if this alone were reason enough for the genocidal war of utter extermination carried out against them! And the only way we can possibly understand this incredible piece of Church history is to coin a somewhat crude but nevertheless apt expression regarding it all. For it must have frightened the hell out of the orthodox Church, a Church which we have to remember felt itself to be the one and only upholder of the absolute truth of the divinity of Christ in the world; it must surely have frightened the hell out of it to think that there was growing up under its very feet another alternative Church which had the possibility, nay, even the probability, of becoming equally strong as itself, but which nevertheless was a Church which denied, or seemed to deny, the divinity of Christ![67] Such a thing was absolutely and literally inconceivable to the mainstream Church especially in view of the hardened dogmatism which permeated it, a dogmatism which was moreover by the decade growing stronger and stronger. Thus out of fear, and fear alone, the Cathars had to be annihilated! It was of little or no interest to the Church dignitary or later, to the Inquisitor, that to an ordinary member of the Cathar movement the divinity or not of Christ mattered far less than the purity by which they lived their daily lives. What mostly only mattered to the dogmatic Inquisitor was whether or not his victim agreed or disagreed with him regarding his conception of the incarnational divinity (or otherwise) of Christ, something about which even the finest of heads, it has to be said, can debate until the cows come home, and yet not get very far with it in the end anyway! And many of the other kinds of (probably spurious) charges brought against individual Cathars would thus have to revolve around this one point – often filthy charges, it must be said, which were in any event more likely to have been the Inquisitor's own fears and hates projected onto his victim, rather than anything else. So what chance does a simple peasant or even an educated gentleman (as many of the *parfaits* were) have in such a situation? Nill! Of course they were dualists and of course they were heretics!

At the end of the day virtually nothing can be really known regarding the finer points of Cathar theology anyway. And even if it actually was the case that they could be regarded as dualists and therefore disbelieving in the divinity of Christ, it was surely the duty of the mainstream Church to enlighten them in this regard if it genuinely felt itself to have known better. But then a familiarity with the Mystery wisdom was a prerequisite for being able to give any such valid instruction, something the orthodox Church simply did not possess, (but which, ironically, the Cathars did!).

In any event the concept of the divinity of Christ, however true it may have been within the strict and narrow definitions of the orthodox theologians, was nevertheless by the 12th century a totally dead concept for them anyway. For they had gradually over the centuries lost all manner and means of teaching or understanding it. And it is obvious the only way of teaching they knew by the time of the Cathars was the way of brute and terrible force.

And by God did they start to use it then!

Inevitably of course there were some enlightened voices in the Church at the time. And one of these was the great St. Bernard of Clairvaux. He understandably became genuinely alarmed at what was building up in the Languedoc, and so in the year 1145 he journeyed there himself briefly to investigate. Bernard however was far more appalled by the activities of his own Church in the Languedoc than he was by the so-called heretics, and he openly said so. He also said upon his return, about the Cathars: 'No sermons are more Christian than theirs'.

The fact is that the Cathars were not concerned at all about hair-splitting theological nuances. What they were concerned about however was with the living of their daily lives as purely and as morally as possible, as is fitting for true followers of the Way as it is outlined in the Gospels and the New Testament generally. And in these matters they were exemplary as even their Inquisitors and accusers were forced to admit on many occasions. Their whole Mystery connection to the Sophia wisdom via the Holy Grail also indicates their deepest cultivation of the inner life, the true life of the spirit, something which knows instinctively how not to overemphasize outward appearances or dogmatic formulas but rather takes the direct experience of the Real Presence as the only or ultimate guide to the religious life. And this they cultivated in its most inner form through their sacrament of the *Consolamentum*, which as far as one can gather, had echoes in it of the 'love-feasts' of the very first Christians. And in this sense they can be seen as representing not only a continuation of the Mystery or esoteric spirit generally within the Church, but also illustrating very clearly the potential this spirit has for emerging as a powerful force for the good in the world.

THE DEVASTATION OF THE LANGUEDOC

For the culture which arose in the Languedoc in southern France in the 12th century is said by most historians to have been the most sophisticated and advanced that Europe had yet achieved, something which was due in no small measure to the purifying presence of the Cathars. They were also of course harbingers of some of the deepest tenets of the ancient Mystery wisdom which had always in any case, from time immemorial, been the wellspring of the very best aspects of culture and civilization. The Languedoc had thus acquired a wealth and a luxury that was, by the 12th century, the envy of many of its neighbours, but especially the northern nobility. The Church unashamedly exploited this greed and envy for its own purposes however, and when one of its Papal Legates to the Languedoc was murdered (not at all as it turned out, by the Cathars) on January 14th 1208, the Church found just the right excuse it needed to set in motion one of the bloodiest episodes of its long history. For immediately after this event Pope Innocent III ordered a Crusade against the Cathars, offering all kinds of enticements to those who joined, enticements like the cancellation of all debts to Jews, the remission of all sins past *and* future, not to mention of course the rich booty to be had, and so on. Needless to say the Pope soon amassed a huge rabble of any army.

Not long afterwards, this rag-bag of an army set out marching. And on July 22nd 1209 they entered the town of Beziers, one of the Cathar strongholds. Then in an evil orgy of violence the entire population of this town was murdered *en masse* on the spot! It is estimated that as many as 30,000 innocent men, women and children were slaughtered on that unimaginably terrible day!

Now this horrible event set the tone and marked the opening of an awful war against these innocent people which lasted for about another 20 years or more, at the end of which the total and vast area of the Languedoc lay devistated, its wonderful culture and its deeply religious people utterly decimated. It is impossible to calculate how many died in the course of this forgotten war.

The extermination of the Cathars and their movement was obviously meant to be total! Not the faintest trace of them was to be left on the face of the Earth! And in this the Church more or less succeeded. Of course it is not possible for history to completely whitewash over the horror of events so vast as this. Something of them eventually comes to light in the general consciousness. And as we piece together more genuine knowledge of the Cathars and their movement it will surely be seen that here we have yet another example of the perversion of Christian truth, the massacre of innocence and goodness for the sake of political expediency, and the triumph of narrow and dogmatic intransigence over what is perhaps the most necessary of all Christian virtues, the virtue of religious tolerance.

Chapter Three

THE DANGEROUS SECRET OF THE KNIGHTS TEMPLAR

Whereas the Cathars represented an esoteric movement which grew up outside the strict paramiters of the Medieval Church, there were nevertheless also within the orthodox body of the Church many signs that this spirit was also active. In passing we may mention a couple of the better known movements like the Fraticelli, also known simply as the 'Spirituals'. Another one was the Brethern of the Free Spirit. There were many others.

However the most successful, widely known and significant, but nevertheless also the most tragic of all these esoteric spiritual movements was the one known as the Knights Templar.

In fact one may say that the spirit of Esoteric Christianity came to a sort of climactic expression in the Church in this great movement which was inaugurated very early in the 12th century. (The year 1118 is the most widely accepted date given by historians for the formation of the Knights Templar).

Now the Templars is a movement which has always intrigued historians, not least of all because of the aura of mystery, legend, and rumour which surrounded them during their lifetime, a mistique moreover which actually continues to this very day! For like the Cathars, the Knights Templar seem to have had about them a certain indefinable 'something', a 'something' which of course has its roots in the fact of their essentially esoteric nature. It is a 'something' however which will always remain not much more than that unless or until an overall framework for recognizing the reality of the sophiacal Mystery spirit is adopted by historians.

However, before developing these points further let us briefly consider some of the outer and more important historical facts regarding the Templars. And in doing this let us try to keep in mind something of the atmosphere of the high Medieval culture which gave birth to this, perhaps the most fascinating of all movements which the Church has begetted in its long 2000 year history.

We have referred previously to the hierarchical nature of Medieval society generally, and also to its highly structured and loyalty-based feudal system of government. But perhaps the most conspicuous of all aspects of this world, and one which is intrinsically bound up with this hierarcism, was the way in which it was almost totally immersed in the Gospel message. For it is a fact that hardly any part of the Medieval world was left untouched by the Incarnation, and virtually all learning and cultural activity centered upon it. Thus at this time of the High Middle Ages, in a very real sense the Church was in fact universal. The general period is for this reason also known as the Age of Faith. We must also remember that the Incarnation was unambiguously taught by the orthodox Church to be a fully *historical* reality and that mythology and the like had nothing to do with it at all. Here in fact lay one of the greatest strengths of the Church's teaching. And for this reason also the far away and mysterious Holy Land, where the Incarnation drama was known to have actually occurred, was regarded as a place of huge spiritual, religious, and symbolic significance in the consciousness of medieval man. Symbolism in fact played into the make-up of this medieval consciousness in an all-pervasive way. For in virtually every aspect of his outer life, as well as deep within the feeling life of his soul, medieval man was, as even the most cursory acquaintance with his world will show, highly absorbed in, and preoccupied with, ritual, gesture and their symbolic significance. His consciousness differed very much from ours in many ways. He or she was for instance far more imaginative and inward in his or her soul-life, compared to our highly abstract and extroverted mode of consciousness. In consequence, his or her religious life had as much to do with feeling as such than with pure conscious or abstract thought. Thus for most people it was simple virtue that was cultivated far more than any kind of deep spiritual knowledge. Notwithstanding this however, those who did pursue knowledge as such could deepen their soul and spiritual life all the more easily if they so wished, and do so moreover in a way that is most difficult for us nowadays, for we have largely lost touch with this feeling aspect of the spiritual life.

MEDIEVAL MAN AND THE IDEAL OF PIETY

For medieval man therefore, his religion played into every aspect of his life, his thought, and especially his feeling. In this way Christianity grew as a great social force in the Middle Ages, out of a powerful, yet simple and virtuous faith in Christ Jesus.

Most particularly however for medieval man it was in the matter of *fealty*, a virtue which in fact provided the moral basis for the entire feudal system of government, that manner and custom was most carefully regulated in his society. Symbol and symbolic gesture thus had far more power, spiritual and otherwise, than they have nowadays. And in this milue we can easily come to understand the religious passion and fervour with which the Holy Places were held by the people in general.

But it weighed particularly heavy however on the minds and hearts of all deep-thinking men and women at this time in Europe, to know that the Holy Land and all its sacred and highly symbolic shrines were in the hands of those who did not at all have the same feeling of fealty for, or anything like the same kind of belief in, Christ, as they did themselves. For it was a fact that by the end of the 11th century, all of the Holy Land had been conquered from the Christian Byzantine empire by those most powerful of all heretics that had yet emerged to challenge Christianity, the Moslems, (or more precisely in this case, the Seljuk Turks). And it was out of these deepest and most pious sentiments of the Christian Europeans that that other most notable feature of the medieval world then emerged i.e. the Crusades.

Of course there were many other factors besides this playing into this extraordinary epoch of the Crusades, factors far more to do with economics, politics and so on, than directly with religion as such. But of the depth of piety, and of the genuine, though often blind, faith practised by these our recent medieval forebares, no one can have any doubt at all. For undoubtedly the High Middle Ages was marked more than anything else by a love of, and a fidelity to Christ that was beyond the questioning of most. That kind of questioning, so natural to our own way of thinking, only came later. For the moment however it was the virtue of piety which most fructified the spiritual soul of Europe. And it was by dint of these very same sweet-loving and pious sentiments that medieval man could only behold in those who did not share similar feelings, nothing but pure *infidelity* towards Christ! And so it was in this manner that the concept of the hated 'infidel' arose and was duely woven into the complex texture of medieval European thought.

Now it would not be far off the mark to say that the Knights Templar represented the very cream of this kind of pious medieval man. Just prior to their formation, the Holy Land had been recaptured from the hated infidel in the first Crusade. And very soon a few of these most highly motivated and pious of men, obviously delighted by this great victory, got together and decided to create an organization dedicated to the protection of the Holy Places and their pilgrims. This was ostensibly the original purpose for the formation of the Templars. And the manner in which they went about this formation indicates very clearly that the deepest of thought and the most careful of preparation, both spiritual and temporal, went into it to ensure that their Order would in fact be comprised of the very best types of men in society. For it is obvious when one looks into the origins of the Knights Templar that from the very start they were intended to be primarily an elietist organisation, but elietist in the best sense of the term. Elietism or hierarcism was, after all, the very dynamic, one could say, that moved all of medieval society. The Templars were thus meant to be an institution that was in strict accord with the prevailing orthodox mentality of the time. Totally unlike the Cathars whose movement was in essence a spontaneous grass-roots expression of the deepest spiritual fervour of the times, the Templars from the beginning intended to harness this fervour into the most disciplined kind of order and the most carefully prepared and thought-out organization imaginable. Though historically they are recorded to have began in the year 1118, it is obvious from a close study of the facts that this is merely the date on which they, as it were, 'came out'. For many years of preparatory work had gone into the creation of their Order, whereby a network of approvals, blessings and fealties from the very highest in society had been obtained before they, as it were, 'turned on the switch'.

It should be noted here that this was also the time in the Church when the Mendicant Orders were coming into play as a vital force. This is quite a seperate issue of course, but the Templars in a sense may be seen as taking as their ideal a sort of marriage of two of the most notable features of the medieval Christian world, 'Friarhood' and Knighthood itself.

THE TEMPLARS AND THE GRAIL CASTLE

The original group of the Templars who gave birth to these ideals was actually very small, less than ten in fact. But something of the depth of the purely esoteric wisdom which inspired them can be gauged from the fact that the Order was not long in existence when one of the most influential and wealthiest counts in all of Europe at the time, the Count of Champagne, joined them. The significance of this may be understood when it is realised that it was at this Count's court in Troyes that there had been flourishing for quite some time a Cabalistic School of esoteric wisdom. It was here also in fact that the Grail romances themselves received their first purely literary airing. This happened chiefly through the poet Chretien de Troyes whose name itself implies the connection with Troyes. Indeed the

Grail connection generally is very strong with the Templars as it had also been with the Cathars, indicating clearly that here, in the heart of Europe, the deepest aspects of the ancient sophiacal Mystery wisdom of the East was being cultivated. Wolfram von Eschenbach, the author of the greatest of the Grail romances, *Parzival*, is also known to have visited the Templars in Palestine, and in his epic poem he accords to them the unique and high distinction of the guardianship of the Grail Castle. All of which points directly to the arcane nature of the Templar's motivation and the deep esoteric inspiration behind the foundation of their movement.[68]

Moreover, in Wolfram's romance, which is actually full of arcane references, the Grail Castle can easily be understood as referring symbolically to that world beyond the threshold of the senses, a world of which those who engage in depth meditation become aware. And indeed the whole of the romance of *Parzival* may be regarded as an attempt by Wolfram to give this mysterious, though often chaotic spiritual, astral, or etheric world, an ordered frame or point of reference based on the Christian Mystery. In this we may also come to understand just why he gave to the Templars the guardianship of the Grail Castle,[69] for he would have been aware of their great reverence for this mysterious world behind the everyday one, an understanding of which they would have continually practised through prayer, meditation, as well as through symbolism and ritual.

Now we have already clearly demonstrated in previous chapters how the whole trust of the Church had been from very early on in its history focussed on a denial of this spiritual wisdom and actively suppressed the cultivation of it. And it was just because of this that the Catholic Church had then no choice but to base its structures of theocratic authority on only a partial image of man. For as we now know they deemed man to be essentially devoid of spirit, making him out to be composed of body and soul only, a terrible blunder (see page 115ff). Strictly speaking therefore the Church had become something of a strange, even headless creature, for it denied the very thing from which it should, by the nature of its supposed authority have gained its greatest strength. After all, its authority was nothing if it was not spiritual, or spiritually based!

The deeply sensitive and truely enlightened ones in the Church's midst however (always very few in number!) saw through this anomaly. And by virtue of their cultivated wisdom and knowledge they automatically acquired a genuine spiritual authority which the mainstream Church possessed, as an institution, only in a brittle or shell-like form. And it was these very same sorts of men who formed the vital backbone of the Templar movement, thus creating an institutionalized and genuine spiritual authority in a Church which did not have it in any deep sense at all, apart from them.

This is the real reason that they were feared and respected throughout the length and breadth of Christendom during their all too short history. And feared and respected they surely were! For only one man, and one alone, was ever above them in authority, and even he feared and actually never crossed them, even when they had been outlawed. This was the Pope himself!

Now in all of this we can easily detect the reason for the Templar's unique standing in the Church. For they were widely recognised as actually having and cultivating genuine spiritual authority and wisdom, in contradistinction to the Church itself which merely claimed outwardly to have this authority, but could not in truth have it. And it was this, more than anything else, which lay at the heart of the Templars' great success in the High Middle Ages.

THE TRINITY OF VIRTUE:
POVERTY, CHASTITY AND OBEDIENCE

The best of the Templars were deeply pious monks. What the Templars had done in fact was to take the already well established Christian institution of Knighthood and turn it into a thoroughly inspired and highly disciplined religious Order dedicated to fighting for Christ, in every conceivable sense of the term. So because it arose within the paramiters of the orthodox Church, and because also of the careful preparations laid for it before it actually became fully public, once it did so it rose very rapidly in power and influence. Though never very great in numbers it nevertheless attracted into its ranks only the most idealistic and pious Christ-inspired men of the time. But many of these were very wealthy also. And because of this the Order soon became very wealthy itself. For when a wealthy individual joined, he put all of his resources, however vast they were, into the hands of the Order. No individual knight was ever allowed to own anything himself, for they were all, as true monks, subject to a vow of poverty, (as well as of chastity and obedience).

Their early insignia indicates this understanding of poverty quite well. It depicts two people on a single horse, only one of whom is a knight. The symbol very graphically indicates the ideal of brotherhood and of helping or loving one's neighbour. It is an especially evocative and potent image when one considers that the whole *raison d'etre* of a young man coveting the status of knighthood at the time (which most of them surely did, for often it was the only possible way for advancement in medieval society, especially for those of lower birth) was to have his very own horse.[70] Thus to have to share it with someone else would surely have seemed to him almost absurd, even repugnant in its piety! Yet this nevertheless was the image that was held up to them if they wished to become one of the cream of all knights, a knight who took no temporal lord or noble as the object of his fealty, but Christ himself. This was a Knight Templar.

It was only to be expected however that as the Order grew in strength, privilige and prestige, it inevitably attracted into its ranks those of a far lesser moral calibre than that of the original founders or its early recruits. And this, coupled with the inevitable envy they stirred up in kings, nobles, and others, who in some cases may have had good reason to resent them and their universal authority and power anyway; all of this began eventually to create something of a backlash against them.

Now undoubtedly like any large institution there inevitably were some of the Templars who abused their authority. This is not difficult to understand, given what we know of human nature. There may even have been some really bad ones in their ranks! But from the very start the Templars had kept up a most rigorous regime of the utmost secrecy[71] regarding all of their activities, activities which moreover grew increasingly numerous and manifold as time went on. For at the zenith of their power these horsemen were in fact, among many other things, the very Bankers of Europe, being put in charge even of Royal treasures. And so despite, or perhaps even because of the fact that as individuals they were not allowed to have possessions, as an institution they nevertheless became extraordinarily wealthy.

It was this very wealth however that paved the path of their eventual downfall, for greedy and envious eyes began to be set upon this wealth by very powerful forces.

THE GREEDY KING

It was in such an atmosphere that malicious rumours about them were spread abroad and began to grow. And towards the end of the 13th century, by which time the Muslems had regained entire control of the Holy Land once more, thus in a sense removing from the Order of the Templars their very *raison d'etre*, the time was ripe for an attack against them by their enemies. This, when it came, was spearheaded by one of medieval Christendom's most vicious and greedy of monarchs, Philip IV of France. It was this cold and cruel king, (also known ironically as Philip the Fair), who, having systematically squandered his people's resources, in the end had left himself and his country in a state of near bankruptcy. Then with his greedy eyes set upon the vast wealth of the Templars he took hold of some of the vacuous rumours circulating about them, concocted some spurious charges against them and laid a meticulous plan to outlaw their organisation and thereby gain for himself their great wealth.

It was a plan worthy in its conception and its precision of execution of say a modern military dictator's harshest crack-down on his strongest opponents. For precisely at dawn on Friday October 13th 1307 all the Templars in France were to be arrested and all their property confiscated in one quick, sharp, and highly organized round-up.

Interestingly, almost as if they knew what was about to happen and were thus prepared for the inevitable, these, the most highly skilled of fighting men in the whole of Christendom, submitted *en masse* to the Royal decree without any resistance whatsoever! And soon afterwards the full force of the Inquisition was brought down upon them. The rumours about all their strange ritualistic activities and the attendant images of devilry and debauchery that the spirit-fearing and spirit-denying Church built up out of these rumours; all of this now began to be ordered and collated into a body of so-called evidence against them. The methods used to get this confessional evidence were of course the usual inquisitional ones of the vilest forms of torture. And many of the Templars admittedly did indeed confess to the strangest kinds of things under such torture.

Much has been written about the esoteric aspects of the Templars in this regard. But perhaps the only truely legitimate thing that can be said in this context is that no matter what they said under such conditions it can hardly be ever more than mere conjecture to use it as a means of ascertaining the truth of what the Templars believed, knew, and cultivated ritually within the highly secretive confines of their Order. To take just one example: There were confessions of the Templar's spitting on the Cross. Now this, obviously, in the mind of the Inquisitor, was the supreme blasphemy! But as is well known nowadays with modern psychological insight, during extreme forms of physical or mental stress the mind produces all kinds of distortions. It seems indeed in many cases that under such conditions the mind or soul actually leaves the body itself and becomes quite independent of it! It requires little imagination therefore, especially if it's an imagination informed with some genuine spiritual awareness, to accept the possibility that in such a torture situation a Templar could actually have left his lower soul or more bodily self exposed to some sort of possession or projection from psychic forces other than his own conscious and purely spiritual ones. The Inquisitor's fantasies in this sense may become a sort of ensouled projection to which the victim responds. In this sense, with this manner of understanding, these types of confessions of the Templars may be easily regarded as examples of them succumbing in some way or other to what may be called the 'powers of temptation', using this term in a deeply Christian/esoteric sense. And in this sense also one could not regard the Templar's true selves as denying Christ. Such a manner of thinking also throws light on their strange confessions. But of course no such kind of understanding was possible either to the Inquisitor or the people at large at that time, who only knew how to take such things at their face value.

There is one other feature of the Templar's confessions however which has received perhaps more publicity than any other, (most of it terribly distorted also for the very same kinds of reasons just indicated). And that was that they confessed in many cases to secretly worshipping a god who bore the name of Baphomet.

BAPHOMET: WHAT BLASPHEMOUS THING IS THIS?

Now this Baphomet seemed like an entirely original creation of the Templars. No one had ever heard of him or it before. And because of this he or it has kept historians and scholars wondering and guessing ever since. Moreover it was also this very strangeness of Baphomet which caused the Templars to be accused of all sorts of idolatrous and indecent practises in relation to him or it. But precisely because this being had no precedent and because also of the Templars total secrecy regarding their esoteric practises anyway, they left themselves totally exposed to every conceivable type of fantasy projection, regarding Baphomet, from their detractors and persecutors.

However a relatively recent piece of scholarship about Baphomet resolves this entire mystery!

Dr. Hugh Schonfield, who has written a number of interesting books on the origins of Christianity, published in 1956 one called The Secrets Of The Dead Sea Scrolls. In this Dr. Schonfield recounts his significant discovery of a cryptographic code which he found had been used to conceal from unworthy eyes the true meaning of certain esoteric names in early Gnostic or esoteric writings. He called this code the Atbash Cipher. It was a system of coding which, he found, was used in various texts including some of the Dead Sea Scrolls, for example.

In another book however, published in 1984 (The Essene Odyssey), he turned his attention to the Templars, and specifically to their worship of Baphomet. And by applying the cryptographic principles of the Atbash Cipher to this enigmatic name he found that it decoded perfectly into the word Sophia!

Now, given what we have so far recounted in this book, this is not actually very surprising. Indeed one can justly say it fits the overall picture perfectly. For it was precisely this Sophia Mystery-wisdom which was most severely anathamatized by the established Church and hence the Templars had absolutely no choice but to keep it all utterly secretive.

The fact indeed that we now know that Sophia lay at the very centre of the Templar's movement is perhaps *the* most generally revealing statement of all that we can make about them in respect of their being a movement which tried to bring to light and life within the highly restrictive atmosphere of the mainstream Church, the perennial or Mystery wisdom. Herein lay their great secret and the source of their great power. They were also nevertheless, it has to be said, far too ahead of their time in trying to bring to light at that particular stage of history the Mystery of Sophia in Europe. They were indeed in many ways attempting the virtually impossible, given the Church's dogmatic and militaristic stance on anything to do with real spiritual insight. And for their efforts the Templars suffered the almost inevitable consequences!

In France the Templars were mercilessly put down, very many being burned as well as suffering imprisonment and torture. And because of the activities of Philip the Fair, who pressurized other monarchs in Europe into suppressing the Templars, in many other countries also they were harassed and imprisoned. Indeed Philip's hatred of them seemed to have had no bounds. And significantly it was also only under pressure from Philip that the Pope himself, who in any case had always been Philip's puppet,[72] agreed to officially dissolve the Order. This happened in 1312. And this it should be noted was done without ever an official pronouncement of guilt being made against them by the Church, something which undoubtedly indicates a deep fear, if not indeed a great respect for them, which lingered on to the bitter end.

The final act in this spectacular and tragic spiritual drama of the Middle Ages came in March 1314 when the Grand Master of the Order, Jacques de Molay and one of his chief colleagues were slowly roasted to death in an horrific *auto-de-fe*.

Just before he actually died however, Jacque de Molay apparently made two very significant statements. One was that his previous confession, which had been extracted under torture, was totally untrue. The other was that he called his two principal accusers, King Philip and Pope Clement, to join him before the Throne of God within one year, to answer for their actions. And both of these men were actually dead within a year from de Molay's prophetic execution!

Although the Templars were officially disbanded in 1312 they continued nevertheless to exert influence in one way or another for many centuries afterwards. In Scotland for instance they were never officially dissolved at all. In other places they joined the ranks of similar types of organisations like the Hospitallers, organisations which they themselves (the Templars) had been the inspiration for in the first place. But Christendom was never to see anything even vaguely like the Templars ever again.

Nowadays however as we travel around Europe we are constantly reminded of them and also of just how widespread their power and influence was during their brief history. For virtually everywhere we come across 'temple' in a place name (and one indeed is never very far from such a place), we can be fairly certain that here the Templars had exercised their power, their influence, and their great authority in the service of Christ, pursuing the very highest of Christian ideals which they cultivated rigorously in the pure light of the great logosophical Mystery wisdom of the Incarnation.

Chapter Four

THE SPIRIT OF THE ROSE CROSS

The defeat of the Templar movement marks the final attempt of the spirit of Esoteric Christianity to find a true expression within the confines of the orthodox Church. For from here on the cleavage between the Church and this sophiacal spirit becomes ever more clearly marked.

At this point also we begin our entry into the modern era with all its attendant complexities regarding the soul and spiritual nature of man and his relationship to the world. For here in the 14th century the stage is being set, as it were, for the later triumph of materialism at the shocking expence of the spirit, a trend which has in a certain sense reached its apotheosis in our very own time now at the beginning of the third millennium.

Up to this point we have been observing how, apart from its very early wonderful flowering in Palestine immediately after the Incarnation, the esoteric spirit of Christianity was gradually eschewed by the body of the Church. This we have seen, occurred because the Church placed virtually all its emphasis on building up the purely temporal body at the expence of the much more significant Mystical Body. This latter aspect, to which the Church normally paid (or pays) only sterile lip-service, represents of course the enduring and true reality of the Mystery of the Incarnation. For indeed it can be said that if this latter esoteric aspect is not cultivated, developed, and proclaimed in a manner at least as dilligently as the outer or exoteric one, the 'body' will quite simply die!

This Pauline analogy between the body and the Church is of course very apposite and instructive here with regard the great tension that has developed between the inner and outer aspects of the Church. For just as the physical human body will soon die of thirst, or something worse, for lack of clean pure water, so too will the temporal body of the Church die if it continues to be denied the 'living water' of the esoteric spirit of Sophia. It is in this manner that we must come to understand what is truely meant by the Mystical Body. And it is after this fundamental manner of thinking also that we may come to truely appraise the current crisis in Christianity generally.

THE RISE OF THE SECRET SOCIETY

Now this split condition of the Church which was in fact cronic from the early centuries, actually only became acute in the High Middle Ages. Exoterically it led eventually of course to the great cleavage we know as the Reformation (see page 172). Esoterically however this cleavage gave rise to a phenomenon which has remained with us in some shape or form ever since. What we speak of here is the phenomenon of the 'secret society', something which, though it features in all epochs of history, actually proliferated in the Middle Ages.

Depending on the reasons for their existence and the methods they deploy to achieve their ends, such kinds of groups can of course gather unto themselves great, though subtle power, regarding the functioning of any civilized society. And undoubtedly they had much more power in an epoch as ordered and controlled as the Middle Ages, in comparison to our own much more open world.

But given what had happened to the Cathars, the Templars and others, it was of course inevitable now in the 14th century that if Esoteric Christianity was to be cultivated in any organized way at all, it had to be done so in total secrecy. For by now it was overwhemingly obvious that the forces behind the Church's orthodoxy, even the Church itself, would go to any lengths to deny the secret riches of esotericism access to the mainstream of Christianity.

Perhaps the best known (to us!) of these secret societies, wherein the ancient wisdom continued to be cultivated within the overall framework of western Christendom, are the Rosicrutians and the Freemasons. Now it is actually very hard to estimate the extent of the influence these Brotherhoods had upon the social and religious fabric of the societies in which the operated. Undoubtedly however such influence was very significant, especially during the time in which such societies were being most true to the spirit of the ancient wisdom.[73]

Nowadays much speculative literature is written about these and other secret societies which by their very nature, we must remember, came into existence in order not only to cultivate, but also to conceal as far as possible from hate-filled eyes, the true nature of the Mystery wisdom. Such a paradoxical situation was inevitable, for as the history of the Church by this time had overwhelmingly shown, there were far too many people around who were hell-bent on destroying altogether this precious jewel of the ancient wisdom, especially in its incarnational or re-incarnational aspect. It had therefore to be cultivated and promoted in the most subtle of ways imaginable, ways which to the average mind nowadays are almost impenetrable by the sheer density of their symbolism. It is because of this therefore that scholarship in this area does little more usually than unearth mysterious puzzle after mysterious puzzle, presenting the researcher and his or her readers with a sort of pandora's box of occult symbolism and allusion, astonishingly rich in content certainly, but also all too often devoid of truely reasonable interpretation.

Any approach to these types of societies however which is not based on a positive acceptance of the validity and veracity of the ancient wisdom, as well as on a clear understanding that there was always afoot an active movement to suppress it, will do little more than add extra speculation to the already dense mystification!

What we will do here therefore, and in order hopefully to avoid any further mystification, is to record merely the salient or most pertinent features (from the point of view of our present study) regarding *one* of these societies, namely the Rosicrutians. By doing this we will be both able to illustrate, as well as get a feeling for, the overall place and significance of these kinds of societies within the ongoing development of the spirit of Esoteric Christianity in western Christendom.

WISE AND HOLY MEN OF GOD

For it is a fact that those who went by the name of the Rosicrutians were the ones who most securely and deeply bore within them the Spirit of the ancient wisdom during this critical period of our Western history. And by gaining some understanding of them, however cursory it may have to be here, we will, as it were, get a flavour of how the sophiacal spirit, now in its movement totally underground, began to work invisibly within the culture and the soul of European man.

The Rosicrutian Brotherhood was established in 1459 through the work of the Initiate known as Christian Rosencrutz who had made contact with, among others, the dispersed representatives of the now moribund stream of the Templar wisdom. What Christian Ronsencrutz did was to give this dying stream of wisdom a great new impetus. For in the teaching and the character of this personality, the ancient wisdom came to a rich and modern maturity. He brought to it a new unity as well as giving it an updated and thoroughly Christianized expression, and was moreover able to organize and inspire the Brotherhood into a powerful esoteric movement.

Conventional historians however have difficulties with the apparent 'invisibility' of the Rosicrutians. Although they are well recognised as having actually existed and what they stood for is also well known, precisely who they were remains quite a mystery. And we must say something in this direction here in an attempt to clear up the confusion.

In one sense the Rosicrutians, if they were going to work at all in the material world, simply had to work invisibly, given the history of the esoteric spirit up to this time. The terrible repression and persecution of previous individuals and movements which attempted to bring this wisdom to the forefront of the Christian consciousness was in itself reason enough for the Rosicrutian's apparent and cultivated invisibility.

There is however yet another reason, equally if not more pertinent than this. And that is to do with the fact that the Rosicrutians were not so much ever concerned anyway with the outer world of nitty gritty politics and so on as with the overall transformation of human thinking and consciousness along purely spiritual lines. Although they were highly active in all kinds of good social work, they saw their primary mission in fact as an antidote to what they astutely observed as the purely materialistic trends in the society of their own time. And they thus, as a foundation of their movement, promoted, more than anything else, the creative and curative powers of the imagination. They were therefore in this sense a utopian movement primarily, and as such did not occupy any particular 'place' [74] on the Earth but rather had their true place in the spirit or the spiritual world. In an archetypal sense this may also be regarded as the world of a purely *divine imagination*. [75] And this latter world, by definition, cannot of course be seen with physical eyes and could only be found through accepting and practising the Rosicrutian's own initiatory disciplines. Historians, needless to say, don't do, or usually don't understand, this! Hence the apparent invisibility of the Rosicrutians to them generally!

Now the initiation procedures of the Rosicrutian Order is actually illustrated or summed up very well in the very name of their founder. For the name Christian Rosencrutz actually means the Rose Cross of Christ. And this Rose Cross was the profound symbol of the Rosicrutian Order.

And it is a measure of just how little is generally understood by conventional or academic writers on the subject of the Rosicrutians that this symbol, itself undoubtedly the key to any esoteric or even exoteric understanding of the Rosicrutians, is usually misconstrued. It is for instance usually referred to as a cross which is rose-coloured, something which does not at all convey the import of its true meaning.

The Rosicrutians were a network of Brothers who went quietly through the world effecting good works of Christian loving service everywhere, and they did so out of a great depth of knowledge and inspiration which they acquired through a spiritual training based principally on a profound meditation on the Mystery of the Incarnation. And for them this was summed up in the symbol given to them by their founder, the symbol of the Rose Cross. This was not a rose-coloured cross however, but actually a black cross with a wreath of seven red roses entwined around the intersection of the two crossbars.

Now in this form this symbol is probably one of the most profound of all Christian symbols and is indeed capable of perhaps infinite elaboration spiritually in meditation. For it summs up the Christian Mystery in a wonderfully pure and simple way. It also however in a very graphic manner throws much light on the fundamental cleavage we have been discussing heretofore, in that it defines the essential difference between the esoteric and the exoteric emphasis in Christianity, which latter of course was the perogative of the mainstream Church. For what is in question here is the essential difference between the esoteric symbol of the Rose Cross on the one hand, and the exoteric symbol of the Crucifix on the other.

THE ROSE CROSS: SYMBOL OF SPIRITUAL RE-BIRTH

Expressed at its most basic level the symbol of the Rose Cross indicates the following: the black cross is representative of the lower or earthly man while the roses are symbolic of the fact that out of this lower, dark, or merely earthly human nature, the higher or spiritual Christ-man grows, essentially through a process of purification of his blood. In this way the Rose Cross depicts the full Christian incarnational cycle of earthly birth, death, and eventual spiritual re-birth. Moreover it also overcomes the severe limitations of the Crucifix itself, which concentrates of course on the death aspect only, with all the attendant consequences that such a one-sided image has had (and continues no doubt to have!) for both our communal history and our individual Christian-formed psychology.

Be that as it may, throughout the 16th century these Brothers of the Rose Cross were deeply inspired by this symbol and were consequently highly empowered spiritually, psychically, as well as physically in their work. They were for the most part very ordinary people, a network of tiny scattered bands, small in number but big in spirit, for they were Christ-imbued. They worked in all manner of ways and in an exceedingly quiet and secretive fashion. They had to! They had no choice! In this way however through their activities they kept alive in the undercurrent of European culture a stream of what may be called the pure spiritual 'living water'. This they managed to do in total opposition and in great contrast to the ever growing might of the forces of militaristically backed materialism, forces in which the orthodox Church unfortunately usually acquiesced, largely through ignorance.

It is important to remember here also of course that by this time that great upsurge and refinement of culture and learning, the Renaissance, had impacted greatly on the folk-soul of Europe. Fundamental and far-reaching changes were taking place everywhere at this time but especially in the development of consciousness itself. For Europe was now emerging out of the faith-imbued strictures of the Middle Ages and into the modern period of scientific enlightenment. That other great revolution was also in full swing, the Reformation. The invention of the printing press around this time also needs to be most carefully marked. For this invention was nothing less than mammoth in its implications. (This latter indeed is an example of one of those rare events in the history of mankind, in the face of which all attempts at verbal articulation of its repercussions usually fails. One can merely draw analogies and parallels: the invention of the computer in our own day is something of similar import and significance for man's development).

Perhaps not quite as complex as our own time, 16th century Europe was nevertheless getting to grips with great new possibilities and ever widening horizons, both intellectual and territorial. From this time, all learning and culture, in fact consciousness itself, was taking on an entirely new dimension. And due to ever expanding possibilities of individual advancement and education, the 'status quo' had to accommodate a huge new input of original, or reinvented ideas from various quarters. A great new sense of freedom was thus arising.

THE DANGERS OF SHARING THE SECRET

It was the printing press especially of course that gave the word 'secret' a totally new dimension too! For in an age when some piece of information or knowledge could be printed and disseminated by the thousands, what indeed could be really secret any more? A situation had actually arisen whereby what formerly had been passed by word of mouth or by carefully copied and guarded manuscripts, could now be printed and circulated *ad infinitum*. And it was in just such a milue that the Rosicrutians moved from being a truely secret society to one publicly known to be concerned with the deepest questions and issues of the day.

Thus it was in the years 1614 and 1615 respectively that the two famous Rosicrutian Manifestos appeared in the form of printed and widely circulated copies in Germany. In these documents a plea was made, on behalf of all those who were deeply influenced by the Christ Mystery and the ancient wisdom generally, for 'the establishment' to take up this wisdom and knowledge in a scientifically applied and consciously responsible manner, with the aim of a wholehearted and truely spiritual renewal of culture generally. Then in the following year, 1616, a third document, the mysterious Chemical Wedding of 'Christian Rosencrutz was published. This document however went very much further than the others in that it gave in an imaginative narrative,[76] an account of the processes which occur in the human soul as it undergoes the various degrees of initiation into knowledge of the soul and spiritual worlds of which the material world is, in terms of the ancient wisdom, but a transient reflection.

Now all of these publications managed to create a huge stir in the public life of Middle Europe at the time. And whether or not they had the primary intention of doing so, they certainly had the effect of both publicising and politicising the erstwhile highly secretive work of the Rosicrutians. And when the excitement thus engendered was blended into the general air of intellectual and cultural freedom of the time, all this managed to raise widespread hopes for a truely spiritual regeneration of mankind too.

170

For this was all happening at a time in which the Roman Church was becoming increasingly recognised as nothing but an obstacle to all such spiritual progress. However, the tragic downside to all of this, as far as the Rosicrutians were concerned, was that now that they had come to the notice of the status quo through the widespread dissemination of knowledge about them, their days were truely numbered. For the fact was that they were no longer 'secret' any more. Ironically now, it was in fact this secretive aspect of their activities which was the author of their downfall. For it was this very secrecy which caused the taps of rumour and villification to be turned fully on regarding them, and the frenzy of the heresy hunters once more was whipped into full swing. And so it was actually not very long after the publication of the Manifestos that the whole movement was, like many other esoteric movements before it, mercilessly crushed.

THE BOHEMIANS' LOVE OF WISDOM

The epicentre of the 'Rosicrutian Enlightenment' had in fact been the ancient and historic Kingdom of Bohemia, a place of the richest cultural heritage in Europe, which had, in the period preceeding the time in question, also gradually become a place of the deepest Christian esoteric studies and of hermetic learning generally. Inevitably therefore it was here also that the Catholic forces of reaction gathered into a fierce momentum against the Rosicrutians and their movement. And beginning with the defeat of the Bohemians at The Battle of the White Mountain on 8th November 1620, these reactionary forces, led here by the Duke of Bavaria, came down with a mighty vengence and cruelty upon this Kingdom. And from this defeat onwards the Bohemian's were 'subjected to the most frightful tyranny and persecution'.

It was in this manner that what has come to be known as the Rosicrutian Enlightenment was very quickly snuffed out and yet another chapter in the history of Esoteric Christianity came to a tragic end.

Before this movement was snuffed out however it did manage to achieve something quite significant regarding the cultural/spiritual life especially of Middle Europe. For it brought to a far greater awareness than would otherwise perhaps have been the case, the significant part that esotericism must play in any genuine spiritual or cultural renewal in society generally.

The Rosicrutians came near to achieving some such renewal in Bohemia and would, if succeeded, have undoubtedly spawned a much more general revival of arcane learning in Europe had they not stirred up the heretic and the witch-hunters.

Like many other movements before it however, the Rosicrutians, once their secrecy had been exposed, were considered to be a threat to the established religion and its orthodoxy of theocratic control. As such they quickly became easy targets for the witch-hunters and they were put down. Not only were they put down however, but the events which followed immediately upon this elimination of the Rosicrutians were such that any similar kind of esoteric enlightenment would never be allowed to return again. Thus very significantly it was at precisely the same time of the Rosicrutians' defeat that another terrible catastrophy was unleashed in Europe by similar spirit-fearing powers. This time however the scale of the destruction was to be even greater, in fact very much greater, than anything that had gone before. For it was a catastrophy which wrought immense cruelty and suffering upon people all over the continent of Europe. And it is known generally as the Thirty Years War.

THE 30 YEARS WAR

Stated at its most basic level the Thirty Years War was a reaction against the progressive movement of the Reformation as such. What the Reformation had essentially done of course was to polarize into a stark clarity the already long existing division within the Western Church, or more precisely, within the soul of Europe itself. The foundation for this division had been laid, as we have seen, way back in the very early centuries of the Church when the sophiacal wisdom had been so tragically abandoned. This in turn led to the eventual denial even of the very spirit itself! (See p 115).

The Reformation essentially was nothing more than an exoteric expression of this esoterically based problem, and though it achieved for the Church some advances, it has, from a larger and deeper perspective, done in fact little more than highlight the crying need in Christianity for the purifying and unifying waters of the perennial wisdom. For only within the framework of the sophiacal wisdom's tripartite concept of Man as a microcosmic reflection of the macrocosmic and divine reality of the Trinity

172

itself, only in this way can a sure basis be found for a true healing of all the growing divisions in the psychological, spiritual and religious life of modern man. This tripartite wisdom has alas been almost entirely lost, as well as much else, to the mainstream Christian Church.

The need for such a return to basics was of course sensed, if not actually consciously recognised, by the reformers of the 15th and 16th century. For inherent in such a return to basics, as far as the Mystery of Christ is concerned, was a breaking free from all law-ridden authoritarianism as such, and allowing the individual the freedom to find his or her own unique way to the blissful truth of the Christ Mystery. It was after all this very freedom which in the first place had allowed Christianity to emerge out of the almost overwhelming legalistic restrictions of Judaism, and so enter into the wider world as the powerfully liberating and purely spiritual force it has since become.

But after the endless repression over the centuries of this most basic of all of the many virtues of the Christian Way, the situation became critical in the 16th century and resulted in the splitting of the Western Church. Put into very broad terms this splitting of the Church, the Reformation, was essentially an outward expression of an inward and deeply felt desire by the individual Christian to assert his true Christian right to know God through the spiritual power of Christ and Christ alone. The Roman, Catholic, or up to then simply the orthodox Christian Church, was now beginning to be perceived as that entity which was actually getting in the way of this pure realization. The Roman Catholic Church thus took on the guise of 'the enemy' in this regard from the Reformers' point of view. The reason for this was that from the time of the defeat of The Gnosis onwards, Christian orthodoxy had always been built on the view that any kind of dabbling in knowledge, spiritual or otherwise, for its own sake by an individual, would or could only lead to misadventure or even worse in the end. The Church therefore took upon itself to make all the rules in this regard. When once it became apparent from the 16th century onwards, that an individual could actually pursue knowledge without regard for the Church's monopoly, or even worse, do so without even its actual approval, and yet somehow claim such pursuits to be Christian – it was this fact more than any other that caused the Church to, as it were, really shake in its boots and eventually crack in half. And simultaneously something very interesting and very revealing happens. For when all this 'unsanctioned' scientific investigation was seen to be threatening the stability and authority of the Church, these scientific pursuits were given the tarnish of devilry by the dogmatic reactionaries. For the extremely limited vision of these reactionaries allowed them to see it in no other way! And so around this time significantly we find an archetypal figure emerging into the imaginative framework of the European consciousness, a figure who, although he is highly cultured and learned, he is also nevertheless branded as being nothing less than a child of the Devil! This is the sinister, dark but nevertheless alluring and majestic figure of Faust. (He got such a poor reputation because he was believed to have literally sold his soul to the Devil). Faust represents nothing less in fact than the individualized expression (in an archetypal image) of all the turmoil that is being engendered in the European soul at this time and of which the Reformation is merely the outward or historical symptom. However, this emergence is very significant in that Faust, though a highly learned man, is also a very sinister one . For what we are now dealing with in fact is yet another re-invention of the oldest of all the skeletons in the cupboards of the Roman Church, the heretic. This time however he is cast in a very different guise, a modern one even. For now he emerges in, one might say, an even grandiose fashion, replete with all the finest embellishments and accoutrements that a civilized and cultured life of the Middle Ages could afford. However, looking behind the scenes of this creation one sees that the whole idea is none other than the very old Roman one which essentially is suspicious, even afraid of knowledge and wisdom and therefore it has to be suppressed.

Thus we may say that in the emergence of this archetypal character, Faust, we find revealed the sinister workings of a manipulative power which has as its ultimate goal the suppression of (spiritual) knowledge but has as its field of action that most delicate and vulnerable of all human qualities, the imagination.

And it is these combined factors which make Faust such an enduring and fascinating character.

Chapter Five

FROM HERETIC TO DEVIL

The birth of Faust in the soul of Europe at the time of the Reformation was, one can confidently assert, an inevitability in many ways. In fact Faust himself and the emergence of his story at this time are indicative of a deep disturbance on two complimentary levels: the individual psyche of European man as well as what we may call his more general folk-soul. For what Faust actually does is to give an individual, artistic or imaginative countenance to a much more generalized or social problem of which the Reformation was of course merely the outward or historic manifestation. Thus in trying to understand Faust or the reason for his emergence at all, we shall at the same time be getting to grips with the esoteric v exoteric nature of the problems which lie at the heart of the true spiritual quest.

And these problems, though in Faust are given a medieval setting, are nevertheless still with us today. They are in other words still totally relevant and as such account for the enduring popularity of the Faust theme.

We will therefore look at this whole Faust phenomenon here now in some detail.

Ever since the early days of the Church when it first took up its evangelical mission to the world in earnest, Faust had in a way been germinating or gestating in the imagination of Western man. He takes in fact his initial conception from one Simon Magus who makes a brief but very significant appearance in the New Testament, (See Acts 8:9-24). Now this Simon Magus was a magician of obviously very great renown throughout the land of Samaria. He had recently turned to the new Christian Way but was not as yet, at the time the incident actually takes place, fully initiated. (This latter point is specifically referred to in the Acts). But he comes to the attention of the writer of the Acts primarily because he tried to *buy* spiritual power from Christ's disciples. Now for this lack of insight he is of course severely rebuked by the apostle Peter.

This incident may be viewed in fact on a number of different levels and actually is one which begs the whole difficult question of authority or power as such in so far as it plays into the ever present tension between the temporal and the spiritual generally. It can be stated with confidence that this polarity represented in fact one of the key tensions in the whole development of the Church. However as the centuries passed and the Church got farther and farther away from this episode about Simon as well as all the other historical events which surrounded the Incarnation, it also lost its ability to discern, in a truely spiritual manner, the subtle meaning contained in much of the Gospel. This situation was of course very much further compounded by the Church's active repression of the ancient wisdom. Dogmatic literalism then began to replace true spiritual discernment as the primary tool in evangelism, and so the written scriptural records[77] in this manner gradually and inevitably became the bedrock of the Church's dogmatically enforced authority. Thus the Church was now at liberty in this kind of situation, to interpret the Gospel, one can say, in whatever way it wished, in order to serve its own narrowed focus best. And so this particular incident regarding Simon Magus, in time became the *ex cathedra* basis for judgment upon the practise of magic and the cultivation of esotericism generally. Moreover this was always a judgement which, as we have seen, was universal in its condemnation and invariably cruel in the extreme in its enforcement.

It was, or is, however, also a judgement which totally misses the mark if one reads the incident in the Acts carefully enough. It is important therefore to look at this Gospel incident in order to see how literalism and dogmatism generally can just as easily lead to confusion regarding the Gospel, as much as to anything else.

A close reading of the incident in question thus reveals that it is in fact not at all Simon's magical powers (or even for that matter the very practise of magic as such) that is being condemned here, but something quite different. For Simon, it appears, despite his newly professed Christianity, had a total misunderstanding of the Christian use of money, or more precisely of gold. Gold in fact had a very special place in the consciousness of the early Christians. For as the sun metal (see page 185f) gold always had, for the practioner of the ancient wisdom, the deepest of magical and alchemical significance.[78] And because of this special relationship to the sun and also because Christ was regarded as the sun God or the Solar Logos in the early Church, how one used this precious substance from now on, especially among the new congregations, was of the very essence of one's worth or measure as a Christian.

176

CAN YOU BUY THE HOLY SPIRIT?

What this incident regarding Simon therefore is attempting to underline is that a new relationship to gold is now needed if one is to find one's way into the Christ Being. One must be prepared even (horror of horrors!) to give it all away for nothing if necessary! There are other parts of the Gospel which stress this point also. But essentially the incident here regarding Simon, more than anything else points up the fact that the Christ-Spirit, when one truely has it, actually gives or should give one total freedom in the world, i.e. freedom in and from the merely temporal world, of which the 'money' aspect of gold is of course the most potent symbol. And it was this very important part of the initiation that had not obviously tweeked with Simon! He brazenly or ignorantly tried to buy spiritual power with gold or money. And in this manner Simon Magus became responsible for a new kind of sin, and even gave his name to it: simony.

The very fact however that he had attempted to buy the Holy Spirit in the first place indicates that he felt his own spiritual or magical powers, from wherever they came, to be of less value than those of the Christians. And undoubtedly he thought he could make up for this deficiency by invoking the mighty power of gold, magically or otherwise! This however was the very rock he stumbled on, for, as the Christians knew only too well, because of the Incarnation everything in the world had to be viewed in an entirely new and spiritual light. And this was especially true of money or gold. Moreover this had to be a purely inner and mystical light and one which was essentially, indeed absolutely, free of all materiality, or in this particular case 'purchasing power' as such. To reiterate: It was not the magic as such that was being condemned in the Acts, but the misunderstanding by Simon of the purely Christian use of gold and also of the whole business of buying and selling as such.

For the early Christians, especially those who were fully initiated, placed the greatest of emphasis on a correct understanding of the spiritual aspects of goods, ownership, possessions, gold, and so on, as other parts of the New Testament very strongly indicate. Simon had not yet arrived at a correct understanding of these aspects. He erred, and was duely and severely rebuked.

The problem was (and still is alas!) very common! It is to do essentially with the communion or the community aspect of Christianity. Originally the 'breaking of the bread' was of the greatest possible symbolic significance in the rites of the Christian gatherings, for it meant there could be no Christ or Christianity at all unless the aspect of sharing was intrinsically part of it.

But the step from bread to gold is, on the other hand, only a small one if one considers the fact that outside of the community of the congregation bread was not at all shared and, quite the contrary, one had to buy it with money or gold. Simon's case however was highlighted in the Acts because he possessed a far greater spiritual power than the average person. And even though he was an accepted member of the congregation, he still felt he could 'buy' anything with gold. He had not in fact learned as yet to Christianize his magic – that was the point! But his status as a magician came to be entirely and erroneously mixed up with his sin of simony in the later development of Church thinking, and in a sort of elaborate and historical version of 'chinese whispers', he eventually ended up as the dark magician Faust who actually did sell his very own soul to the devil! (Such is an example of the workings of the 'rumour machine' of bad history).

The truth of the matter of course is that the very early Christians themselves were also wonder workers, magicians even, but magicians of a new and very different colour than any that had gone before! For it would be entirely in keeping with the spirit of the times in which the first followers of the new Way lived to say that they were people who were practising, in every little detail of their productive lives, the white magic of pure spiritual love, a love which poured into their inmost being through their sublime Christ-initiation.

Once however the Church lost sight of this initiation aspect of the Mystery, any possibility of ever really understanding the white magic of Christ inevitably got lost to it also. It was however essentially this magical and Mystery aspect of Christianity which was kept alive in the various esoteric movements, the history of which we have been tracing up to now. And one can say indeed that a sort of Faustian thread runs through all of them.

We will look therefore at the Faust story itself now and try to discern something of this elusive thread.

THE STORY OF FAUST

The gist of the story is that Faust, a supposedly real individual who lived in the 16th century, was a highly learned man, accomplished in many of the arts, including and especially of course, magic. But the implication is that because he could not get fully to grips with the essence of a purely Christian faith and its truth, he decided to sell his soul to the Devil instead. Part of the bargain was of course that the Devil would duely give Faust the power and possibility to indulge indiscriminately in all his appetites and desires. But his precious soul was the very expensive price-tag!

Now from the point of view of Esoteric Christianity it is in fact of no great concern at all how much or how little of the medieval story of Faust is actually historically true or not. There is no doubt however that there actually was a real Dr. Faustus who provided the inspiration for what gradually evolved into the legend of Faust. Legends and myths always have some basis in fact anyway, but is it not true that their interest lies as much in the form of the consciousness which gave rise to them in the first place, as in the immediate details of their expression? And in the case of the Faust legend we have a literary phenomenon indicating the kinds of tensions which had in fact long existed in the soul of Western Christendom but which however never achieved any form of true and meaningful expression. Many and varied were the forces which worked both psychically and physically to prevent this from happening ever since the denial of the essential inner aspect of the Christ Mystery, a denial which took place in the early centuries.

It was certainly however a very real Dr. Faustus who provided the bones of at least an attempted resolution of this great psychological deficiency. And whatever may have been his character in real life, this now proceeded to be embellished imaginatively and ingeniously out of the deepest of Western man's soul-disturbances and spiritual longings. Thus we can see that whatever else he was, Faust was certainly a creature with a very long period of gestation behind him. For when he finally emerges onto the stage of Europe, what we have is a character in which all these conflicting elements in the human soul culminated into a highly moral tale of woe and wonder. The tensions that have now to be dealt with are deep, manifold and perennial, those for instance between the lower and the higher man, between light and dark, between good and evil, etcetra. But in the case of the Faust creations, once one understands something of the background and history of esotericism generally, the tensions depicted in him are also very much to do with the spiritual crises that was becoming increasingly manifest in Europe at this time. For as we have indicated earlier, the Reformation was merely the tip of the iceberg of a far deeper spiritual and religious problem, the origins of which went way back to the early Church's eschewing of the real Mystery nature of Christ. The tensions which this denial engendered within the body of the Church were manifold but were such that they sounded their deepest note in the psychological conflict between man's inner and outer experience. And this at bottom is also of course representative of the cleavage between esoteric and exoteric Christianity.

FAUST: SYMBOL OF THE SPLIT PERSONALITY

Herein lies the fascination with Faust and the 'reason' for the emergence of the whole Faust phenomenon at this time. For once the Church's moral, spiritual and religious authority began to come under the greatest of pressure in the 16th century, there also got under way a vital and potentially powerful reappraisal of the ancient wisdom generally. Such a reappraisal lay in fact at the very heart of the Renaissance. Concomitant with this development however there also arose within Christendom a kind of fear and suspicion of intellectual endeavour generally and of scientific investigation in particular. Up to then the Church had been a sort of protective Mother, acting in all aspects of individual human endeavour as a caring guide and a loving teacher. But an understandable fear of the unknown duely arose in the soul of Europe once the individual began to cut himself off from the certainty about the world and the universe that the Church had hitherto provided him with. And it was out of this kind of mood that a picture of the Devil then crystallized as a strange yet somehow familiar kind of being, a sort of *doppleganger* who prodded and goaded the human body and soul down all kinds of questionable avenues, tempting him in the process towards the most dangerous kinds of accomplishments and freedoms.

The great popularity of Faust in other words rested squarely on the fact that he was in a sense a picture of Everyman, in so far as he (Faust) was a representative of a newly emerging type of consciousness in Europe at this time.

For with the termination of the Age of Faith, with in other words the release of the soul from the cocooned certainty of a simple loving faith in Christ which had been up to then its mainstay and most cherished possession, a new power, as if in compensation, was then acquired. In retrospect this new 'psychic' power can be seen as part of an ongoing and natural development of the totality of man's being. Even more than that, it may indeed be regarded as one of those occasional but very big evolutionary 'jumps' in human consciousness of which social anthropologists are aware, and which always bestow on man new possibilities and give him new horizons. And in this particular case it released into the soul a very significant, new, and vital power, one which simply *had* to be reckoned with, whatever the cost. For what we can observe at this time in Europe was nothing less than the widespread taking hold of the power of objective thought as such, and even more to the point, the pursuit of scientific investigation for its own sake, something which inevitably followed on from this objectivity. A new god even, one could say, had arrived on the scene, the god of Reason. A god certainly to be reckoned with, but one however not, at that particular point of time anyway, entirely to be trusted! (Even Luther for instance, the greatest of the progressive reformers of the period, is said to have regarded reason as nothing less than the Devil's whore!).

Faust can thus be seen as evidence of a sort of archetypal preparation which was percolating in the soul of Western man at this time, a sort of imaginative or artistic attempt to get to grips with the huge, even frightening possibilities that the new way of thinking seemed to open up for human beings, especially regarding the material world. Any meddling with God's creation now began to take on a whole new mantle of uncertainty and fear, especially in the souls of those who for far too long had been steeped in the fogs of ignorance and superstition.

Small wonder therefore that that band of industrious men who now began to emerge at this time and of whom perhaps Faust can be regarded in a sense as a prototype, if not actually a role model, came in for such great misunderstanding and villification. These were the Alchemists who may correctly be looked upon as the genuine recipients of the ancient wisdom and whose movement (in so far as it may be regarded as such) now became the newest or latest vechicle by which the spirit of Esoteric Christianity would continue to work in the world.

Chapter Six

THE TRUTH ABOUT THE ALCHEMISTS

The origins of alchemy can be traced way back to the latter part of the first millennium. It was an art however which did not, as it were, peak until the 16th and 17th centuries, during which time the greatest of its adepts flourished. Perhaps the best known of these nowadays is Paracelsus who was active in the early 16th century. He died in 1541.

The Alchemists as a general rule were wise, practical, and often very devout men. What distinguished them from other kinds of philosophers or wise or holy men however was that they were the very first to start applying their wisdom in a systematic way, with the aim of gaining a more direct, as distinct from merely theoretical, understanding of Nature as such. They were in fact the first to put the experimental method into practise in a sustained and ordered manner. In their own day they represented the progressive element in many of society's most important and necessary disciplines, including and especially medicine. (Paracelsus' diagnostic method, which took the whole man, body and soul, into account, is undergoing a revival in our own day).

But as individuals they could in fact be adept in many different arts or disciplines at the same time. This broadness of their vision and ability was indeed one of the principal features of the Alchemists. They were moreover extremely industrious and laid in fact the foundation for modern chemistry physics and science generally.

As materialism advanced in later centuries however their reputation as a body fell into disrepute, and they came to be regarded or even discarded as dilettants or merely muddled astrologers, quacks, and the like.

Now there were undoubtedly, as there always are in any profession (especially those of the nature of the Alchemists) dilettantes and frauds. This element was inevitably blown up however by the repressive forces within the Church and society, and was used, in familiar fashion, to discredit, victimize and, in some cases, even to execute them! So that even during their own lifetime they had to exercise extreme caution regarding their practises, for fear of the dreaded Inquisition which was still very active at this time and whose employees were literally never far out of sight! The great Elizabethan mage, John Dee for instance, had his fabulous library, museum and precious instruments tragically ransacked by a mob because they believed he (like Faust!) was conjuring up the Devil!

By the time of the Alchemist's hey-day of course the printing press was in full swing. So there is a vast spectrum of alchemical literature available, much of it, it has to be said, impenetrable in its symbolism and its allegorical nature and content. Indeed it is often suggested that much of what the Alchemists wrote was in fact purposefully obfuscated so that their knowledge would not become known to the heretic-hunters. And indeed there must be some truth in this. What is certain nowadays however, thanks to modern scholarship and a resurgence of a genuine interest in the alchemists, in their lives and work, is that by and large they were anything but dilettantes. Quite the contrary! They were in fact the most serious minded, cultured, and genuinely spiritual people, in an age when much uncertainty existed regarding man's purpose in life and his future on Earth. The Alchemists represented in fact the true spirit-seekers of their new age, an age we must remember in which Christianity was undergoing the greatest break-up in the West it has so far experienced. Indeed these two factors, i.e. the break-up of the Church and the emergence of Alchemy are entirely inter-related.

The Reformation was fundamentally a progressive movement, one of the essential features of which, as the 'Rosicrutian Enlightenment' clearly shows, wished to keep the mutually reinforcing disciplines inherent in Religion and Science fully integrated. The Rosicrutian Manifestos are in fact only fully understood when they are regarded as entirely visionary documents issued more or less spontaneously at a time when there was a widespread perception abroad that Science and Religion was now poised to merge into a great new power for the transformation of the world. Up to this time it has to be said of course that the complimentary nature of science and religion had always been nurtured by the Church anyway, however unconscious or inarticulate this may have been. But then prior to the 15th century, the modern idea of science as such did not really exist in any event. The Alchemists however, as recipients of the ancient and perennial wisdom, were entirely in tune, both psychologically and philosophically, with the new mood emerging in the human soul at this time. Essentially this was a mood that began to look at nature in an entirely new way, one of discursive, objective and experimental interest.

THE ALCHEMISTS AND THE ANCIENT WISDOM

Alchemy actually arose out of a blending in the soul of this new mood of objective and scientific interest in the world with the deepest tenets of the ancient and by now fully Christ-imbued esoteric wisdom. The ancient wisdom, because it is also the perennial wisdom or philosophy, is always of course thoroughly alive and does not fail to move with the times ever. (Contrary to popular opinion esotericism is always in fact ahead of the times rather than behind!) How one became an Alchemist therefore was by taking hold of the esoteric wisdom as the initiates of old had always experienced and elaborated it, but in an entirely new way. A higher harmony needed now to resound in the soul of those who wished to be foremost in the possession of the esoteric wisdom if it was to yield really good fruit for the future. More than any others therefore it was the Alchemists who attempted to cultivate this sweet harmony in every detail of their lives and work. That this was in fact the case can be easily deduced from the mode of expression they used in many of their writings, which are often full of the most pious and devout sentiments.

Anyone who approaches the Alchemists with an awareness and some appreciation of the ancient wisdom generally, will have little difficulty understanding that they were in many cases initiates or seers themselves, and cultivated assiduously the 'Great Work' of esoteric initiation into the hidden worlds of Nature, as well as being scientists in the exoteric sense. One can say that these first scientists (for that is what in truth the Alchemists were), regarded their very own soul as the true laboratory. And it was there, more than anywhere else, where all the most illuminating experiments actually took place! For the Alchemists were attempting, to express it in another way, to heal the divide between the inner and the outer experience of the world as they perceived it in their individual Christian souls, a division which they felt all the more acutely by dint of the Church's virtual total denial of the esoteric or inner aspect of the Christ Mystery. They were undoubtedly aware (and with varying degrees of understanding) of this anomalous and repressive aspect of the Church's position, and their lives and work were duely tempered by it. It was a problem however which they did not succeed in overcoming. Indeed given the scope of the problem they could hardly have overcome it! For it is true to say that their overall cause was in fact the very bulls eye in that target at which the latest of the Church's reactive programmes, the Counter-Reformation, was aiming. The Roman Church especially, given its entrenched and absolutist position regarding the limits of knowledge, could only see in any kind of experimenting with nature's secrets a transgression into God's private territory, a domain in other words unfit for mortal investigation.

Such activities were thus necessarily regarded as immoral and sinful. And the end result of all this was that the Church now parted company once and for all with science as such. And the disappearance and later discrediting of the Alchemists is entirely due to the fact that the Counter-Reformation, whatever else it may or may not have achieved, certainly did achieve the complete and tragic separation of science and religion. This indeed is one of the chief 'legacies' of the Counter-Reformation. For it well and truely paved the way for the eventual triumph in Europe of the materialistic way of thinking. And so this one-sided mood which duely engulfed Europe in the wake of Newton, tended to regard these amazing people, the Alchemists, as being nothing less than a bunch of looney gold-diggers or mad moon-struck magic-heads!

Unfortunately this sort of image still clings to the Alchemists even in our own day. But the real truth about them nevertheless is slowly emerging as more careful, sensitive, and less materialistically driven minds turn towards them, their work and their world. It must be stated of course that none of these three latter aspects of the alchemical phenomenon can be understood in isolation, a common and mistaken approach to them which perhaps explains some of the myths and misunderstandings which have evolved about the Alchemists through the centuries. Their main work for instance was and is still generally understood to have been the transmutation of base metal into gold. And this aspect, taken in isolation, does undoubtedly seem to us a form of utter silliness. A familiarity with the lives of the Alchemists and the milue in which they worked however, will soon reveal that this simple way of depicting them does not in the least do justice to their great intellectual sophistication, their genuine and deep interest in the material world, and most importantly, the spiritually-imbued consciousness out of which they experimented. For in comparison with the Alchemist, the modern materialistic mind finds in the glitter of gold nothing but a decoy as far as the spirit is concerned. To the Alchemists on the other hand, gold was as much a sun-symbol indicating a profound, inner, and essentially spiritual transmutation, than an attractive material thing to be sought after for its own sake.

THE ALCHEMISTS SEARCH FOR THE TRUTH ABOUT GOLD

For the Alchemists were able to understand something of the evolution of the universe by dint of an intuitive and intimate investigation of the various metals and mineral substances which they understood to be fundamentally related to the different planetary or heavenly bodies. Thus in so far as the Earth itself is obviously part of the overall cosmic evolutionary scheme, all of the substances which it contains, and especially the metals could, by an occult law of correspondences, be related by the Alchemists to the other planets or heavenly bodies. In this way gold was considered to be a sun metal. And just as the sun itself was felt to contain nothing less than the key to the entire enigma of the microcosm and the macrocosm, something which was of course entirely in line with the deepest secrets of all the ancient wisdom paths, so gold represented to the Alchemists the key to the mystery of the universe and of man's true relationship to it. We may thus come to understand that the Alchemists had as much interest in the material metal itself as they had in the Logos-Mystery of the sun-Being (Christ) whom they held the gold to symbolically represent. In this way the 'transmutation' which they so earnestly sought may also be regarded as a high degree of initiation into the sun-Mystery of Christ. In the 'Chemical Wedding of Christian Rosencrutz' (which is essentially an alchemical document) for instance, there is a scene where Christian Rosencrutz receives an initiation, and through this he becomes a 'Knight of the Golden Stone'. In alchemy gold and stone are in fact always profoundly symbolic of the esoteric aspects of the Christ Mystery.[79]

All of this however is not to suggest either that the Alchemists did not in some cases perform the 'ultimate miracle' anyway, and actually transform a base metal into gold. The erudite turn-of-the-century scholar A.E.Waite, who investigated these and related matters very closely indeed, does not exclude this possibility. But the material transmutation of base metal into gold was not however the central issue as far as the Alchemists were concerned, something it tends to become in the minds of those who are motivated by a one-sided concern with material existence only. Waite sums up the Alchemist's claim for our renewed and deepest attention, and put them into their correct overall perspective, when he says (regarding the actual transmutation of metal) '...it is by no means a point of importance to the discriminating student of occultism. But they (the Alchemists) have left behind them a theory which is wholly true in its application to that one substance in Nature which we know to be capable of indefinite perfectibility; and the splendour and glory of the accomplished Magnum Opus, when the young King issues from the Everlasting East, from the land of the Morning and of Paradise, "Bearing the crescent moon upon his crest", though it be a dream, say even, which no one can actually affirm, though it be an impossibility for the metal, is true for the man. And all that is beautiful and sublime in alchemical symbolism may be rigorously applied to the divine flower of the future, the young King of Humanity, the perfect youth to come, when he issues from the Spiritual East, in the dawn of the genuine truth, bearing the Crescent Moon, the woman of the future, upon his bright and imperial crest".[80]

Here the imaginative, creative, and ultimately the spiritual aspect of the Alchemist's goal shines through.

✳ ✳ ✳

It was this *deeply spiritual* aspect of their work however which, as the Counter-Reformation spread, and with it the rise of Newtonian and materialistic science generally, placed the Alchemists entirely under suspicion. For the Reactive forces are always, as we have by now hopefully clearly illustrated in the course of this book, set entirely against the spirit and the work of acquiring any kind of true spiritual knowledge and wisdom, a work which invariably draws from them their most resentful and hateful tendencies. It was however the eventual almost total triumph of materialism in the 18th century, rather than any implied success of the Counter-Reformation as such, which lost the day for the emergence of a real spiritually based science of which the Alchemists were the forerunners.

Chapter Seven

THE ARTISTS KEEP THE TRUE SPIRIT ALIVE

As the 17th century progressed and as learning and education generally became ever more widely cultivated and available, something which was due fundamentally to the increasing supply of printed books, the materialistic bias also became more and more the determining factor of the mass consciousness of Europe. But then, following on the heels of this development, especially from about the 18th century, something else also begins to happen which can be rightly regarded as a fundamental reaction against this materialism. For full blooded spirituality, as distinct from mere piety, mysticism, or religiosity as such, now becomes the pursuit of the artist more than any other type of individual. The Church had always of course up to this point been the primary patron of artists generally. But as the whole loosening process of the Church's universal grip developed, the artists also took unto themselves more and more freedom of individual expression. (The French Revolution was pivotal in this whole development). And stepping back from the Church, the artists could now see more and more clearly not only the truth regarding the Church's relationship with the spirit as such, but they also felt an even greater freedom and urge to express their feelings in this regard.

So, freed from the restrictive influence of the Church's patronage, the artists in this changing climate began to find new outlets for their voice. Book illustration was one of the best of these new 'markets'. And the earliest illustration known of the printing press itself (in the *Danse Macabre*, printed by Mathias Lyons in 1499) testifies quite well to this emerging trend in respect of the artist and his growing sense of responsibility towards the spirit and spirituality as such. For in this illustration it can be seen that it is Death himself in fact, rather than any other kind of spirit, who is the real inspirer of this new education. The illustration clearly shows how Death is trying to seduce the printers.[81] The presentiment artistically depicted in the illustration is quite clear. In effect Death is saying to the book-loving compositors: 'You printers have the pious belief that you are spreading knowledge and wisdom through your books and pamphlets, don't you, ha, ha, ha. But in fact you're doing nothing of the kind! What you're really doing is making us much more alive, ha, ha, ha'. For the artists' begin to feel very deeply at this time that what materialistic science was doing and indeed could only do, was merely to dissect Nature, and in the process turn her into nothing more than a machine, or worse still, a corpse. Her truely living aspect was being, they felt, completely disregarded. Vitalism had little or no place in this emerging philosophy.

For Life itself was being denied. And genuine spirit-seekers, which real artists virtually always are, are usually the ones who suffer most from this kind of denial. Indeed it is the very articulation or expression of this denial which has often been the *raison d'etre* of art, good, bad or indifferent, since the abandonment of the spirit by the Church.

In short, the artists were alert to an evolving situation in which they certainly could see that materialistic science was discovering genuine secrets of Nature and applying them (for good or ill) to the social sphere. But these secrets however, they could also well understand, were of only one side of Nature, her corpse aspect in fact, secrets that is, even of Death itself. This perception, in whatever way, macabre or otherwise, the artists may have begun to articulate it, was of course an inevitable outcome of the abandonment of the alchemical principle of 'inner transmutation'. For this principle, which represented the kernel of the Alchemist's work, was based on a study not only of the sub-natural or purely chemical forces contained in the dead material itself, but more importantly on how those forces could stimulate into soul-filled life what was formerly only latent. The Alchemists did not in this sense treat Nature as a corpse but rather as a partner in their 'Great Work' of transmutation, a process which was in any event everywhere apparent to their inherently spiritual mode of comprehension. For when they surveyed the outer world, everywhere the Alchemists could see this archetypal process of transformation or metamorphosis at work in Nature's manifold forms. It was a process however which, more than anything else, they desired to take effect within the crucible of their own individual souls. For the 'Great work', the 'Magnum Opus' of the Alchemists always had the ultimate aim of transforming the lower, material, or purely sense-bound man, into a higher and truely spiritual one.

But now, within the matrix of 18th century European society, everywhere this alchemical mode of comprehension was being denied. This state of affairs was of course long simmering. For in fact it had its theological and philosophical beginnings in the dogmatic declaration at the Council of Constantinople in 869 (see page 115) which denied the very existence of the spirit. Now however, with the newly emerging and very powerful domain of materialistic science gaining ever greater currency in the 17th and 18th centuries, something even more dangerous and sinister was happening. For now the life-giving properties of the very soul of man himself, as she experiences herself in her intimate communion with Nature, even this was now coming under the greatest of suspicion.

Not only the spirit, but now the soul of man also was being denied!

ISAAC NEWTON IS CAPTURED BY THE MATERIALISTS

The materialistic-motivated culture which was solidly laying its foundations in 18th century Europe was as dry and as soul-less an affair as one can possibly imagine, a milue in fact where only those totally devoid of imagination and given up entirely to pedantry and the like, could hope to make any kind of headway in society at all.

Isaac Newton (1642 –1727) has long been regarded as the great inspirer of this new highly utilitarian and mechanistic trend in science and society. But though it is now becoming increasingly obvious that Newton himself was anything but a pedant, his discoveries in the scientific realm were nevertheless pressed by his followers into the service of this dry culture which became ever more obsessed with one thing, and one thing only, the power and the possibilities inherent in the machine. Thus Mechanism as a general and popular philosophy, took hold of the European mind at this time, and the effects of this have remained and been developing ever since, not just in Europe but all over the world.

Now it was the artistic movement known as Romanticism which provided the vital antidote to this crass situation, crass that is as far as genuinely felt soul and spiritual values were concerned. And the Romantics felt there was only one way to deal with this soul-destroying mechanism, this paralysis that was gripping Western society. And that was to create one great big hell of a stink about it all! Stir it all up was their fundamental philosophy! Make cracks in the system anywhere and everywhere you possibly can they said, and then maybe, just maybe, some fresh air might get in! Just prior to Romanticism there was an artistic movement in Germany known as the *Sturm und Drang*, which means in effect Storm and Stress! This sums up the mood of the Romantics very well. Get enthusiastic, get excited about whatever you can, was the message. It's the only hope. And they did!

Romanticism may not have had much of an effect on science and religion as such. But what it did in fact do was instigate a revolution in aesthetic sensibilities, the implications of which are very far-reaching and long-term. In a sense this movement has only just begun to colour our individual modern lives and souls in any kind of deeper way. It still nevertheless effects our outlook on life to a marked degree. Take just one facet of modern life for instance for which the Romantics are largely responsible: eroticism. Prior to the Romantics this was largely unheard of to the mass of western society. Now it should be stressed that it played only one smallish part in the entire Romantic Movement also. But it is nevertheless perhaps the most acutely obvious legacy of Romanticism in our own culture.[82] But there are many others.

The Romantic Movement is in fact notable in very many respects. In terms of the inner life of Western man however it is actually to this movement that credit must go for the survival of any genuine sense of the true spirit which we may still possess after all the suppression. For in a world otherwise utterly devoid of spirit, those who longed for its pure and refreshing draught were able to find something of it here in the Romantics, especially in its poets. And in so far as a sense of true Romanticism resides in the modern psyche at all, there still resides also a true sense of the spirit.

The Romantic Movement coalesced and developed around a relatively small number, but of very significant individuals. From the point of view of our present study we will restrict ourselves to mentioning just a few of these. Most notably we must point to Novalis who, due to a recognition by those who knew him of his profound sense of, and familiarity with, the spirit and the spiritual world, he was actually regarded as the Prophet of the whole Romantic Movement. He was perhaps all the more highly regarded because of the fact that he died so young. He was only 29 when he died in 1801. However the profundity of the small body of work which he left behind has yet to make its full mark on the literary consciousness of man. And this of course has largely to do with its deeply spiritual nature, which when set against the prevailing materialism of our time is not capable of being properly evaluated. Nevertheless his nearness to, indeed his deep intimacy with, the Sophia-Christ, shines clearly through both his life and his work.

THE TITANIC FIGURE OF GOETHE

But perhaps the full implications of this artistic movement of the

Romantics will only be fully recognised in the decades or even the centuries to come when another of its luminaries comes into his own, which he has by no means as yet fully done, certainly in the English speaking world at any rate. This is the titanic figure of the German, Johann Wolfgang von Goethe, (1749 –1832), whom we may rightly regard as the greatest of all the geniuses of modern times.

Goethe is best known today as a poet and particularly as author of the most profound of all treatments of the Faust theme. He worked in fact on his dramatic poem, Faust, virtually all his life, completing the very complex second part only just before he died. Goethe however was much more than a poet. He was many things. And it is moreover entirely true to say that Goethe's life and work were perfectly in tune with the spirit of Esoteric Christianity. He was in fact deeply interested in, and influenced by, alchemy all his life, and from the sidelines, as it were, vehemently opposed the materialistic trends in the sciences of his day. For apart from being an aesthete, novelist, and poet, Goethe was also an active and productive scientist all his life. His scientific work however, which drew heavily upon the principles of the ancient wisdom, was not regarded with any real credibility by the establishment of his time, simply because he adopted an approach to Nature fundamentally at variance with the entrenched Newtonian position. His scientific work was in fact actively repressed. Nevertheless it is true that Goethe performed the most careful and meticulous of scientific experiments which unequivocally proved many important things which the materialists did not want to hear. To take perhaps the best example: he proved that Newton's theory of optics was, or is, fundamentally flawed.

Now apart from anything else that one can say about this, it is in fact one very good example of the sort of materialistic 'mythology' which we labour very much under still to this day, a kind of hangover one can say from the 18th century. For although Goethean science is in our own day undergoing a long and overdue revival and reappraisal, Newton's optical laws are still regarded almost universally as being correct and Goethe's as totally wrong! Interesting maybe, but wrong! What all of this really amounts to however is just another case of historical 'chinese whispers'. None of those who assert, for instance, that Goethe is wrong, ever bother to check him out! If they did they would see that he is in fact correct! What we have here is largely a case of an untruth or a half-truth being taken up and put out by the establishment (for whatever reason), then passed on and on from one person and one book to another, with the inevitable consequences that always are attendant upon untruths or half-truths of this nature. For Goethe's *Theory Of Colour*, perhaps *the* most accomplished of his contributions in the realm of science, unequivocally proves that colours are not at all exclusively contained in pure white light as is the Newtonian hypothesis. This is in effect only *half* the picture. In working with the age-old principles of polarity, and the fundamental relationship of the lower to the higher, of the microcosm to the macrocosm, Goethe proved categorically that colours emerge in their truest nature from the polarity of black and white and not from the pure white light alone.

Thus it can be seen that Goethe's method of scientific investigation differs fundamentally from the orthodox method, principally by virtue of the fact that it does not exclude the whole phenomenon for the sake of the expedient particular. The primary trend in materialistic science is always in fact towards isolation. In Goethean science however the trend is towards unification. Even more importantly Goethe does not sacrifice the aesthetic element to the purely utilitarian one, which latter is also a primary feature, and a very decadent one, of modern science. It is decadent because the true ideals of Science as such are compromised through it to the service only of profit-motivated capitalism, and not very much else. In the personality of Goethe however the sublime synthesis of Science and Art is in fact accomplished, and it is for this reason that his life and his work are, and will continue to become, an object of the greatest interest to all who wish to pursue a genuine and fully modern spiritual path through life. Indeed Goethean science can in fact be correctly regarded as genuine spiritual science, an idea or a concept which of course materialists have the greatest of difficulty getting their heads around. However, the validity of this assertion regarding Goethe's method can be ascertained from a wide variety of angles, once even a little familiarity with his life and work are gained. But its validity is perhaps best ascertained, in general terms at least, from the fact that in his work Goethe was able to prove scientifically to himself the existence of something which the later psychologist and psychoanalyst Carl Jung (1875-1961) was to call the universal spiritual 'archetypes'. These may be regarded as those forces or powers residing in the human soul, a study and an understanding of which throws great light on all the wonderful array of Nature's forms that manifest themselves to us through our physical senses.[83]

GOETHE: MODEL FOR THE FUTURE SCIENTIST

The Goethean method of scientific investigation is thus seen to be holistic in the very broadest meaning of this term. And it is rich beyond measure, precisely because it affords a true spiritual insight into Nature. And though it has in recent years just begun to be looked at seriously by the scientific establishment, its long-standing principles are ironically very much in accord with the more progressive ideas that are now generally fertilizing this scientific establishment.

One of the principles of the Goethean method of scientific investigation for instance is that the investigator must take into account any effects the experiment he makes has on himself (or herself). These effects can in fact never be left out of the overall result of the enquiry. Not only that but the whole phenomenon of the 'after image' was the subject of the most careful and precise study by Goethe. And once it begins to be at all understood scientifically, the significance of the 'after image' has powerful potential for thawing the icy grip of materialistic thinking, and allow the breath of a pure spirit to flow back once again into science, and by extension into life generally also. The importance of this holistic approach to all scientific investigation is now slowly becoming recognised and indeed there is no other way in which conventional science can ever rid itself of its bedevilling 'uncertainty principle' except through it!

Now all of this, it may very well be argued, seems quite a bit removed from Christianity as such! If however we are able to appreciate the underlying mood of the Romantic soul, we shall in fact find that Goetheanism is not at all as far removed from the true spirit of Christianity as we may think it is at first sight. For considering the situation more closely we will see that there is a spirit at work in all of this which is entirely in accord with the tenets of esotericism. It is also a spirit totally in tune with the basics tenets of the Gospel. For the Gospel is about nothing at all if it is not about total and absolute freedom of the divine Spirit as it comes to expression in man. The Romantics for their part most certainly perceived a great threat to this Spirit. For it was a movement that was, as we have already said, deeply concerned with, in fact a direct reaction to, the strait-jacket into which the whole intellectual life of Europe was forced as the prevailing mechanistic philosophy paved the way for the Industrial Revolution and its horrors.

Romanticism was in fact nothing less than a revolt of the human spirit against all these soul-destroying trends in which they (the Romantics) saw nothing but an almost total denial of the great hopes and ideals of the Gospel message. Christianity as such of course necessarily took a very different form of expression in the Romantics in comparison with the orthodoxy of their day and *its* type of spirituality, which was inevitably tied up with, and deeply tainted by, the ascendant capitalistic and utilitarian mood. Thus at this time it can be said that never before was conventional or orthodox spirituality more removed from its true esoteric roots.

The Romantics however felt otherwise. In fact it was now, paradoxically, the case that only they could give the deepest expression to the true Christian spirit. For during their time it was the Romantics who managed to suffuse Christianity, through their art, with the revivifying breath of true Mystery, without which it (Christianity) inevitably dries up, an element which moreover was now virtually totally absent from conventional religion.

WILLIAM WORDSWORTH

The great English Romantic poet William Wordsworth (1770 – 1850) captures something of this Christian Mystery element of Nature in his wonderful poem *Ode To The Intimations Of Immortality* from which the following verse is taken. In the poem the poet is able to elucidate with great charm, and put into a deeply Christian context, the common but nevertheless archetypal process of physical child-birth and growth, death, and eventual spiritual re-birth. The poem is a profound meditation on the familiar, but nevertheless truely enlightening facts of Nature's great cycle:

> Our birth is but a sleep and a forgetting:
> The Soul that rises with us, our life's Star,
> Hath had elsewhere its setting,
> And cometh from afar:
> Not in entire forgetfulness,
> And not in utter nakedness,
> But trailing clouds of glory do we come
> From God, who is our home:
> Heaven lies about us in our infancy!
> Shades of the prison-house begin to close
> Upon the growing Boy,
> But he

Beholds the light, and whence it flows,
He sees it in his joy;
The Youth, who daily farther from the east
Must travel, still is Nature's Priest,
And by the vision splendid
Is on his way attended;
At length the Man perceives it die away,
And fade into the light of common day.

This superb poem, of which this is only part of one of eleven equally evocative verses, is excellent for anyone who wishes to capture something of the real 'flavour' of Esoteric Christianity, an introduction as it were, to those who may not already know much about it, to the foundation of this ancient spirit of wisdom, wonderfully and creatively reasserted here through the inspired utterances of this poet for a modern audience.

The poem captures something of the true mood of Esoteric Christianity. It also illustrates very well the deep and genuine spiritual concerns which lay at the very heart of the Romantics and their movement. For the whole turning away from the soul of Nature, a trend which had reached point nadir in the 18th century, this denial of the pure life in Nature by the materialists – all this was total anathema to the Romantics. For the eventual outcome of this materialistic mentality they could well perceive was going to be nothing less than the very death of the soul and spirit itself.

The Romantic Movement was in fact a direct response to a gnawing and growing presentiment about the destructiveness of materialism inherent in its attitude to Nature. And moreover the Romantics presentiment has been proved entirely correct. For from our retrospective viewpoint, as we today survey the mass destruction of the ecosphere, we are witnessing an unsurpassable tragedy which can be entirely blamed upon the widespread and prevelent spiritual ignorance we have inherited and which has culminated in our own greed-driven consumer culture. Now this true and redemptive love of Nature, so dear to the Romantics, is or was entirely in keeping with the Sophia aspect of the Christian Mystery. For Sophia may be regarded as an intrinsic and vital aspect of Nature herself. And it is she who always comes to the fore in any true spiritual revival. This is so because she is, apart from anything else, representative of the true Soul of man. And in so far as a man searches for his soul and for true meaning in life, he or she searches for Sophia also.

196

She has been known by many names. For instance her Mystery also figured very strongly in that other great post-Medieval movement, the Renaissance, a movement in which esoteric philosophy generally played a vital and a major role. There however she was given the Latin name of Natura, perhaps a better or more accessible name for her, for it indicates how closely connected she is with the wisdom of Nature.[84]

And it is also very evident that that towering genius of the Romantics themselves, Goethe, also fully comprehended the vital importance of incorporating this feminine wisdom into Western man's consciousness, if he was to form a true and holistic image of himself and his God. Goethe recognized fully that Sophia lay at the very heart of man's spiritual quest and was the object of the fulfillment of all his deepest and purest desires. The truth of this can be fully gauged from the ending of his monumental and majestic work, Faust.

In this work Goethe deals with the whole problem of evil in the most comprehensive and imaginative way possible, and from a deeply Christian viewpoint. Thus Faust goes through his great trials and testings on the Earth, but by the time we reach the wonderful final scene:

> The noble Spirit now is free
> And saved from evil scheming:
> Who'er aspires unweariedly
> Is not beyond redeeming.

Faust is now being borne upwards to the heavenly spheres by the angels and is free at last from all materialistic entanglements, and this is what he experiences:

> Free is the view at last,
> The spirit lifted:
> There women, floating past,
> Are upward drifted:
> The Glorious One therein,
> With star-crown tender,
> The pure, the Heavenly Queen,
> I know her splendour.

Highest Mistress of the World!
Let me in the azure
Tent of Heaven, in light unfurled,
Hear thy Mystery measure!...
...Virgin, pure in brightest sheen,
Mother sweet, supernal,
Unto us Elected Queen!
Peers of Gods Eternal!

And then the closing lines of the entire poem are:

Penitents, look up, elate,
Where she beams salvation;
Gratefully to blessed fate
Grow, in re-creation!
Be our souls, as they have been,
Dedicate to Thee!
Virgin Holy,[85] mother, Queen,
Goddess, gracious be!

All things transitory
But as symbols are sent:
Earth's insufficiency
Here grows to Event:
The Indescribable,
Here it is done:
The Woman-Soul leadeth us
Upward and on!

In this manner Goethe uttered his final and most mature words (for he completed his great work only just before he died, having worked on it throughout his career) in order to be able to give adequate expression to the great Mystery of Sophia and thus compose his beautiful hymn to her.

Chapter Eight

THE DARK AGE ENDS AND A NEW AGE BEGINS

The coming of the 19th century saw materialistic science reach its highest, or (depending on how one wants to look at it), its lowest point. The work of Charles Darwin (1809–1882) and the subsequent effect of Darwinian thinking, had a profound impact on the life and culture of the West, and especially on its spirituality and religion. Whereas previously man had always, by virtue of his myths and his traditions, even by his very nature, looked upwards to God or the gods and spiritual beings generally for an explanation of his origins, he now turned his thoughts and instincts in the opposite direction and looked for his origins in the natural world only. And so it was that in this mood very clever minds soon began to cast their critical attention upon the Bible and on scripture generally, and particularly of course on the Gospel itself. And it then began to emerge, in the face of a great lack of historically verifiable information, that most of what was taken as absolute fact in the Gospels could not at all be proven 'scientifically'. The materialistic/scientific method of investigation was now, in other words, getting its sharp mechanical claws into the subtle art of history as well, and the result was nothing short of a complete debunking of Christianity. A sceptical, satirical, even a downright ridiculing of Christianity now became the order of the day in much of the intellectual, artistic, and cultural life of late 19th century Europe. And in such an atmosphere it became virtually impossible, even sinful (!) to profess oneself a Christian! For Christianity, and indeed religion generally, was now becoming regarded as merely something for the poor, the ignorant, or the oppressed, a sort of 'opium of the masses' as the greatest and most influential of all the materialists of this period (Marx) put it. In this kind of situation it is not surprising therefore that intelligent, articulate, and deeply searching people in the West now began to seek spiritual nourishment not only outside the Church, but even outside Christianity itself.

The Orient and the treasures of its spiritual wisdom had of course long been known to students of esotericism. But with communications and traffic all the time increasing between East and West, it was now the case that this Eastern wisdom began to make an impact on the West generally. And in the process the Western mind began to wake up to the fact that conventional Christianity was not after all the be-all and the end-all of religion as such. The general mood among the intellectuals regarding

Christianity accentuated this East-looking trend of course. But it nevertheless now became generally obvious that there were vast treasures of spiritual wisdom in Eastern religions quite apart from anything that Christianity could ever offer, treasures moreover which any true and genuine spirituality could not possibly afford to ignore any longer.

MADAME BLAVATSKY, THE GREAT RUSSIAN CLAIRVOYANT

Now one of the most remarkable public figures of this period was Helena Petrovna Blavatsky (1831-1891) who was, as well as many other things, a very gifted clairvoyant, and who, out of this clairvoyance, wrote some very interesting and controversial books which she packed to the hilt with arcane and occult knowledge. Her works are in fact a veritable encyclopaedia of esoteric knowledge, but an encyclopaedia which is also alas very haphazardly arranged, and because of this, tended, and still tends, to scare a lot of order-seeking intellectuals and scientifically minded people off reading. The publication of these books was nonetheless something of a milestone in the history of esoteric literature generally and they were (still are!) a source of the greatest curiosity and interest to anyone even vaguely interested in the fascinating subject of the ancient wisdom.

Now the unprecedented appearance of Blavatsky's books at this time, and indeed her overall motivation, can in fact be explained in a certain way, out of the ancient wisdom itself. For up to her time esoteric knowledge, when it was published at all, always tended to be allegorical or highly symbolical in form and content, as anyone who peruses it will soon discover. However, the time we are speaking of here, the end of the 19th century, is a point in human evolution when a great Cycle of time is actually coming to an end. These Cycles, known as Yugas in the Eastern form of the wisdom, where knowledge of them was and is deeply cultivated, run in set periods of time (5000 or more years) and are known as (to give a couple of examples) Tetra Yuga (Silver Age) and Dvapara Yuga (Iron Age). These two are in fact those Ages that immediately preceeded the one which was deemed to be ending in the year 1899 and which was known as the Kali Yuga or the Dark Age. So with the Dark Age (spiritually speaking of course) now ending, and a much more light-filled age dawning, students of the esoteric wisdom generally could, as it were, feel much freer to broadcast to the world their spiritual knowledge and spiritual secrets, indeed felt it incumbent upon them to do so, precisely because of this new age. And this is exactly what Blavatsky did!

She also set up in 1875 a general Society with the goal of disseminating as far as possible the principal tenets of the ancient wisdom. This was the Theosophical Society and it is still in fact in existence, though like all the other esoteric societies mentioned so far, quite devoid nowadays of the spiritual quality of its original impulse. In its heyday however the Theosophical Society attracted very large numbers and very bright people too, and had branches all over the world. It caused in fact a great stir generally, but of course particularly among real spirit-seekers. And in a *certain sense* one can say that if Esoteric Christianity was being cultivated anywhere at this time and in any kind of organised way, it was here under the aegis of this Society. Given the general climate and attitude which existed towards Christianity during the Society's heyday however, it is not difficult to understand why the Society overtly disavowed any kind of a purely Christian bias. Whereas there was a rich cultivation of the esoteric and ancient wisdom generally within the Society, there was in fact no real willingness at all on the part of theosophists to look at the Incarnation in such a way that its true meaning might be revealed by this ancient wisdom.

For Christ was seen by them as merely one of a long line of avatars, no different basically from any of the many other great sages and initiates who appear on Earth from time to time. Thus the essential aspect the Incarnation, its uniqueness, was for them never given any genuine consideration. And it was this very lack of goodwill towards the deepest core of Christianity which in fact spelled the ultimate demise of the Theosophical Society.

Another and directly connected factor in this demise was that one of the leaders of the Society, C.W.Leadbeater, became entirely and totally misled by his clairvoyant faculties. This is something which can, and in fact often does occur, if a fully adequate spiritual training is not earnestly undertaken by those seeking genuine esoteric knowledge. Clairvoyance alone is by no means a fool-proof method of acquiring genuine spiritual (or indeed any other kind of) knowledge. For if it is founded upon false concepts acquired through the ordinary consciousness, the results of clairvoyant knowledge will also be erroneous. This happened with Leadbeater regarding Christianity. And the resultant downfall of the Theosophical Society thus occurred in the following way.

Leadbeater was walking in the Indian countryside one day when he came upon a remarkable Hindu boy. And the more he observed the little boy the more engrossed he became with him. Now eventually Leadbeater's faculty of clairvoyance led him to believe that in the young boy's spiritual aura he was actually 'seeing' a reincarnation of Jesus! He then proceeded to evolve in his mind a great, a mega-plan even, for this boy, and not only for the Theosophical Society, but for the whole world also! He duely brought the boy before the Society which in its turn went ahead with plans to educate the boy in a certain way in the West. The overall strategy was to eventually announce the boy to the world (when he reached a certain age) as the fulfillment of the Second Coming! Now this boy, once he became a bit mature, found all of this extremely difficult to take or to understand. He then went through the greatest of inner spiritual trials and intense psychic agony in trying to come to terms with it all. However he eventually won through to a stable and clear understanding of himself and his place in the world and 'saw through' the Theosophist's megalomaniacal plans for him. He then denounced these plans and declared publicly that he was not Jesus at all but a perfectly ordinary person like everyone else! This happened in 1929. The Society's reputation, needless to say, began to fall utterly and tragically apart after this. (The boy, when he grew up, became known as Krishnamurti, and was a highly respected spiritual teacher in his own right, up to his death in 1986).

Now from the point of view of Esoteric Christianity this episode regarding the Theosophical Society is, in a sad sort of way, very instructive. For it indicates very clearly just how very misguided people can become regarding Christ and Christianity in general, if the essential points of the Incarnation are not properly understood, or even worse, if there is insufficient goodwill towards the Incarnation which would allow such a true appraisal to evolve.

The Krishnamurti episode was in a way foisted upon the Theosophical Society and this could only have occurred in a situation where there was a lack, regarding Christianity, of the kind just indicated. Leadbeater in fact had no real understanding of Christianity at all, despite his renowned clairvoyant faculties. For if he did have such an understanding he would have known that the physical incarnation of the Christ Being at the Incarnation was a once only and unique event in the entire history of the Earth planet. And what is spoken of in the Gospels as the Second Coming and so on, is entirely to do, not with the physical body at all, but with the Mystical or etherial body as such. This basic understanding of Christianity is crucial if error regarding the true nature and the Real Presence of Christ is ever to be understood. The Theosophists however, in their hot pursuit of Eastern wisdom, eschewed any path that would lead them directly to such a pure Christian enlightenment.

This is not to say that there were none within the ranks of the Theosophical Society who sensed the fact that Christianity and the ancient wisdom were entirely capable of blending into a new and more enlightened understanding of Christ as was generally available in the West at this time. Whereas there may not have been in the Society any keen discernment of the precise nature of the Incarnation in its purest spiritual essence, there certainly was a sense of something very spiritual in the air. And this 'sensing' moreover was not one that was confined merely to the Theosophists either. It had broader repercussions in the artistic and cultural life of the period as well.

THE CELTIC REVIVAL

It was after all the ending of the Kali Yuga, the Dark Age! And this also coincided very significantly with the blossoming of what we have come to know as the Celtic Revival. Now there were many enlightened personalities connected with this spiritual/mystical/literary revival of the Celtic soul and its traditions; Fiona MacLeod in Scotland, and George Russell (AE) in Ireland to mention but two.

But of course the chief protagonist of the Celtic Revival was the great Irish poet William Butler Yeats, and from the point of view of our present study it is Yeats who provides us with the most interest.

Yeats of course is such a broad and complex personality that one hesitates to make any definitive statements about him. For like all of the greatest artists he is only truely revealed through his artistic work, in this case his poetry; and any attempts to add to that, regarding his personality, risks, one fears, the censure of his very ghost! For although it has up to recently been intellectually fashionable to downgrade the well known 'mystical dabblings' of Yeats, it pays to remember that it was to these very 'dabblings' that he himself attributed all of the inspiration for his work. And that in itself is something of a mystery worth contemplating!

Now Yeats joined Blavatsky's Theosophical Society in 1887. He found however the Madame a bit hard to take, and was later expelled! This, as it

203

turned out, was no great problem for the young William. For he was already a member of another, even more select, group of esotericists, and he immediately set about developing his arcane pursuits with them. This was a Society or an Order of practical and theoretical magicians known as the Golden Dawn. And in this Order Yeats found a rich repertoire of myth, symbol and ritual, through which he could enthusiastically set about satisfying his deep thirst for spiritual knowledge and awakening.

And for inspiration also! For poetry was, after all, the most important thing in life for him, and always was.

True to the intellectual climate of the time however, Yeats never made much overt use of Christianity as such in his writing. But this does not in the least suggest that he was not 'christian'. In fact it may not be far off the mark to suggest that his leaving of the Theosophical Society had quite a 'christian' impulse to it. For as we shall presently show below, it is obvious that he was deeply interested in the mystical side of Christianity and indeed placed it, at one stage, at the very centre of his ever and deeply searching spiritual quest.

The Hermetic Students of the Golden Dawn, to give the group Yeats joined its full title, was founded in 1888 in London, and its repertoire of magical rites and rituals was a sort of pot-pourri of various mystical and esoteric traditions which had long bubbled under the surface of exoteric Western Christianity. It also took on board some of the extant esoteric knowledge regarding Christian Rosencrutz, as well as cultivating a sort of latter-day alchemy. In an oath that Yeats took for instance as part of one of his 'initiations' in the Order, he had to 'solemnly promise and sware that with the Divine permission I will from this day forward apply myself unto the 'Great Work' which is so to purify and exhalt my spiritual nature that with the Divine Aid I may at length attain to be more than human, and thus gradually raise and unite myself to my Magus and Divine genius, and that in this event I will not abuse the great power entrusted to me'.[86]

As we can see from this, the young Yeats was certainly aiming high! However, that he deeply sensed the crucial importance of the Mystery of the Christ as being central to all genuine esoteric and spiritual pursuits, can be deduced from the fact that in 1893 he 'attained the inner order of the Golden Dawn and in the initiation of the Path of the Portal, he lay down in the tomb, died a symbolic death, and rose reborn in spirit, Christified'.[87]

Fired by his interests and pursuits in Theosophy and the Golden Dawn, Yeats later went on to conceive of a purely Irish esoteric Order which would, he hoped, unite the radical and esoteric truths of Christianity to those of the ancient wisdom. The order would be called 'The Castle Of Heros'. He went on to develop his plans for this Order in fact to quite a considerable degree, and had even earmarked an unoccupied castle in the middle of Lough Key in Co. Roscommon as its headquarters. He went so far as to work out various rites and rituals for the Order and even had some of his friends doing the same. To this Order he hoped to attract the finest specimens of Irish lads and lassies, where they would duely receive a thorough esoteric education as well as a deep spiritual training, and in this manner become fit and worthy leaders of their country.

Yeats' plans were of course highly idealistic and the Order never in fact materialized. But the rites and rituals he so cherished then proceeded to take on more dramatic or purely artistic leanings in Yeats' imagination, and they soon evolved into the concept of an Irish Mystical Theatre. And while neither of these spiritual projects of Yeats ever really took of the ground, they did in fact bear some excellent fruit. For in time these ideas led to the birth of the world famous Irish National Theatre, the Abbey, which still flourishes.

There is little evidence however that as Yeats grew older he deepened his connection with Esoteric Christianity. Rather the contrary seems sadly to have been the case, and he ended his life with a very cold relationship to the life of the spirit as, perhaps more than any other fact, his epitaph clearly reveals:

> "Cast a cold eye on life, on death.
> Horseman! Pass by!"[88]

SOMETHING IS 'IN THE AIR'

The period around the turning of the 19th into the 20th century was one filled with expectation and anticipation. The beginning of any new century is always perhaps a bit like that anyway. However, at this particular turning point there was something 'in the air' which marked it out, certainly from a spiritual point of view, as something quite special. In many ways it was similar to that short period of anticipation and excitement brought about by the Rosicrutian Manifestos when they were initially put into circulation in

205

Bohemia about 400 years previously. But each new cycle of time has its own distinct flavour, its own particular characteristics and impulses. And at the turning of the 19th into the 20th century, with the ever increasing efficiency of communications both physically and electronically, a brand new element made its appearance in the mass consciousness of men: globalization. This feeling, this concept, now began to colour virtually every aspect of life, and the result was that a new way of thinking was fast emerging.

Now especially in esotericism this new outlook could be felt in the West as a drawing closer of the East with its rich treasure of spiritual wisdom. Students of esotericism generally were also well aware of course that the new century represented the ending of the dark age of Kali Yuga, and by virtue of this a new age of light was now being ushered in. George Russell (AE), the Irish visionary, writer and poet, who was an avid student of the ancient wisdom and a very highly regarded individual in his own day, felt this dawning perhaps more deeply than most. Russell, who was a great and lifelong friend of Yeats, was one of those rare individuals possessed of a profound though atavistic clairvoyance which allowed him a very special, if idiosyncratic, insight into the true nature of the world and the spiritual beings which underlie it all.[89] It must be said however that his temperament caused him to clothe his visions in a deeply romantic/Celtic way. And unlike Yeats who kept abreast of the times AE lost credibility largely because of the stark realism of the progressing century. In his own lifetime however his was a way very much in tune with the overall esoteric/spiritual mood of the time.

Indeed the whole 'Celtic Revival' of this period, something in which Russell was deeply involved, was very much connected into this awareness of the new post-Kali Yuga age generally. And in so far as it can be said that the 'Celtic Revival' was concerning itself with a now almost forgotten age some 1500 to 2000 years or more before, it can in fact in many respects be understood as a modern reappearance of the spirit of Esoteric Christianity. And if the great friendship between Yeats and AE at this time can be seen in any kind of clear light at all, it must be in the light of the fact that they were both equally deeply imbued with, and inspired by, the pure Sophia or Mother Spirit of their native land. And reviewed in the light of the great Mystery wisdom, what else had this ancient land of Hibernia been but a sort of magic cauldron, a Holy Grail even, in which the living wonders of the ancient wisdom had fused so wonderfully to produce the prototype, if nothing else, of a great new Christian enlightenment?

Nevertheless the Celtic Revival was only *one* aspect of a much broader interest in esotericism and spirituality which was 'in the air' at this time. We have already mentioned the very successful Theosophical Society. But this period also saw the setting up for instance of the Society for Psychical Research which attracted a lot of interest. And also at this time there was the big ghostly stirring in more conventional religious circles known as the Spiritualist Movement. There were others.

THE ANTHROPOSOPHICAL SOCIETY

The Theosophical Society was at this time a worldwide Society with a very large membership, but it was particularly strong in Europe. In Germany however, where the strongest, clearest, and deepest of philosophical thinking had always been cultivated, and where christological studies were often very profound, it was only to be expected that the debacle with Krishnamurti would have had the most serious of consequences for the Theosophical Society there. And so eventually the German Branch seperated itself off into a distinct body, under the leadership of the great German-Austrian seer and philosopher Rudolf Steiner. This new entity later became known as the Anthroposophical Society[90] and it was in *this* Society, more than anywhere else, that the most progressive awareness of Esoteric Christianity was now being cultivated. In fact the true community and healing aspect of this esoteric spirit can be seen to be fully at work here in this group, right from its inception. For during the first major global catastrophy, the Great War, Rudolf Steiner, on the neutral soil of Switzerland, got together hundreds of people from the various warring nations and there instructed them in the building of what may be rightly regarded as a modern Mystery Temple.

The building was named, significantly, after Goethe: the Goetheanum. Even a limited acquaintance with this building, the foundation stone of which was laid in September 1913, leads one to conclude that it must have ranked as one of the most fascinating buildings ever conceived and constructed in modern times. It was a huge building made entirely of wood and incorporated, among much else within its complex double-domed structure, the whole concept of the microcosmic/macrocosmic relationship of man to the planets and the wider universe.

It was however burned to the ground on the night of New Year's Eve 1922!

And although the cause of the fire was never actually established, arson in fact has always been suspected. And given the opposition that Rudolf Steiner met with during his life (there was at least one attempted assasination) it would not be in keeping with the whole history of the spirit of Esoteric Christianity in the world, if it were totally ruled out that the forces of Reaction were responsible for it.[91]

As the century progressed however these forces became ever stronger. And by the turning of the middle of the century, when yet another great global catastrophy, the 2nd World War had run its course, the entire world became so physically dejected and so mentally numbed that any talk of spirit or spirituality was met with little but disdain. For this war, together with its spawning of the Holocaust and the atomic age, combined to effect in the global consciousness-soul an acute and awful awareness of the evil of which man was capable, once he had turned his back absolutely upon the Spirit of God.

And in such an atmosphere, genuine spiritual movements, especially esoteric ones of course, had little or no place. By now the promise of an esoteric spiritual renewal, so widespread at the turn of the century, had totally dissipated. For virtually all of man's energy, psychic or otherwise, now became focussed on mundane needs alone. To preserve even the barest conditions necessary to the survival of some scraps of genuinely human and physical freedom was all that could now occupy the soul of man. An 'Iron Curtain' came down between the riches that East and West had to offer one another, and the whole world held its breath as a cold war of purely materialistic ideologies got under way.

THE SWINGING SIXTIES

The 1960's however brought a change to all of this, in the West at any rate. For as the threat of total atomic annihilation receeded somewhat, a new and youthful sense of freedom duely arose with it. A great reservoir of psychic and spiritual energy, long held in check, diverted, or simply repressed due principally to the great global wars, was now released in a young, peace and freedom-loving generation. And the war-mongering materialistic shell which had temporarily suspended or cocooned the soul's spiritual longings, now burst open once more, this time into a veritable circus, a riotous carnival of new hopes and possibilities.

The swinging '60's had arrived! What the deeply searching poets and writers of say, the Celtic Revival had, in the latter part of the last century, understood as the ending of the dark Kali Yuga, now took on a whole new extra dimension here of colour, chaos and spiritual possibility. And the New Age was born!

Since then there has been a rich flow of spiritual and other interchange between East and West, and, especially since the recent lifting of the Iron Curtain, this augurs well for the future.

A note of caution however needs to be sounded amidst the rising tide of a genuine revival of interest in things spiritual. For although the demise of the God-denying ideology of Marxism must, from the point of view of spirituality generally, be seen as an excellent thing, it must also be coupled with an awareness of the rise of fundamentalism in the great world religions, something which most certainly does *not* augur well for the future!

With the spiritual release of recent years however, a rich possibility also is now at hand for the emergence once more, and development to a new stage, of Esoteric Christianity, something which is under way to some extent in any event. But given the aforementioned rise of fundamentalism, if confrontation on a much greater scale between individuals, communities or nations, resulting from religious ideology, is to be avoided in the future, it can only be done through a much wider dissemination of the basic tenets of Esoteric Christianity. For there is no other spiritual philosophy which can unify mankind in the way this ancient philosophy and wisdom can. Through it, all are enabled, without prejudice, to tap into and utilize the vital thread of pure spiritual wisdom, the perennial philosophy, that lies at the heart-core of *all* religions. This in fact is what Esoteric Christianity is. And moreover this is what it *does*. Thus one can justifiably plead that Esoteric Christianity be taken up seriously, and as much as possible be incorporated into the mainstream of Christianity. If this is done the Church can once more become what it once was in the past, i.e. that vessel through which the visionary faculties latent in the human soul can be awakened and nurtured, to the common good of all mankind. This awakening is something indeed which the Church never fails to do or to promise, once the image of the Mystical Body is kept alive before the mind's eye.

But of course the question may rightly be asked: What is the Mystical Body?* Many people however, brought up within the paramiters of the

* See Page 164

Christian Church, will have some inkling, however unformed, as to its real meaning, and therein lies a true basis for the real spiritual renewal, the need of which has been spoken of at length in the course of this book. Any attempt here however at a development of this concept, or this image, which emerges out of the depths of the 'spiritus mundi', would take us too far. Such an elaboration would require at least a volume to itself if it were to be properly addressed and put within the framework of the esoteric renewal of Christianity.

That there exists however within the Church a deep awareness of the need, and thirst for a genuine spiritual renewal of Christianity is nothing at all new to say. The awareness of this need has been there for decades at least, but becomes in fact acute the more time passes. But a combination of many factors have merged in our own day to create a clearly discernible, a veritable audible spiritual sighing and longing.

THE SAD MUSIC OF OUR TIME

The soul is the instrument of this sad music. And the note it sounds for Christ is in fact but one in a great cacophony of spiritual strings sounding within the chaotic music of the New Gnosis, or the New Age in which we live. The Christ-tone however is one that echoes deeper than all others. For it is the sound, one can say, of the very soul of Sophia herself as she goes about her lonely search for her murdered Beloved. In another sense she may be seen or understood as seeking a body in which to incarnate her divine Wisdom. And it is in this sense that the Church may best now regard itself as a single body. In yet another and broader sensed this sound of the Sophia-Christ may be regarded as the 'thin small voice' crying in the apocalyptic wilderness of 'the growing murderousness of the world' (W. B. Yeats). And though this murderousness has reached a crescendo in our own time, the coming of this crisis has long been felt. For we live right now in spiritually desperate times where the power of the spirit of Deception has never been more active.

W.B.Yeats felt all of this very deeply indeed, and in his highly inspired poem The Second Coming (1921) he certainly captures the mood of our time:

> Turning and turning in the widening gyre
> The falcon cannot hear the falconer;
> Things fall apart; the centre cannot hold;

Mere anarchy is loosed upon the world,
The blood-dimmed tide is loosed, and everywhere
The ceremony of innocence is drowned;
The best lack all conviction, while the worst
Are full of passionate intensity.

Surely some revelation is at hand;
Surely the Second Coming is at hand;
The Second Coming! Hardly are those words out
When a vast image out of Spiritus Mundi
Troubles my sight; somewhere in sands of the desert
A shape with a lion body and the head of a man,
A gaze black and pitiless as the sun,
Is moving its slow thighs, while all about it
Reel shadows of the indignant desert birds.
The darkness drops again; but now I know
That twenty centuries of stony sleep
Were vext to nightmare by a rocking cradle,
And what rough best, its hour come round at last,
Slouches towards Bethlahem to be born?

With the current debasement of human sexuality, the all-pervading aggression and decadence, the desecration of the environment and much else besides, who can not discern for themselves, however dimly, what Yeats did here for the world in this poem? For how else indeed can the human soul respond, in the face of the current state of the world, except in tones that may in truth be termed apocalyptic? Yeats was indeed right in his intuition! Right in what he felt at any rate. For in the absence of a spiritual centre, the physical and the purely instinctual appetites will necessarily take over. And this is largely the reality in which public and much of private life is now lived.

Yeats of course could write his apocalyptic poem out of the depth of an intuition and a feeling that come as second nature to an artist of his standing. And to be sure Yeats was only too well acquainted with the age-old human dilemma of the spirit 'fastened to a dying animal'.[92] But he was not at liberty perhaps to try to deal with the great tensions this terrible dilemma increasingly engenders, by cultivating Christianity as freely as he may have wished to, deep down. The fact is however that these great tensions are resolvable! For to believe otherwise would be tantamount to denying all truely human, and especially Christian ideals, something which of course philistines are always only too ready to do. For at bottom a philistine believes only in himself or herself, and not much else besides. And the increasingly trivial mono or mass culture of our time sadly is one made mostly for and by the philistine.

Purely human ideals however need a centre outside of the selfish personal self if they are to be truely good. Christianity, esoteric or otherwise, actually provides that centre. And certainly from the point of view of Esoteric Christianity it has to be said that this centre can and does hold!

For there is no doubt at all that the Sophia-inspired wisdom contained within Esoteric Christianity allows one to discern the true meaning and purpose of human life on Earth. Esoteric Christianity can do this because it contains the key to the proper unravelling of the complexities of the fact of the Incarnation, revealing it to be a true and fully redemptive spiritual Deed of God, done once and for all. Through it, all human conflict, whether inner or outer, whether spiritual or physical, is seen to be brought to a peaceful resolution. And all men of goodwill may discover this fact according to their own particular lights, whatever, whoever, or wherever they are.

I AM = GOD

Everyone nowadays has free access to this key! It may be used in an infinite number of ways in the outer world as well as in the world of soul and spirit. It leads one to one's true spiritual centre, bestowing great confidence and strength for all the increasingly difficult tasks of life on the Earth. From the point of view of modern spirituality it is not a question at all whether this key exists or not. Such questions can well be left to those content with mere intellectual debate. For modern spirituality, that is, a spirituality that takes into account the condition of the modern soul, is entirely or purely concerned with one thing, and that is the enlivening of this heart-centre.

In esoteric wisdom this sacred heart-centre is called the I AM. By its very name one can immediately sense both its individual and its universal nature. The fact that the name CHRIST and I AM are the same (see Appendix I) actually reveals very much about the Mystery content of the incarnational wisdom. Discerning the reality of the Incarnation is not at all in other words about definitions, theological debates and so on. But it *is* about hard work, inner work on oneself, about that kind of spiritual endeavour which polishes the mirror of one's own soul so that the reality of this incarnational spirit of the I AM can be truely seen, felt, and reflected there. Moreover it is true to say that the task of all spiritual renewal, whatever outward name or context it may have or be given, is synonymous with the enlivening of this centre in the human soul.

Now the individual can of course go a long way in this soul work on his or her own. And meditation, prayer, spiritual discipline, moral conduct, etcetera, all play an important part in this progress. But the fullest awareness of the centre spoken of here, and its proper awakening, can only truely come about in genuine communion with others. This community aspect is vital to any true discernment of the real nature of the Incarnation. It has been said that there can be no Christianity without community and no community without Christianity. And it is this community, 'communion-al', or communal aspect of Christianity which is the business of the Church *par excellence*. One indeed may rightly regard 'the Church' as none other than the building and the enlivening of true community, of community spirit, something which is becoming ever harder to create as the effects of the historical spiritual denial, delineated in this book, become ever more apparent in modern life.

There are of course thousands of ways of creating community in a purely temporal setting. There is however only one way which truely fertilizes community in a purely spiritual way and without which community need not be properly called 'Christian'. So just as at the very beginning of the Church the Love Feast (see page 135) was at its very centre, so too in the spiritual renewal of the Church the Communion should be at the very centre. And in terms of pure Christianity, especially Esoteric Christianity, a renewed understanding and appreciation of 'communion' must be regarded as crucial. The root reason for this is that it is only through the Communion that the Holy Grail aspect of the Sophia Mystery is really understood.

And the secret of the Grail of course lies at the very heart of Esoteric Christianity (see page 137ff). What this means ultimately in fact is that it is only through the sacrament of the Communion, and all that this implies, that the essential consecration of man and Earth[93] can be fully understood to have in reality taken place. This incarnational act of consecration may be said to take effect through man's participation in the Earthly working of the logosophical spirit-power; and it is through the images contained in the rite of the Communion that this fact is most easily portrayed and most fully discerned. Hence its importance.

One can thus see from this brief exposition that Esoteric Christianity has the capacity to inform and enliven all aspects of the Church's activities. We have only mentioned the Communion because of its central importance. For in the act of *sharing*, symbolized in the Breaking of the Bread, the most profound of all spiritual laws is indicated. Every other aspect of spiritual life, in the truely Christian sense, can only grow and improve if this spirit of sharing represents its foundations.

WHICH WAY SHOULD I TRAVEL?

We live in a time of great uncertainty in many aspects of our lives, not least in the vital spiritual aspect. And instinctively we know that spiritual uncertainty leaves us open to uncertainty in all other areas of our life as well. As with other more mundane aspects of life however, we only reap results in our spiritual life in accordance with the *work* we do regarding it. In our own time real soul certainty only begins to dawn for us once we undertake some fully conscious endeavour in this regard. For well and truely gone are the days when we were happy to accept dogmatic truths and 'articles of faith' handed to us readymade on a silver plate! The times demand that we are pro-active regarding the health of our soul if we wish, through it, to keep our total organism truely alive, vital and well.

Many are the paths we can take and many are the spiritual choices on offer nowadays. How therefore can we discern which one is right for us? For like any long journey which we may undertake in the outer world, spiritual journeys harbour certain risks also. So against what do we measure the worth of anything we may learn, see, do, or hear along the way?

But whatever path we may decide to take, one thing may be taken as certain. If the path is to be of any worth at all, some kind of activity or work aimed at enlivening the soul and spirit-centre of our being is essential. For in our modern world this centre is becoming increasingly caked over with the death-dealing effect of technology and materialism. In its outer aspect it is in fact true to say that the centre *is* losing its hold. But we all, at least those of us with even a modicum of genuine sensitivity left for the Good, the True and the Beautiful, need to do something to help awaken and renew our spiritual capacities if this is to change. These are capacities which everyone in fact has, but which merely lie dormant in most.

Some people may undoubtedly have misgivings and fears about such efforts, psychological barriers which can have many causes. Some may quite simply have a natural fear of 'the occult' etcetra, a sort of hangover one could say from the Middle Ages.

Anyone however who acquires spiritual capacities which are built upon the foundation of Esoteric Christianity will not run the risk of being misled in this regard. For in Esoteric Christianity there is, as outlined above, the vital star-point of guidance for our barque as we sail through the physical world towards our true spiritual home. This is none other than the pure heart-centre of the cosmos that does in fact always hold, no matter what we may encounter. This is an indestructible spiritual centre that outlives and outshines all other phenomena we may experience in our lives, whether physical or psychical, and it certainly outlives and out-shines all purely material and temporal manifestation, giving us a certainty, a joy and, most importantly of all, a sublime peace. For this is that peace which can only come from the One true God and is the peace 'which passeth all understanding'.

Chapter Nine

THE THIRD MILLENNIUM: POINTERS

'All that was conferred upon human evolution through the coming of Christ, has been working in it like a seed. Only by degrees can the seed ripen. Up to the present, no more than the minutest part of the depths of the new wisdom has found its way into physical existence. We are but at the beginning of Christian evolution. In the successive epochs that have elapsed since his appearance, Christian evolution has been able to unveil only so much of its inner essence as men and nations were capable of receiving, capable also of assimilating to their power of understanding. The first form into which this recognition could be cast, may be described as an all-embracing ideal of life.'

As the centuries progressed this ideal was nurtured and fostered by the Church as best as it knew how. One may say in fact that the always rather nebulous or etherial entity known as 'the Church' *is* what constituted or constitutes this very process.

The early Church emerged as a fully independent entity out of the spiritual and philosophical matrix which flourished in the Middle East generally in the epoch after the decline of the ancient Mystery Religions (see early chapters). And in what has become known as the Gnostic Church there was a concerted effort to incorporate this ancient wisdom into the new Christian body. For highly complex reasons however this effort failed. The history of Esoteric Christianity is in fact a history of the ongoing battle by the orthodox Church against the re-emergence of the ancient Mystery wisdom within the Church's paramiters. And what may be termed spiritual fear was the root cause of all this. For this was a fear founded upon ignorance of a great spiritual treasure, the abandonment of which led to so much hatred, heresy, war, and even genocide over the centuries. Perhaps in the Inquisition of the Middle Ages this fear came to its most forceful and horrible expression.

Looking around us today it is not difficult to see that we have only taken the first tentative steps in reaching the true Christian human ideal. We are still very far removed from its realization. We are furthermore nowadays in danger of even losing this ideal altogether. Our contemporary world demonstrates this in manifold ways. For while great advances have been made in many fields of human endeavour, huge numbers of modern human beings also experience tremendous lacks, and suffer acutely from feelings of emptiness and desolation, despite the apparent 'fullness' of their lifestyles.

The reason for this is that no amount of activity, of material comfort or possessions, of distractions or entertainments, can compensate for a loss of soul. And this latter state represents in fact the true picture of modern life. If truth be known we live with, or in, an IT, rather than a him or a her! Our experience of life is of the machine rather than of true being as such. IT, information and technology is everywhere, but virtually nowhere is true living wisdom to be found, a wisdom that unequivocally affirms the spirit of, and in, life, over and above everything else! This state of affairs is in fact the end result of a process that began a long long time ago. And it cannot indeed be otherwise as long as wisdom is denied access to the well-springs of the 'easy' life we have managed to create, especially in the West.

Information or knowledge is undoubtedly a very useful thing. By its very nature however information is highly fluid – it's content changes from one period of time to the next according to the prevailing conventions. Genuine wisdom however is not like that. For wisdom is, by its nature, always both ancient and modern; and if it is spiritual wisdom it becomes, like God, the world's truest constant, and for this reason also, it is called perennial.

Genuine spiritual wisdom differs fundamentally from other kinds of knowledge. It has a different and opposite source to mundane knowledge. The latter comes from below, the former from above; one is material or physical, the other spiritual. And if the spirit is left out of *any* reckoning, one is dealing in fact with something even worse than a falsehood, i.e. a half-truth. The modern consciousness-soul is immersed in this latter state.

In a recent statement His Holiness Pope John Paul II gave a very significant utterance when he apologized on behalf of the Church for some of its former errors. Those Christians, Catholic or otherwise, who listened to this announcement most carefully, could not help but get the strange feeling that they were somehow apologizing to themselves! For the statement begged the whole question of just who or what 'the Church' really is. Who was apologizing to whom? The statement does however point clearly to the fact of an awakening within the Church, an awakening, that is, to past spiritual error, to a communal sense of what is wrong or went wrong, and of where to go from here? And this truely is a big step in the right direction.

For in so far as great injustices have been done in the past out of fear and ignorance in relation to the true spirit of man, in so far as this is true, we are all to blame to some extent, for we all share in the same spirit.

We all at the end of the day confess in other words to the One Spirit who informs or indwells our understanding of the Incarnation. And this Spirit is nothing but God himself, the One Supreme God, the Divine Ground of All Being, known and revered to all people everywhere, ever since time began. Thus it can truely be said that the Incarnation as it presents itself in its truest light, the light of the ancient or perennial wisdom, is totally communal in the broadest possible meaning of this term. It stands, as we have said, in the world as a representative and redemptive Deed of the Spirit of God for man. In this sense the true claim of Christianity lies not so much in its teaching as in its Deed. And it has a 'mass' application surely, as well as providing the individual with the safest possible spiritual ground he can ever find in the world. This is the reality. But the gradual rise of spiritual fear and error within the Church in past times was in direct proportion to its abandonment of the ancient wisdom. And the rise of the concept of the 'universal' or 'catholic' Church was directly linked into this, in so far as separation from the communal aspect or the 'communion' was regarded as dangerous. The history of the Church however, despite this effort to form a coherent united body of believers, has led, as we are only too well aware of today, not to a unified body at all, but sadly to a disjointed one of competing or even warring minorities, cults and sects, in virtual or total antithesis to the original and true intention.

The reasons for this are clear. The centre of the Church did, or does not in fact hold, precisely because the sublime truth of the Incarnation was submerged, or even washed away, by a widespread spiritual fear engendered by the hocus-pocus with which the ancient wisdom got branded by weaker minds within the Church's orthodoxy. The Mystery element thus became totally misunderstood. This uncertainty led to fear, and so the Mystery element was eventually abandoned altogether. Hardly a shred of it exists in the conventional Church today. The renewal of the Church calls however for a complete reversal of the fact of this historical error. The concept of the Mystery of Christ, in the totally real sense of the renewal of the ancient Mystery wisdom – this is what is required. The concept of a 'slimmed-down' Church, recently voiced by one of its highest and most influential dignitaries, in which the Church is seen as sort of tightening up its dogmatic weaponry and fighting it all out in its own diminishing little corner, is in fact a *complete travesty* of all that the true concept of the universal Church has ever stood for! For its Mystery is expansive and all-inclusive, even cosmic, and can never be regarded as anything other than this.

What the Church truely needs in other words, is to awaken to the reality of the esoteric and etherial Christ, whose Presence it has for far too long been unable or unwilling to give due attention to.

POSTSCRIPT

I realize that I have only sort of 'skimmed the surface' of a very difficult and highly complex set of issues in the course of this book. My intention was not however to elaborate or expound in any detailed way on what I have referred to continually as the ancient wisdom, etc. Rather my intention was, as I said at the outset, to provide an overall historical framework for a phenomenon the perception of which is dimly felt by many but only rarely if ever addressed because of this. The articulation of this phenomenon however shows how it came about that something which was once so vital to the Church's very existence has gradually been sidelined, suppressed, and eventually almost forgotten about.

But never quite!

For the wonderful flame of the esoteric spirit, at bottom the only thing through which the Holy Spirit of the Church may be fully comprehended or understood, cannot by its very nature be put out! It was basically my intention to 'prove' that this spirit was lit in the world through the Incarnation and it *can* only go on becoming stronger as time passes, despite, indeed perhaps because of the obstacles. I realize fully that I may have raised a thousand questions in the minds of my readers for every one I may have answered or posed myself. But, paradoxically, if such be indeed the case then I would gladly consider my task to have been successful. For if the spiritual renewal necessary to the Church, a renewal to which this book is intended as a genuine contribution, if this is to truely come about, then an awful lot of questions indeed will have to be posed and properly answered. My intention was merely to show the kind of thinking, the line or direction of thought these questions must take, if they are to be properly addressed and answered. I hope others, perhaps more qualified than I, will take up this challenge, or specific aspects of it, with goodwill, honesty, and humility in the near future. That it is a very difficult task I am only too well aware! However it is also a task I would most easily vouch for as being a joyful one, and sweet beyond measure in the fruit it is capable of producing.

Sean Byrne
St. John's Tide
July 2000

APPENDIX

APPENDIX 1

I AM

In the Jewish religion the name of God was the most sacred of all its knowledge and possessions. It was known, but only in written form. It was never spoken.

In the Burning Bush episode (see Exodus, chapter 3), attention is drawn to just how special a person Moses is, for he is given a supreme initiation into the secrets of God by actually hearing his (God's) name *spoken*. Only God could speak his name. This was the essence of the Jewish religion, especially in its Logos aspect.

This name in the Jewish scriptures is known as the tetragrammaton, i.e. the four letters which make up this name of God. They are the Hebrew characters: yod, heh, vau and heh, or in English IHVH. When translated into English the word indicates 'that I am'. (Translators or philologists will slightly alter the emphasis according to their own lights, but the essence of the matter is the I AM). And Jehova is how the word is most commonly rendered, phonetically, into English.

Now all of this is highly significant spiritually from a number of angles. For essentially what we are dealing with is a universal sound which in fact transcends the ethnicity of individual language types. We may therefore justifiably think of a transcendent Word which points to the universal Logos, especially since we are looking at a scriptural incident in which God himself is making an appearance. Thus we are concerned with not only a universal sound or word but also with the Word in its purely creative aspect.

The I AM in this context is a very useful sound for meditation and it can be explored quietly in a number of highly enlightening ways. In the Eastern wisdom it is the same as OM or AUM which was always recommended for meditation because it was believed to be the universal creative sound of God. Which of course points precisely in the same direction as does Jehova, when considered in the correct light. It is therefore a very ancient sound. But it is also a perennial one. And thus even to this day people still commonly use it in their spiritual life. They do this unconsciously however, out of habit mostly, thus largely nullifying its value.

Nevertheless when praying, the word AMEN, which usually terminates a prayer, is the same sound, with the same universal origin as OM or AUM. Furthermore if one looks at the well known Sanskrit doctrinal formula 'Tat Tvam Asi', which translates as 'Thou Art That', you get very much the same sense of meaning: (I AM) THAT I AM : THAT I AM = THOU ART THAT!

In the tetragrammaton the first of its letters, Yod, can easily be seen to have come over into the English as simply God. (Yod, in Hebrew, is the dead letter I which of course when given life becomes I AM = God). This is interesting to note, for it emphasises the tragic separation of knowledge of God from the other part of him, his trinitarian emanation, or Creation, represented by the other three letters, heh, vau and heh. The development of the English language was of course concomitant with the suppression of the ancient wisdom and this analysis of the Hebrew name of God underlines this.

Christ Jesus, in the Gospel of St. John especially, calls the reader's attention to this OM or AUM aspect of his Logos Being when in this Gospel he refers to himself fully seven times as the fulfillment of the I AM nature of God: I AM the Door; I AM the Way the Truth and the Life; I AM the Light of the World, etc.[94] Also in the Book of Revelation, Christ says of himself: 'These are the words of the Amen'. (Rev. 3:14). The profundity of the Logos aspect of Christ is thus underlined. And by bringing this creative I AM centre fully alive in ourselves through prayer and meditation, something which has been made possible by the Incarnation, we discover the 'Christ in me' or the 'Christ in you', in the sense indicated so clearly by St. Paul. (See especially Gal. 2:19-21 and Col. 1:25-27).

APPENDIX 2

THE RESURRECTION

What is referred to simply as the Resurrection is perhaps that aspect of the overall Incarnation Mystery which is most difficult to understand. This perhaps goes without saying. Nevertheless the whole of the Mystery of Christ hinges upon the Resurrection. There is in fact no such thing as the Christian religion or Christian faith without it. (See St. Paul's first letter to the Corinthians, chapter 15). It is precisely this aspect which seals the uniqueness of the Event of the Incarnation, thus turning it into that spiritual Deed via which the entire course of human history is altered forever and for the good.

In our modern highly scientifically minded world however it is precisely this aspect of Christianity, more than any other, which has proved to be so embarrassing, and has been the subject of much controversy in religious and theological circles. It does nothing however for the truth of the Incarnation to in any way diminish or play down the Resurrection. And it is in fact a virtual debunking of Christianity to deny it.

However, the current, often sceptical, attitudes towards the Resurrection, even within the Church, are in many ways understandable. For without such concepts as only an acquaintance with the ancient or perennial wisdom can give, this aspect of Christianity will always be the prime target for sceptics and materialists generally. It is therefore all the more necessary to be able to think clearly, constructively and logically about the Resurrection, and in what follows an indication is given as to how this can be done.

Needless to say the Resurrection is an enormously complicated phenomenon. And it has to be pointed out that what is said here is no more than the briefest possible indication of the general line of thinking which must be adopted if some kind of clarity regarding it can be arrived at. Thus while the thoughts given are brief, they are however also deep and complex. But they may be fruitfully approached by anyone with an unprejudiced mind, and are moreover capable of being elaborated to whatever degree it may be felt necessary by anyone wishing to do so, through the esoteric or the Sophia inspired wisdom.

Now the first point concerns the communal meal or the Communion of Christianity. This, we can justifiably say, is one of the vital pillars of Christianity. It came about because at the Last Supper the archetypal Form was given for a new cosmically creative ritual which later evolved into this fundamental sacramental act of Christianity, the Eucharist. And it was through the 'real-ization' of this Form that the new higher or 'spirit-man' was to emerge in due course out of the old lower or 'animal-man'. This older image of the lower man is reflected macro-cosmically in the Zodiac and its predominantly animal images, and the Twelve present at the Last Supper are representatives of this cosmic division. (Leonardo da Vinci, who was totally immersed in the ancient wisdom, in his masterpiece, The Last Supper, gave to the Twelve Apostles physiognomies and gestures which can be regarded as expressing the qualities of these twelve Zodiacal signs). This older Cosmos, out of which man was born, was based on a divine Wisdom which in its turn was reflected in the form of this lower microcosmic man, the human being. This older creation was in fact what is known esoterically as the Cosmos of Wisdom. The new 'spirit-man' however is based on a divine Love made incarnate by Jesus Christ, and through him man thus now participates in the creation of a new Cosmos, the Cosmos of Love. At the Resurrection one part (Love) of this new creation, through the bodily or physical, was effected. Christ is in this sense the blueprint of the future fully evolved spirit, yet also physical, man. The other part comes about through the resurrection of Wisdom or Sophia. This latter resurrection is of course yet to happen. And it is the very process in fact by which the new Cosmos of Love takes effect. It does so through man's own individual and free efforts. The individual physical resurrection can only take place if the resurrection of Sophia is effected in man by man himself. This obviously occurs only over great expances of time. However the 'communion' is the deepest power available to man in this respect. For through it he was given the miraculous spiritual power to re-enact the Death and Resurrection of Christ. And this re-enacting is also a way of 're-membering' the Sophia-Christ. The technique involved in the ritual is that by which the animal-related desire nature of purely human blood is purified and turned upwards or transformed into a purely spiritual 'desire' for God instead (see page 132ff).

Thus at the Communion the first Christians were merely doing what they had been told or shown, so that they could in this way learn to 'see' (or ritualistically 're-member') for themselves the miraculous power of the Event that had recently taken place. In this way also they could learn to participate fully, even down to their physical body and blood, in its 'resurrecting' properties. This therefore is the tremendous power that is handed down sacramentally and spiritually through the Eucharist. And this also indicates the vital role the ancient wisdom plays in it all.

NOTES TO THE TEXT

1. Gnosis is the Greek word for knowledge. Whereas the general term 'The Gnosis' refers more to a period of time, the Gnostic Church of course is quite specific, and this latter designation will be used also during the course of this book. The whole of The Gnosis is a fascinating historical period, spiritually speaking, but unfortunately not a lot is known about it, mainly because of all the book-burnings which represent one of the chief hallmarks of Church history generally. A lot however can be inferred about Gnosticism from what we do know, as this book intends to illustrate. It is an area of investigation however which needs certain ingrained prejudices against it to be fully overcome before this exhilarating period of Church history (and pre-history) can be of deep and lasting benefit to the Church itself, both now and into the future.

2. 'Logos' is the Greek for 'word'. This Logos aspect of the Jewish, and of ancient religions generally, will become clearer as the principal tenets of this book unfolds.

3 . The 17th century German philosopher, Leibnitz, elaborated in his work the concept of the 'Perennial Philosophy' (*perennis quaedam philosophia*), which, he believed, constituted a primordial basis for linking science and religion into a unity higher than that which they possess as seperate disciplines. In this book this term, and other similar ones, (most frequently the 'ancient wisdom') are used, and have this fairly general meaning given by Leibnitz. A definite sense for this meaning can be gained once certain aspects of this wisdom are accepted without prejudice. And these basic tenets should become clear in the course of this book. The intention however is not to give a specific or detailed resumé of the ancient wisdom in the book (which can be done via the bibliographical list, or in other ways), but rather to call attention to it in a certain light or highlight it from a particular angle.

4. The word 'spiritualism' in its use here and in other parts of the book, is not intended to convey any similarity with its use in the Spiritualist Movement which began in the 19th century.

5. It almost goes without saying that one cannot transmit any knowledge at all about something unless there is a recognised concept regarding the 'something' as a basis for this transmission. Otherwise there is merely muddled thinking! This latter is largely the situation nowadays with regard to spirit and spirituality as such. The whole of this book is intended as a contribution towards a renewal of this conceptualizing ability which has been lost through ignorance, as well as through

a sustained programme of repression of the spirit or of genuine knowledge of the spiritual world. The other side of the process of achieving certainty regarding knowledge (of anything, including spirit), i.e. actual perception, can come about once the thought processes regarding knowledge generally and its acquisition are directed in a proper way. See *The Philosophy of Freedom* by Rudolf Steiner.

6. Philosophy as yet in the time of Pytagoras still had a Mystery or initiation element to it. Plato (b. 427 B.C.) took this process a big step forward by discussing philosophy and wisdom much more openly and casually with his students and friends in the gardens of the Academy outside Athens. Hence the birth of 'academic' learning as such, as distinct from Mystery knowledge.

7. "Know thyself, and thou wilt know the Universe and the Gods". – Inscription on the Temple of Delphi.

8 See Acts 7:22. The first Egyptian name of Moses, according to the Egyptian historian Manethon, was Osarsiph. See *The Great Initiates*, by Edouard Schure, p. 178ff.

9 *The Great Initiates*: Edouard Schure, p. 171/2

10 For the sake of conceptual clarity, in the male/female divide of the Trinity of the Godhead, male is considered equal to pure divine spirit as such, and female spirit is equal to what is determined as soul, i.e. the mediating, as opposed to the primal spirit.

11. In the Egyptian trinity the Father, The Solar Word, or Osiris, was also seen as the Sun God. Isis can be regarded as a moon deity; and their progeny, Horus, pre-eminently became the child of Earth, albiet a sun-child.

12 *The Great Initiates*: Edouard Schure, p. 124/5.

13 A more popular expression of this knowledge was the manner in which the Greek Sun-God Helios was identified with Christ in the early Church. There is a mosaic in the necropolis under St. Peter's in Rome, dating from the 3rd century, which is known as Christos-Helios. In it Christ is depicted as the God Helios, driving his sun-chariot across the sky.

14. 'And God said: 'Let us make man in our image'. (Genesis I:26). The plural is explained by the fact that God cannot be seperated from his Creation.

15 The traditional symbols for the four Evangelists indicate quite well the presence of this initiation knowledge in the early Church. The symbols are Matthew (Man), Mark (Lion), Luke (Bull) and John (Eagle). These symbols have zodiacal and astrological significance and appertain to different types of initiation into the ancient Mysteries. The Gospel in this sense is seen to unify or bring together various aspects of the initiation Wisdom through Jesus Christ.

16. See Acts 22:1-21.

17. See Acts 17:23.

18 The Church Father St. John Chrysostom (b. aprox. 347 A.D.) addresses 'the initiates' directly in one of his recorded sermons telling them that they must now learn to deepen their marvel at the Mysteries through the new light and power of Christ.

19. See note 4.

20. As the Church gained ground in the civic world (towns and cities) at the beginning of our era, it gradually came to be regarded as the principle vechicle capable of mollifying the more robust habits of the countryside dwellers, or even worse, those living on the heaths (hence 'heathens' or 'pagans'). In comparison to the often severe strictness and virtuousness which the Christians imposed upon themselves, the country people with their rich and colourful, though often licentious habits, thus appeared fearful. And so if they did not join up with the Christians they gradually became disparragingly regarded as mere 'pagans'! In this manner however we have another classic example of the baby having often been thrown out with the bathwater!

21 Constantine was initiated into a pagan sun-cult of Syrian origin called the Sol Invictus. Through this solar cult he was able to approach Christianity with far more understanding than would otherwise have been the case, hence his eventual legitimizing of the Christian religion.

22. This is indicated in a number of ways in the New Testament but perhaps the word 'Church' itself, which is derived from the Greek work *Kurios* meaning Lord, is the best illustration.

23. See Mark 11:15-19; Luke 19:45-48, etc.

24. See Matthew 26:67.

25. See Stephen's Defence in the Book of Acts of the New Testament (specifically Acts 7:48).

26. See *Mystery Knowledge and Mystery Centres* by Rudolf Steiner.

27 See 1 Peter I:12.

28. See *Mystery Knowledge and Mystery Centres*, by Rudolf Steiner p. 128/9.

29. This is adapted from the version given in *Celtic Myths and Legends*, (Rolleston).

30. Attention should also be drawn here to the famous Wounded King motif which is a definitive aspect of mythic vision and racial memory worldwide. It is interesting however here to note that the wound in the Irish version is much more spiritually explicit, compared to other versions, where the wound is in the side or even more pointedly in the genetalia.

31 See *Celtic Myths and Legends* (Rolleston), p. 103.

32 This is probably the reason, incidentally, why St. Brigid was regarded as the patron saint of milkmaids!

33 Martyrdom in the Celtic Church consisted of not only actually dying for Christ physically (red), but also of a green one which meant the practise of severe austerities, and a less severe white one practised by neophytes. (The severity of the red in the tricolour was obviously diluted with a bit of white to make it a more reconciliatory orange (!), and also to distinguish it from other similar national tricolours).

34 Pronounced: sof-ee-*ah*-cal.

35. Patrick's dream can easily be interpreted as an intuitive or inward realization of the Johannine principle of spiritual re-birth as being a necessary condition for knowing Christ. For in the dream he clearly realizes how he is to become, or indeed has already become, re-born. The 'great rock' can easily be interpreted as the burden of the spirit-killing, death-dealing Law, which so heavily tinged the Roman Church with which Patrick was familiar in his upbringing in Britain. In Ireland this found no place at all! For the spiritual re-birth necessary to knowing

Christ (see John 3:1-8) by release from this law written in stone ('stone to flesh') Patrick had come to know or feel as something at work in the very atmosphere of Ireland, and this magical quality was never to let go of him until he returned to fulfill his destiny there many years later.

36. Essentially, what we are trying to get across here is that in Patrick's consciousness (or more specifically perhaps in his unconscious), the ancient sun-wisdom, though Christianized, was still highly active. From this point of view alone Patrick's writings are hugely important, for first-hand accounts of this nature are extremely rare. Patrick does us a huge service by giving us a glimpse of the transition which had to take place in consciousness because of the Incarnation. And his own struggle typifies the inevitable psychic difficulties involved in this whole process for more mythic-orientated man. It is very obvious from reading Patrick's Confession especially that he was struggling very hard to express his purely Christian consciousness as clearly as possible. Although obviously not illiterate, Patrick nevertheless was at pains to point out that he was not learned, and the style of his Confession itself proves this. He also appears to be familiar with only one book, the Bible, particularly the New Testament. Thus the influence of St. Paul especially is very obvious on Patrick's struggling articulation. For Patrick of course the centrepoint of this struggle was the problem of how to correctly seperate pure sun-worship (which was widespread in Ireland) from worship of the incarnated God who had emerged from the sun to live upon the Earth. For this, the Incarnation, was also the dividing line between the old and the new religion. Patrick however obviously achieved great success in this work, for the purely Christian type of consciousness was, soon after his arrival to preach to the Irish, to sweep the entire country.

37 *The Great Initiates:* Edouard Schure, p. 415.

38 This is taken from the wonderful treasure-trove of early Christian spirituality, the *Carmina Gadelica*. This is a huge work of collected songs, hymns, incantations, etc., which was carried out in remote parts of Scotland by Alexander Carmichael and published initially in 1900. All of the material was collected from oral recitation by the peasants. It's actual origins therefore can not be accurately dated, but obviously much of it goes way back to the very earliest period of the Celtic Church.

39 *Sun And Cross*: Jacob Streit, p. 201.

40 ibid. p. 206.

41 ibid. p. 206.

42 The sense of self consciousness which we in our time take for granted is actually a relatively recent intellectual or psychological advance. For the farther one goes back beyond aproximately the 15th century, the more apparent it is that people's sense of identity came far more from their ancestral or tribal relationships than from their own individual souls.

43 See note 15.

44 The old saying 'money is the root of all evil' does not quite hit the mark. St. Paul's statement in 1 Timothy 6:10 is probably the origin of this old saying. But Paul does not say however that money is the root of all evil. Rather he makes the point that it is *greed* for money that causes evil. And this kind of greed of course only exists in human beings.

45 Erigena means 'Irish born' and the term 'scot' was also used to donate Irishness at this time.

46 Polycarp was one of the apostolic Fathers of the Church in Asia Minor and was said to have known John the Evangelist personally.

47 See *The Battle For The Spirit* by Canon A.P.Shepherd, p. 80.

48 ibid. p. 73. This is Photius whose name means 'The Enlightened One'. He was 'one of the most famous scholars of the Middle Ages and was regarded by post-Renaissance philosophers and philologists as the one most responsible for making available to Western Europe the knowledge of Greek and Hellenistic culture'.

49 Taken from the Cannon. See note 47.

50 Avicenna (980 – 1037) and Averroes (1126 – 1198) to name but two.

51 Note that the word 'quest' is directly related to the word 'question'. Also it is apposite to note here that Parzival, the Grail winner in Eschenbach's romance, is regarded as a dimwit or a fool initially. The implication is that purely intellectual knowledge, or an over-development of the intellect, can often act as a barrier to true spiritual knowledge and wisdom. One is thus in a sense better off if one is a fool!

52 See *The Ninth Century and the Holy Grail*, W.J.Stein, p 54.

53 Here it is apposite to mention that the name of the Grail winner, Parzival, means 'piercing the veil'.

54 See Hebrews 7:15-19.

55 It is important to point out here that in the King James Bible (The Authorized Version) the word 'meat' is normally used for 'food'. Here however, (Genesis 14:18), despite the fact that other Bibles use 'food', the King James version actually uses the more correct word 'bread'. Bread in fact is one of the most significant and important 'metaphors' used in the whole of the Bible. And the 'authority' of the King James Bible is shown up very clearly here in this verse.

56 This was the original gathering for prayer inspired by the Gospel where Christ says that 'if two or three are gathered in my name I AM there with them', (Matthew 18:20). It was known as the feast of the 'agape' (= Greek for the purest form of Christ-inspired Love). Hence these gatherings have become known as Love Feasts, and the extant celebration of the Eucharist is in a direct line of descent from this gathering.

57 The 'twelve' in Acts 19:1-7 indicates of course how the macro-cosmic forces of the twelve sections (houses) of the heavenly sphere (Zodiac) ray into the organism of the congregations via the individual and micro-cosmic man.

58 Good literature on this difficult aspect of esoteric knowledge is particularly scant, mostly confused, and often hopelessly misleading. However, *Enlivening the Chakra of the Heart* by Florin Lowndes is to be recommended.

59 See chapter 9 of *The Reappearance of Christ in the Etheric* (see bibliography).

60 See Romans 5:9. This is the deeper meaning of the divine blood sacrifice which constitutes the core Mystery element of the Deed of the Incarnation. And truely all other talk (of which there is much) about the blood mystery of Christ is of little significance when compared with the insights these facts can give. Also see Appendix 2.

61 The continued existence of the Low Mass and the High Mass are echoes of this early division.

62 The name Cathar is a generic term and can be applied to a variety of sects,

including the Albigenses, active in Europe at this time, especially in the general area of southern France, but also in places as far away as Italy. We will thus use the term 'Cathar' from here on to include all of these variations.

63 In the case of the extreme West however, i.e. in ancient Hibernia, things were different. It is well known, for instance, that the Druids knew about, studied, and taught reincarnation. This reincarnational wisdom of course would have assisted profoundly in the later assimilation of the 're-birthing' aspects of the new Christian incarnational knowledge.

64 For a fascinating account of how the Holy Grail may become an object which can stimulate not only the deepest of spiritual responses but can also, in contrast, be used to to excite the baser elements of the human psyche through greed and black magical practices, read the masterly novel by Charles Williams, *War in Heaven.*

65 See note 62.

66 The Inquisition was set up by the very ascetical order of the Dominicans in 1233, initially to root out the last vestiges of this 'foul leprosy' of the 'pure ones'. But of course, as we now very well know, the case of the Cathars was a mere practise run for what was to become over the next few centuries perhaps *the* most fearful and demonic of all organs of institutionalized terror that man has ever yet been able out of his hatred, to invent, i.e. the Holy Inquisition.

67 It has to be said of course that the orthodox Church had in a sense little or no choice in the matter of its absolute authority in regard to Christ's divinity. For it saw the Incarnation as having no unique or indeed any particularly different significance from other similar historical occurrences if Christ's divinity was doubted or denied. Furthermore it also saw itself as the very temporal embodiment of this truth of his divinity in the world. It had however put itself in an impossible position by denying itself the means by which this Mystery could be understood; for it could, or can, only be understood in the light of its fulfillment of the ancient Mystery religions.

68 It was also at Troyes in a specially convened Church Council in January 1128 that the Knights Templar were officially recognised and incorporated into the Church as a religious/military Order.

69 The Grail Castle can also of course be understood as relating to the whole

broader story of the Temple as such, as it figures in the history of both esoteric and exoteric wisdom generally. And in this regard it is relevant to note that the full name or the Templars (rendered into English from the Latin) is: The Order of the Poor Knights of Christ and the Temple of Solomon. Their first establishment was also on the site of the original Temple of Solomon in Jerusalem.

70 The French term for a knight, 'chevalier' means a horseman.

71 Here of course it must be remembered that the Templars were engaged in activities which by their very spiritual nature would have most likely brought them into serious conflict with the orthodoxy of the Church were they open to being questioned in this regard. By this time anyway there was a growing fear of, and an increasing alienation from, anything whatsoever to do with the genuine spirit on the part of the mainstream Church. Thus from the Templars' point of view any kind of investigation of their methods had to be avoided at all costs for they owed, after all, their power primarily to the approval of the Church in the first place. Without it they would have quickly disintegrated, would indeed never have arisen in the first place as a universal institution. For the Catholic Church was the supreme power in the Middle Ages, especially when it came to determining what was orthodox or what was not, as the horrific Albigensian Crusade so forcefully proved. And for this reason also the Templars could never in fact openly approve of the Cathars, although it is well known that they sympathised with them.

72 Philip, during a quarrel about taxes with the Church, had actually gone so far as to imprison the Pope in Rome! This was Boniface VIII who died soon after this outrage. Philip then installed his own Pope (Clement) in Avignon and thus started what has been called the Babylonian Captivity of the Papacy which lasted from 1309 to 1377.

73 The two particular Societies mentioned here are still in existence, though obviously not 'secret' anymore! However it has to be said that they nowadays bear very little, if indeed any resemblance at all in character, function or spiritual content to the old or original societies from which they take their names. See, in this regard, especially *The Rosicrutian Enlightenment* by Francis Yeats which gives an extremely broad historical overview of the profound influence and significance of the original Rosicrutian Brotherhood.

74 The word 'utopia' is from the Greek and actually means 'no place'.

75 See note 76.

76 The word imaginative or imagination in this special context is not intended to convey the usual meaning of something unreal or of the nature of fantasy and so on, but rather that form of consciousness only by which truely spiritual realities may be apprehended.

77 A distinction can and must be made here, from the point of view of Esoteric Christianity regarding the use of the terms 'the Gospel' and the 'Living Word'. From this point of view the *written* Gospel is merely an outward confirmation of a truth or a reality which, in its deepest essence, is only fully perceived inwardly or spiritually. Thus in this sense there is only *one* Gospel. And this is the one which is written directly into the human heart through Christian love and virtue, the one that is rightly called the Living Word.

78 In this regard it may be apposite to recall here how the three wise priest-kings or initiates, the Oriental Magi, brought, among other gifts, to the new Christ-King Child, the gift of gold!

79 It is also relevant to point out here that the Holy Grail is regarded in Eschenbach's *Parzival* as a stone, the *lapsit exellis* or the 'stone that came from heaven'. All these are pointers to an inner transmutation whereby the real Mystery is comprehended. (See page 132).

80 *The Alchemists Through The Ages* by A.E.Waite, p. 33.

81 In the beginning of printing the printer mattered infinitely more than the author of the book.

82 As may be quite obvious to anyone who can reflect upon this subject objectively nowadays (difficult!), the reason why eroticism has taken such a strong hold on modern society is entirely bound up with the huge and powerful business of advertising which is a key factor in our modern capitalistic economic system. The exploitation of femininity in the form of eroticism and the success of modern capitalism are intimately linked together, a situation which may in fact be regarded from the point of view of Esoteric Christianity as a fundamental abuse or corruption of the entire Sophia Mystery. For this one isolated aspect of Romanticism has been taken and inflated to a ridiculous and even psychologically dangerous degree, in order to serve the demands of the most popular current 'philosophy' which has iron- gripped the Western mind, consumerism.

83 Proof according to the methods and assumptions of conventional science is of course not possible regarding these archetypes. The primary reason for this is that this science does not acknowledge the existence of the human soul. Jung's psychoanalytical science has always been regarded with not a little suspicion by orthodoxy because of this. Goethean science however is a far more exact one than psychoanalysis could ever hope to be, for it was, or is, not restricted to the mind only, but concerns itself with the whole vast observable world of manifestation in Nature. Most students of Goethean science are very familiar with what Goethe called the *urpflanze*, the archetypal plant. This however, unlike Jung's archetypes, he did not regard merely as an hypothesis, or as something not quite definable or observable in a totally real way. For it was something he could in fact see in reality due to the training he undertook in or for his experimental method: He had learned in other words to observe the spiritual blueprint, or the Being of plants, through which all earthly plants are created!

84 The name Pansophia was also coined in the 17th century by one of this period's most enlightened minds, Comenius. This is an excellent name also for it joins the male god of nature, Pan, with the essentially feminine or soul-wisdom of the natural world, giving us the more inclusive and 'Europeanized' Pansophia.

85. The Holy Sophia was also known as the Virgin Of Light.

86. *Yeats - The Man and the Masks*, R. Ellman, p.99.

87. ibid. p. 99.

88. This is inscribed on Yeats' tombstone in the church graveyard at Drumcliff, Co. Sligo.

89. For a wonderful and moving account of how Russell's clairvoyant faculty opened, and how subsequently through this awakening he gained such a splendid vision and insight into the spiritual world and its angelic inhabitants, read his lovely book *The Candle Of Vision*.

90. This Society is still flourishing and directs a growing worldwide Anthroposophical Movement through which genuine spiritual impulses are being brought to bear on the arts, sciences and religions of various cultures and peoples. It is a movement dedicated to the ideal of the spiritual regeneration of modern civilization. See *Rudolf Steiner: Herald of a New Epoch* by Stewart Easton.

91. A new Goetheanum, built entirely of reinforced concrete, was commenced

soon after the fire in the same place, and this building now ranks as the initial prototype of an entirely new style of spiritually-inspired architecture and is of increasing interest to progressively minded architects.

92 See Yeats' poem *Sailing To Byzantium* .

93 The *lapsit exellis* (see page 132) as the Holy Grail is the 'living stone'; this may also be understood as the consecrated Being or Spirit of the Earth.

94 The other four I AM affirmations are: I AM the Bread of Life; I AM the true Vine; I AM the Good Shepherd; I AM the Resurrection and the Life.

SELECT BIBLIOGRAPHY

Adamson, Ian, *Bangor; Light Of The World*, Pretani Press, 1987.

Adomnan's *Life of Columba*, (Ed.) A.O. and M.O. Anderson, Thomas Nelson and Sons Ltd., 1961.

A.E. (George William Russell), *Candle of Vision*, Macmillan & Co. Ltd.

Archiati, Pietro, *The Great Religions*, Temple Lodge, 1998.

Baigent, Michael, and Leigh, Richard, *The Elixir and the Stone*, Viking, 1997.

Bamford, Christopher and Marsh, William Parker, (Eds.), *Celtic Christianity: An Anthology*, Floris Classics, 1986.

Bennell, Margaret, & Wyatt, Isabel, *The Chymical Wedding of Christian Rosenkreutz*, (*A Commentary*), Temple Lodge, 1989.

Betti, Mario, *The Sophia Mystery in our Time*, Temple, Lodge 1994.

Blavatsky, H.P., *Isis Unveiled*, Theosophical University Press, (USA), 1960, 2 vols.

Carmichael, Alexander, *Carmina Gadelica*, Floris Books, 1992.

Christie-Murray, David, *A History of Heresy,* London, 1976.

Curtayne, Alice, *St. Brigid of Ireland*, Sheed & Ward (USA), 1954.

DiCarlo, Russel, E., (Ed.), *Towards a New World-View*, Floris 1996.

Easton, Stewart, *Rudolf Steiner: Herald of a New Epoch*, The Anthroposophic Press (USA), 1980.

Ellmann, Richard, *Yeats: The Man and the Masks*, Penguin Books, 1979.

Emmerich, Anne Catherine, *The Dolorous Passion of Our Lord Jesus Christ,* Burns and Oates, 1956.

Emmerich, Anne Catherine, *The Life of the Blessed Virgin Mary*, Burns and Oates, 1954.

Erigena, John Scotus, *The Voice of the Eagle,* (Trans. Christopher Bamford), Lindisfarne Press, 1990.

Eschenbach, Wolfram Von, *Parzival*, Vintage Books (USA), 1961.

Frieling, Rudolf, *Christianity and Reincarnation*, Floris Books, 1977.

Goethe, Johann Wolfgang Von, *Faust,* Parts 1 & 2 (Trans: Bayard Taylor), Sphere Books, 1969.

Goethe, Johann Wolfgang Von, *Theory of Colours*, (Trans: Charles Lock Eastlake), Frank Cass & Co. Ltd., 1967.

Guthrie, Kenneth Sylvan (Compiler and translator), *The Pytagorean Sourcebook and Library*, Phanes Press (USA), 1987.

Head, Joseph and Sranston, S.L. (Eds.), *Reincarnation: An East-West Anthology*, The Julian Press (USA), 1961.

Holms, Edmond, *The Holy Heretics*, Watts, 1948.

Lowndes, Floris, *Enlivening the Chakra of the Heart*, Sophia Books, 1998.

Marsden, John, *Sea-Road of the Saints*, Floris Books, 1995.

Matthews, John, *The Grail – Quest for the Eternal*, Thames and Hudson,1981.

Naydler, Jeremy, *Goethe On Science – An Anthology*, Floris Books, 1996.

Novalis, *Hymns to theNight & Spiritual Songs*, Temple Lodge Press, 1992

O'Donohue, John, *Anam Cara*, Bantam Books, 1999.

Oldenburg, Zoe, *Destiny of Fire*, Penguin Books, 1969.

Proskauer, Heinrich O., *The Rediscovery of Colour – Goethe versus Newton Today*, Anthroposophical Press (USA), 1986.

Pseudo-Dionysius; The Complete Works, Trans: Colm Luibheid, Paulist Press (USA), 1987.

Rolleston, T.W., *Celtic Myths and Legends*, Studio Editions Ltd., 1994.

Ryan, John, *Irish Monasticism*, Four Courts Press, 1992.

Saint Patrick, (Ed.) Iain McDonald, Floris Books 1992. (This book contains the Confession).

Schure, Edouard, *The Great Initiates*, Steinerbooks (USA), 1976.

Schure, Edouard, *From Sphinx to Christ*, Rudolf Steiner Publications (USA), 1970.

Seddon, Richard, *The Mystery of Arthur at Tintagel*, Rudolf Steiner Press, 1990.

Shepherd, Canon A.P., *Battle for the Spirit*, Anastasi Ltd., 1994.

Stein, W.J., *The 9th Century And The Holy Grail*, Temple Lodge Press, 1988.

Steiner, Rudolf, *The Philosophy of Freedom*, Rudolf Steiner Press, 1988.

Steiner, Rudolf, *Mystery Knowledge and Mystery Centres*, Rudolf Steiner Press, 1973.

Steiner, Rudolf, *The Reappearance of Christ in the Etheric*, The Anthroposophic Press (USA), 1983.

Streit, Jacob, *Sun and Cross*, Floris Books, 1993

Tagore, Rabindranath, *Gitanjali (Song Offerings)*, Macmillan and Co., 1914.

Underhill, Evelyn, *Mysticism – The Nature and Development of Spiritual Consciousness*, Oneworld Publications Ltd., 1993.

Van Der Post, Laurens, *Jung, and the Story Of Our Time*, The Hogart Press, 1976.

Waite, A.E., *The Alchemists Through The Ages*, Rudolf Steiner Publications (USA), 1970.

Welburn, Andrew J., *The Truth of Imagination*, McMillan, 1989.

Williams, Charles, *War in Heaven*, William B. Eerdman's Publishing Co., (USA),1949.

Wordsworth's Verse (Selected by R. S. Thomas), Faber and Faber, 1971.

Yates, Frances A., *The Rosicrutian Enlightenment*, Routledge and Keegan Paul, 1972.

Yeats, W.B., *Collected Poems*, Macmillan and Co., 1952.

NOTES

NOTES

NOTES

NOTES

NOTES

NOTES